SEEDING BUDDHISM WITH MULTICULTURALISM

ADVANCING STUDIES IN RELIGION

Series editor: Christine Mitchell

Advancing Studies in Religion catalyzes and provokes original research in the study of religion with a critical edge. The series advances the study of religion in method and theory, textual interpretation, theological studies, and the understanding of lived religious experience. Rooted in the long and diverse traditions of the study of religion in Canada, the series demonstrates awareness of the complex genealogy of religion as a category and as a discipline. ASR welcomes submissions from authors researching religion in varied contexts and with diverse methodologies.

The series is sponsored by the Canadian Corporation for Studies in Religion whose constituent societies include the Canadian Society of Biblical Studies, Canadian Society for the Study of Religion, Canadian Society of Patristic Studies, Canadian Theological Society, Société canadienne de théologie, and Société québécoise pour l'étude de la religion.

Seeding Buddhism
with Multiculturalism

The Transmission of Sri Lankan
Buddhism in Toronto

D. Mitra Barua

McGill-Queen's University Press
Montreal & Kingston • London • Chicago

© McGill-Queen's University Press 2019

ISBN 978-0-7735-5656-0 (cloth)
ISBN 978-0-7735-5657-7 (paper)
ISBN 978-0-7735-5759-8 (ePDF)
ISBN 978-0-7735-5760-4 (ePUB)

Legal deposit second quarter 2019
Bibliothèque nationale du Québec

Printed in Canada on acid-free paper that is 100% ancient forest free
(100% post-consumer recycled), processed chlorine free

This book has been published with the help of a grant from the Canadian Federation
for the Humanities and Social Sciences, through the Awards to Scholarly Publications
Program, using funds provided by the Social Sciences and Humanities Research
Council of Canada.

Funded by the   Financé par le
Government   gouvernement
of Canada   du Canada

Canada Council   Conseil des arts
for the Arts   du Canada

We acknowledge the support of the Canada Council for the Arts, which last year
invested $153 million to bring the arts to Canadians throughout the country.

Nous remercions le Conseil des arts du Canada de son soutien. L'an dernier,
le Conseil a investi 153 millions de dollars pour mettre de l'art dans la vie des
Canadiennes et des Canadiens de tout le pays.

Library and Archives Canada Cataloguing in Publication

Title: Seeding Buddhism with multiculturalism : the transmission of Sri Lankan
Buddhism in Toronto / D. Mitra Barua.
Names: Barua, D. Mitra, 1976– author.
Series: Advancing studies in religion ; 5.
Description: Series statement: Advancing studies in religion ; 5 | Includes
bibliographical references and index.
Identifiers: Canadiana (print) 20190055154 | Canadiana (ebook) 20190055235
| ISBN 9780773556577 (paper) | ISBN 9780773556560 (cloth) | ISBN
9780773557598 (ePDF) | ISBN 9780773557604 (ePUB)
Subjects: LCSH: Buddhism—Ontario—Toronto. | LCSH: Buddhism—Sri Lanka—
Colombo. | LCSH: Buddhists—Ontario—Toronto. | LCSH: Sri Lankans—Ontario—
Toronto—Religion. | LCSH: Sri Lankans—Ontario—Toronto—Ethnic identity.
| LCSH: Immigrants—Ontario—Toronto. | LCSH: Multiculturalism—Religious
aspects—Buddhism. | LCSH: Intergenerational communication—Ontario—Toronto.
| LCSH: Toronto (Ont.)—Religion.
Classification: LCC BQ749.O585 T67 2019 | DDC 294.309713/541—dc23

This book was typeset in 10.5/13 Sabon.

*Gratefully dedicated to Ajahn Phongeun Vongkoth,
his multiethnic Buddhist community in the Kitchener-Waterloo
area, and dedicated dhamma teachers worldwide*

Contents

Figures and Tables

Acknowledgments

This book has been long in coming. I would not have been able to complete this book had I not received kind nudges from many people since my graduate studies in the Laurier-Waterloo joint doctoral program on religious diversity in North America. The theme for this book was germinated by a conversation with my doctoral supervisor, Kay Koppedrayer. The program itself necessitated its PhD students to locate their chosen research topic in North America and to address the issue of religion and diversity. Within these broad and yet limited foci, Kay advised me: "Mitra, think of a topic that would keep you interested and engaged for a long time coming." Although I have been engaged with the topic of this book longer than I should have, I am grateful for that insightful advice and all the support Kay provided throughout my graduate studies. I could not ask for a better supervisor. She was kind yet firm with deadlines. She warned me not to get fooled by the self-delusional and procrastinating mental statement: "it is all in the mind." Her advice – "there is no paper or chapter of your dissertation until and unless you put it in written words" – helped me to complete the dissertation in time. I am extremely grateful for her superb mentorship. Kay was the epitome of responsible and effective academic mentoring.

Let me also express my gratitude to others who helped me complete my graduate studies, from which this book emerged. Janet McLellan and Darrol Bryant served as members of my PhD committee. With much appreciation, I recall their kind advice and commitment to my success in the doctoral program. I also enjoyed talking with and/or learning from Michel Desjardins, Ronald Grimes, Carol Duncan, Chris Ross, Lorne Dawson, Doris Jakobsh, Mavis Fenn, Jeff Wilson, and David Seljak during graduate school. The latter in particular was very kind in offering me a one-on-one lesson on the various aspects of the secularization process in the West. Let me also acknowledge the moral support I received from my PhD cohort members, as well as a few others who were in the program. In particular, I am indebted to Siobhan Chandler – a great friend, a supportive colleague, and most of all a patient cultural ambassador (as I call her "Madame") who taught me a lot of North American colloquial expressions and cultural idioms. She patiently listened to many of my rambling research observations that eventually developed into the pages of this book. Her friendship, moral support, and encouragement certainly enabled me to survive the rigour of graduate school.

What made the above graduate school experience possible was a list of well-wishers. The Sinhalese, Bengali, and Lao speaking Buddhists in the Kitchener-Waterloo-Cambridge region welcomed me to their communities. I was able to observe the dynamics of Buddhism in diaspora as I repeatedly crossed the ethno-linguistic borders of these communities. I am deeply grateful to Ajahn Phongeun Vongkoth and his Lao Buddhist community of the Kitchener-Waterloo who helped me to call Canada home. Ajahn stood solid as a father figure and took pride in my academic aspirations; he encouraged and assisted me in every possible way to complete my higher studies. When I took time off from school to serve him as a primary caregiver when he was diagnosed with an advanced stage of lymphoma in 2010, he whispered in my ear not to allow his illness to interrupt my school. His deep interest in formal dhamma education and relentless effort with Soutsada (Mem) Vongsaly to introduce the practice to his fellow Laotian Buddhists in Ontario inspired me to conduct research on the practice. Ajahn wished that the Laotian Buddhist tradition had the practice of formal dhamma education that Sri Lankan Buddhists have enjoyed for more than a century.

I am thankful to the Sri Lankan Buddhist community in southern Ontario for many things, particularly for their cooperation in my research project. The chief incumbents of both temples under study permitted me to conduct the research. Ven Kulugammana Dhammawasa Nayaka Thero of the West End Buddhist Temple and Meditation Centre and Ven Ahangama Ratanasiri Nakaya Thero of the Toronto Mahavihara Buddhist Meditation Centre kindly allowed me to study the archival sources at their temples. Ven Bhikkhu Saranapala, the principal of the West End Dhamma School, Ven Udipihille Wimalabuddhi

Thero, the principal of the Toronto Mahavihara Dhamma School, and Ven Hakmana Sumanasiri Thero, the principal of the Maharagama Sri Vajiragnana Dhamma School, encouraged their staff members to participate in the research. Without their blessings, I do not think that I could have received the overwhelming support from dhamma teachers and dhamma students. The veteran dhamma teacher Alloy (Mahaththaya) Perera was instrumental in providing me the information about the history of the Sri Lankan community in Toronto. I wish I could name all the dhamma teachers in Toronto and Colombo (Sri Lanka) who contributed to the research, but the space does not allow me to do so. I am also grateful to all the first- and second-generation members of the Buddhist community at both temples in Toronto for their participation in the research. Had it not been for their participation in the surveys and interviews, the research project that produced this book would have been unthinkable.

I recall conversations with many people during my time (2011–14) as an instructor of South and Southeast Asian religions at the University of Saskatchewan: Braj Sinha, Heidi Epstein, Kristine Michell, Ulrich Teucher, Alexander Ervin, Satya Sharma, Richard Julien, Veronika Makarova, Bettina Spreng, James Mullins, and George Keyworth. I am grateful to the latter in particular for broadening my academic association and highlighting the importance of my research on Buddhism in Bengal. Beyond academia, the mindfulness meditation groups led by Jeanne Corrigal, Jennifer Keane, and Ken Sailor provided me with a sense of community in Saskatoon. Jabunnessa Chapola and her family, the Barua family, and the Bengali speaking community in Saskatoon reconnected me to my cultural roots. Coralea Ens, a former student from my "World Religions" course, has been much interested in my success in academia and has kept me updating her with her nagging question: "how is your book coming along?" I am impressed by familial warmth extended by the Ens family (Coralea's husband, Vic, and their children) that made cold and sunny Saskatoon home for a while. Although a heavy teaching load did not allow me to revisit the book manuscript in a substantial way, the conversations with the people mentioned above kept me thinking about how to transform the dissertation into a monograph.

The dissertation-to-book transformation phase had its own ups and downs. Only the people and institutions that brought this book into fruition deserve this acknowledgment. The first and foremost place in that list of acknowledgment belongs to Anne Blackburn at Cornell University. She was rock solid in the revising phase of the manuscript. Her support and recommendation enabled me to secure postdoctoral research funding to devote myself to the revision. The major revision of the book manuscript took place at Cornell's Asian Studies Department during my first year of a H.N. Ho Family Foundation Postdoctoral Fellowship (July 2014–June 2016) in Buddhist Studies. Anne was very kind and generous with her time, energy, and comments. She read the whole book manuscript and provided me with many suggestions that immensely improved the academic quality of the book.

During my time at Cornell University, I also benefitted from conversations with many people: Nick Admussen, Bronwen Bledsoe, Daniel Boucher, Thamora Fishel, Magnus Fiskesjo, Chiara Formichi, Daniel Gold, Bandara Herath, Yufen Lee Mehta, Viranjini Munasinghe, Sreemati Mukherjee, Swe Swe Myint, Lucinda Ramberg, Keith Weller Taylor, Erick White, and others. I here acknowledge the institutional support received from the Asian Studies Department, particularly Sheila Haddad and Erin Kotmel, who took care of the logistics of my appointment at Cornell.

During my graduate studies and the fieldwork that led to the production of this book, I received generous funding from Canada's provincial and federal government agencies. The Ontario Graduate Scholarship (OGS) from Ontario's Ministry of Training, Colleges and Universities took care of my expenses during the 2006–07 academic year. The generous doctoral fellowship from Canada's federal funding agency, the Social Sciences and Humanities Research Council (SSHRC), during 2007–09 enabled me to conduct fieldwork in Toronto and Colombo. These forms of financial support certainly contributed to the completion of my PhD degree on time, but they also enabled me to provide the cancer treatment to my ailing mother diagnosed with thyroid cancer in Bangladesh. The medical attention added another decade to her life. I justified the latter use of the money as it freed me from my moral obligation, and more importantly it gave me the peace of mind to dedicate myself completely to my graduate studies. I am disclosing these intimate details to remind the funding agencies that the financial support for education goes farther and the impacts are wider than is usually intended.

To transform my dissertation into this monograph *Seeding Buddhism with Multiculturalism*, I also received the Robert H.N.

Ho Family Foundation Postdoctoral Fellowship in Buddhist Studies administered by the American Council of Learned Societies (ACLS). This fellowship has been crucial to conclude this research project and commence another brand new one, this time on Buddhism in wider Bengal, particularly at the Bangladesh-Myanmar borderland. I express my gratitude to the Ho Family Foundation as well as the ACLS for making it possible. I would like to remind both agencies that their funding enabled me to publish a few articles on the Buddhism in Bengal project, and I am working on a separate monograph on the same project. I am also happy to learn that the press' application for a publication grant has been approved.

These acknowledgments would remain incomplete without a reference to the efficient service I received from McGill-Queen's University Press. I cannot overstate the huge relief I experienced making step-by-step progress in the labyrinthine path of publication. Thanks go to Christine Mitchell, editor of the Advancing Studies in Religious Series, and acquisition editor Kyla Madden for believing in the project. Two anonymous reviewers were also instrumental in advancing the quality of this book. Finn Purcell was efficient in determining the corresponding pictures included in the book. Kathryn Simpson was very patient and helpful in getting the idiomatic expressions right. I am impressed by her excellent editorial skills and grateful for every suggestion she made to improve the quality of this book. I am sure that more people worked behind the scenes in the publication of this book. I thank you all for your service!

Finally, let me wrap up these long acknowledgments by expressing gratitude to my family. During the final revision of the book, I locked myself in the study room for many long hours. It certainly gave the impression of my ghostly presence (present but unavailable) to my family – particularly to my son, Adi, who often banged the door crying: "Daddy, Daddy, knock (he meant open) the door!" I am more than grateful to my wife, Aparna, for single-handedly consoling Adi by providing him with motherly and fatherly love altogether. Without Aparna's moral support, constant encouragement, and most importantly love, this book would not have seen the light of publication.

SEEDING BUDDHISM WITH MULTICULTURALISM

1

Introduction: Studying the Intercultural and Intergenerational Transmission of Buddhism

It was a Sunday afternoon. I arrived at the Rick Hansen Secondary School in Mississauga to have a first-hand experience of the Sri Lankan Buddhists' most-demanded temple service: Sunday *dhamma* school. Parents were rushing along the corridor to the assembly hall accompanying their children. A few female dhamma teachers were helping a group of students arrange candles, incense, flowers, and beverages to be offered to the Buddha. Other teachers, parents, and students formed a line standing side-by-side facing the stage where a Buddha icon was temporarily placed on a table covered with a white cloth. The teachers were in white dress, students were in white T-shirts with the dhamma school logo, and parents were in casual clothes. Holding a microphone in between his joined palms, the principal monk started to chant the virtues of the Buddha in the Pāli language. All others joined him intoning the Pāli chanting: *Namotassa Bhagavato Arahato Sammā Sambuddhassa* (Honour to Him, the Blessed One, the Worthy One and the Fully Awakened One). The students who arranged the *pūja* (offering) formed a line one after another, each holding one of the pūja items in their both hands with devotion and care. Everyone in the assembly hall touched the pūja items and then their foreheads. One after another, all pūja items were respectfully placed on the table in front of the icon. All bowed to the Buddha. They then took refuge in the Triple Gem and observed the Five Precepts in Pāli by repeating after the monk. Then all including the monk chanted together the virtues of the Buddha, the dhamma, and the *sangha* again and recited the Pāli verses referring to the pūja items. Afterward, one of the senior students came forward, took the microphone, and recited the ten promises of dhamma school students. All other students took the oath by repeating after the senior student. Then the monk shared the words of wisdom for the day. At the end, students and teachers went to their own classrooms for an hour and a half period. While the students were leaving, the parents circled around a monk in the assembly hall to learn and discuss the teachings of the Buddha.

This 2009 scene illustrates Sri Lankan Buddhists' transmission practices in Toronto. It evokes one of the important concerns that occupy many immigrant communities in diaspora[1]: the transmission of the immigrant religious tradition to successive generations. At Sri Lankan Buddhist temples in Sri Lanka and in diaspora, one can witness this dynamic Buddhist educational ritual that brings monastics and laity, parents and children, as well as teachers and students together on any given Sunday or, in some cases, Saturday. This weekly program called dhamma education[2] has become the most sought-out temple service in Toronto. The survey that I conducted in 2008 indicates that 75 per cent of Sri Lankan Buddhists rated dhamma education as the "most liked" temple service.[3] Many Sri Lankan Buddhist temples across North America (except the few that serve Caucasian Buddhists) administer some sort of dhamma education. In the context of Sri Lankan Buddhists in London, UK, Mahinda Deegalle (2008, 27) notes that dhamma education has been one of the main motivations for providing financial and material support to the monks and temples. Three of the four Sri Lankan Buddhist temples in Toronto provide weekly dhamma school services. The fourth, a representative of the Sri Lankan forest tradition (*Asapuwa*), does not conduct a formal dhamma school but does offer a monthly meditation practice geared toward youths and children. Dhamma education's focus on the intergenerational transmission of Buddhism has made it the most popular of all temple services. With the absence of the extended family and ambient Buddhist cultural environment, Sri Lankan Buddhist immigrant parents depend on dhamma education as a primary – and at times the sole – means to pass Buddhism on to their children.

Figure 1.1　The West End Dhamma School principal with dhamma school students

Note: The Dhamma School logo (at the back) contains a white swan, representing the Buddhist child, and a red maple leaf, representing Canada.

Source: The West End Buddhist Temple and Meditation Centre

This intergenerational transmission has interested other Asian immigrant Buddhists as well. Victor Sogen Hori (1994, 50) observes: "Ethnic Buddhists are not concerned with converting Westerners. Their interest in Westernizing Buddhism is limited to preserving their own ethnic culture and identity in North America. 'How will we transmit our culture to our children?' is perhaps the most important issue in every ethnic community." Hori implies that the act of preserving an ethno-specific Buddhist culture in the West itself entails a process of "Westernizing" – albeit a reluctant one. In other words, as the Buddhist tradition is transmitted from the first generation to the second in diaspora, it undergoes cultural changes that are willingly or unwillingly accepted, or even forcefully resisted, by both generations. These cultural changes can be troubling to the parent generation, who are uncertain about the future of their respective traditions (McLellan 1999, 2009; Smith-Hefner 1999; Cadge 2005; Suh 2004). They are concerned about the transmission of their form of Buddhism to their children born and/or raised in the West, and they worry about how their religious identity and values will be transmitted to their children. The parent generation faces the challenge of preserving their inherited cultural values while being pressured to adapt to a new cultural setting.

The desire to preserve wrestles with the pressure to accommodate; that dynamic interaction is, perhaps, nowhere more explicit than in the process of education. An education system simultaneously preserves and accommodates the subject in question. Peter Hershock (2006, 173) observes: "Education serves both conservative and creative ends. On one hand, education serves to transmit historically embedded patterns of understanding and practice. Or, put somewhat differently, it conserves the particular traditions through which people shape their often complex and distinctive identities. On the other hand, education provides resources and insights relevant to adaptively responding to changing circumstances. In practice, *education both transmits and transforms understanding and practice* [emphasis added]." As education transmits the knowledge, understanding, and practices of one generation to the next, it also modifies the objects that are transmitted to suit the receivers and their current cultural context. Education simultaneously holds both the conservative and the transformative impulses of transmitters and receivers. A study of religious educational endeavours therefore offers an important vantage point to discern what is happening between the first- and second-generation Buddhists. Thus this book is about understanding the practice of dhamma education – how it is conducted, what it entails, the materials used in it, its history, and the parents, students, and teachers who engage in it. Such comprehensive analysis of dhamma education in Toronto will, I suggest, shed light on the reconfiguration of Sri Lankan Buddhism in Toronto.

The Sri Lankan Buddhist community in Toronto offers a good case for an in-depth study on a reconfiguration of Buddhism manifested in formal Buddhist education. Community members have developed a system of formal religious education based on a Toronto-specific curriculum, and they claim to have "the largest Dhamma School in North America" (Wijesundara 2008, 16; Attygalle 2009, 8). Their dhamma education program is informed by a century-long history in Sri Lanka, where Buddhist revivalists pioneered a formal Buddhist religious education program for children since the late nineteenth century (Bartholomeusz 1994, 61; Bond 1988, 48–52, 85–8, 111, 117–18; Gombrich and Obeyesekere 1988, 205, 211, 235; Prothero 1996, 101–6). As an outcome of that historical experience, dhamma education has become a salient feature of Sri Lankan Buddhism in Sri Lanka as well as in diaspora, including Toronto. Moreover, Sri Lankan Buddhists in Toronto are among the early Theravāda Buddhists to have settled in post-Second World War Canada, and historically they make up a vibrant Buddhist presence in Toronto with significant contributions to the larger community. In July 1978, they established the first Theravāda Buddhist temple in Canada. Since early 1980s, they have galvanized other Buddhists in Toronto for the Vesak celebration, an annual inter-Buddhist event to mark the public Buddhist presence in Toronto. Nevertheless, Sri Lankan Buddhists remain relatively under-researched (McLellan 1999, 2009; Boisvert 2005; Matthews 2006; and Harding, Hori, and Soucy 2010). This work seeks to further knowledge of that influential community.

The two earliest Sri Lankan Buddhist temples in Toronto – the Toronto Mahavihara in Scarborough and the West End Buddhist Centre in Mississauga – and their Buddhist practitioners are the focus of this book. Over 160 individuals contributed to this study. I identify them either as the first generation (the parent generation) or as the second generation.

Table 1.1
An overview of research participants

	First generation (between 30–70 years of age)		Second generation (between 16–30 years of age)	
Surveys	96	Male: 57	65	Male: 28
		Female: 39		Female: 37
Interviews	25	Male: 15	25	Male: 11
(individual and group)	(7 dhamma teachers included)	(4 monks included)	(6 dhamma teachers included)	
		Female: 10		Female: 14

The first generation refers to those who migrated to Canada as adults, and at the time of data collection (2008–09) through interviews and surveys, they were aged thirty or over. Monks, lay dhamma teachers, and the parents of students of dhamma schools make up this group. The second generation refers to those who were born in Canada or migrated to Canada at a formative age. At the time of this study, the second generation ranged in age from sixteen to thirty years. A few youths who could be classified as 1.5 generation (those who were born in Sri Lanka and came to Canada during their adolescence, when they were between thirteen and sixteen)[4] also contributed to the study; however, they were not sufficient enough in number[5] to be treated as a separate category. As such, I classified them in the second generation. Their engagement with Buddhist beliefs and practices contribute to reconfiguring Buddhism in Toronto.

THE TRANSMISSION AND RECONFIGURATION OF BUDDHISM IN TORONTO

The main concern of this book is to delineate how a religious tradition is transmitted from one generation to the next in a new cultural setting, and what happens to the tradition in the process of transmission. I probe how Buddhist immigrants influenced by collective Buddhist culture in Sri Lanka transmit their Buddhist tradition to the next generation in Toronto, which is defined by multiculturalism and influenced by an individualist cultural ethos, and I also examine how the successive generation growing up in multicultural Toronto receives the Buddhist tradition that is passed on to them. This is a story of intergenerational and intercultural transmission: the reception and reconfiguration of a living religious tradition comprised not only of abstract doctrines, attitudes, and practices but also followers who uphold and at times wrestle with its aspects. Cultural anthropologist Talal Asad (2003, 194) states: "to discover how these followers instantiate, repeat, alter, adapt, argue over, and diversify them (to trace their tradition) must surely be a major task." The dynamic interaction between religious practitioners and aspects of their religious tradition is historically situated, depending on time and space. This book documents what has been retained, altered, left out, and added to the Sri Lankan Buddhist tradition in Toronto's multicultural setting. Therefore, it is also a story of Toronto, and of Canada by extension, because the reconfigured Buddhism discussed in this book closely reflects Canada's signature feature, i.e., multiculturalism.

As I assess the ways in which first- and second-generation Buddhists in Toronto perceive, practice, and personify (embody) the Sri Lankan Buddhist tradition, I observe that dhamma education allows them to simultaneously reflect on and deflect from their religious tradition in Sri Lanka to redefine who they are and how they practice Buddhism. In that process, I contend, Buddhism emerges as an inclusive and harmonious religion for a Canadian-born generation reimagined as Sri Lankan Canadian Buddhists. Such reconfigured Buddhism and Buddhist identity do not necessarily make Buddhism Canadian;[6] they rather claim that Canada is home for Buddhists and Buddhism. In other words, Buddhism is no longer a foreign religion in Canada, and it is going to stay here for generations to come. This reconstructive claim demonstrates the sensibilities of Sri Lankan Buddhists in Toronto toward Canada's multiculturalism discourse and individualistic and egalitarian North American culture. Multicultural themes like harmony, inclusivity, mutual respect, and peaceful co-existence work at an abstract/philosophical level in reimagining what Buddhism and Buddhists should be in Toronto. But at a practical level, Buddhists engage in an intercultural negotiation that enables them to integrate cultural traits, attitudes, roles, and responsibilities from both collective Sinhalese culture and individualistic North

American culture. These philosophical (multicultural) and practical (intercultural) strategies transform and transmit Buddhism from the first generation to the next. The success of intergenerational and intercultural transmissions of Sri Lankan Buddhism in Toronto call into question a recent study (Beyer and Ramji 2013) that argues that Buddhists in Canada have failed to pass their religious tradition onto the generation born in Canada.

The preceding research findings remind us that a triangular dialogue plays out in dhamma education, as Sri Lankan Buddhists in Toronto wrestle with the contents of their religion in the context of Toronto's multicultural socio-political reality. Buddhism as an inclusive and harmonious religion emerges from that dialogue among living Buddhists, the foundational teachings of Buddhism, and the socio-political imperatives in Toronto. Sri Lankan Buddhists have reinterpreted Buddhism as inclusive and harmonious but they are conditioned, if not compelled, to do so by the Canadian multiculturalism policy. To maintain the integrity of Buddhism, they also had to buttress their reinterpretation with canonical references. As Asad (1993, 4) reminds us, "people are never only active agents and subjects in their own history." Socio-political and economic structures and systems hold "a mode of human agency ('real people doing real things'), one that conditions other people's lives" (6). Asad contends that adherents relate to their religious tradition according to the "discursive structures" of a particular time and space that condition the limitations and possibilities in people's lives (1986, 10). This means practitioners alone do not determine what a tradition looks like. The ambient socio-political system is also at work in shaping a tradition. Historical conditions like social and political economies shape how people exercise their agencies, i.e., motives, perspectives, behaviour, and utterances (Asad 1993). In other words, socio-political and economic systems stimulate practitioners to respond to the foundational teachings and practices in certain ways. They sometimes condition practitioners to perceive, practice, and personify (embody) their tradition in a particular manner. Thus what we witness in Toronto is a discursive formation of Buddhism; as such, it evokes Talal Asad's (1986) concept of "discursive tradition."

Talal Asad explains how and why a tradition becomes a *discursive tradition*. Drawing upon Alasdair MacIntyre's ([1981] 2007, 222) definition of "living tradition" as "an historically extended, socially embodied argument," Asad refers to tradition's emphasis on a particular past that had shaped its sense of moral tone expressed in practice(s). Practitioners discursively engage with the tradition, so that tradition's moral message, originating in a different place and time, makes sense at present. In the following definition Asad (1986, 14, emphasis in original) delineates not only what constitutes a tradition, but also what its functions are, and how and why it functions in a certain way: "A tradition consists essentially of discourses that seek to instruct practitioners regarding the correct form and purpose of a given practice that, precisely because it is established, has a history. These discourses conceptually relate to *a past* (when the practice was instituted, and from which the knowledge of its point and proper performance has been transmitted) and *a future* (how the point of that practice can best be secured in the short or long term, or why it should be modified or abandoned), through *a present* (how it is linked to other practices, institutions, and social conditions)." Asad highlights that tradition's discourses or a connected series of utterances embodied in a practice(s) stem from a particular past and orient toward an envisioned future through a vibrant present. Therefore Asad suggests that it is worth considering the social contexts of a religious tradition as "overlapping spaces and times," which reveal the converging nature of religion (1986, 11). I find this suggestion instructive, as religion in diaspora demonstrates – perhaps at an optimal level – that spaces and times do overlap. In fact, diasporic consciousness is often characterized as translocative (across locations) and transtemporal (across time) (Tweed 1997). We will see in this study that dhamma education in Toronto traverses Sri Lankan Buddhists across time to Sri Lanka and beyond. It enables Sri Lankan Buddhists to envision a new Sri Lankan Canadian identity and to redefine Buddhism congruous to that identity.

Newly emerged inclusive and harmonious Buddhism in Toronto prescribes Sri Lankan Canadian Buddhists to behave in a certain way. It also has left out certain discourses and practices associated with Buddhism in Sri Lanka. Its inclusion and exclusion are justified and rationalized with reference to the Pāli canon; and they demonstrate the moral tone of a discursive tradition. Asad suggests that the discourses – specifically those that relate to the founding principles of the tradition – instruct the faithful what the *right form and purpose* of a practice are. The faithful often debate what makes a practice "right" and what they should intend from the practice. That means getting it "right" in both practice and intention is important for a religious tradition. We will see that the "right" attributes like harmony and inclusivity are social constructions as much as they are Buddhist doctrinal norms. They discursively emerge from Buddhist textual references as well as from Toronto's multicultural context. The past of Buddhist tradition is appropriated in the present for an imagined Buddhist future identity: Sri Lankan Canadian Buddhists. This hermeneutic dance across times echoes Asad's following observation: "a discursive tradition ... connects variously with the formation of moral selves, the manipulation of populations (or resistance to it), and the production of appropriate knowledges" (1986, 7). Here, Asad refers to the cognitive, affective, and behavioural impacts a discursive tradition has on its practitioners. We will see that Sri Lankan Buddhism in Toronto cognitively defines Buddhist doctrines and peaceful co-existence as "appropriate" knowledge and practices, and it identifies with them. On the other hand, it distances itself from "inappropriate" ones like Sinhala Buddhist nationalism and spirit worship. It also generates emotions that motivate adherents to do certain things while resisting others. In other words, the inclusive and harmonious Buddhism in Toronto instructs how its practitioners should perceive, feel, and behave. The first- and second-generation Buddhists have engaged with those instructions variously.

To consider Sri Lankan Buddhists' dhamma education as a discursive practice required me to understand its historical circumstances that have enabled it to emerge, maintain, and/or transform across time and place. My aim has been to document Sri Lankan Buddhists' efforts to "achieve coherence" (Asad 1986, 17) as they strive to transmit Buddhism to a Canadian-born generation in Toronto. As such, I have employed historical, comparative, and ethnographical methods.[7] I locate the origin of dhamma education in late-nineteenth-century British Sri Lanka (Ceylon), and I discuss its different phases in twentieth-century Sri Lanka. I examine the Buddhist catechistic literature and discuss how various imaginations of the Buddhist child reflect the socio-political and cultural situations of the time. From a comparative approach, I discuss the similar and contrasting contents of dhamma education in Sri Lanka and in Toronto. I also highlight the similarities and differences in the ways in which the first- and second-generation Buddhists approach Buddhist beliefs and practices. In order to discern intergenerational dynamics and cross-cultural understanding, I conducted a comprehensive ethnographic research with four components: two separate surveys (one for each generation), observation of participation, focus group interviews, and in-depth audiotaped interviews. I realized that my decision to conduct the fieldwork as a doctoral student in Buddhist monastic robes itself illustrated the discursive nature of the Buddhist tradition. It generated the discussion about the role of monastics and what constitutes "proper" Buddhist studies. My position of power and intimacy vis-à-vis the tradition in question conditioned the situation, and required me to develop a distinct mode of being in the field.

BEING IN THE FIELD *AND* BEING THE FIELD

Initially, I started field research with participant observation; I observed the roles and deeds of others but also my own. My monastic and academic roles forced me to see my own inescapable religious role as a monk within the community. This shift from participant observation to observation of participation echoes J. Shawn Landres' (2002, 105, emphasis in original) argument that "the ethnographer *is* 'the field' – and quite literally. That is, ethnographers do not just *represent* and *define* 'the field'; they *become* it." In the following paragraphs, I discuss how I became the field while being in the field.

In the following section, I discuss how my decision to be in the field in the monastic robes of a Theravāda monk compelled me to negotiate and navigate two distinct roles and duties: those of an ethnographer and also of a Buddhist monk. In these negotiations and navigations, I myself gained a new identity as a monastic ethnographer. The ethnographic strategy that I used reflects Landres' (2002) phrase "Being (in) the field." The new identity and strategy in the field demonstrates a discursive relationship not only between the researcher and the researched, but also between two scholarly traditions (Buddhist monastic scholarship and ethnography) that I happened to represent.

Born in Bangladesh, at an early age I travelled to Sri Lanka where I studied Buddhism in the stream of textual studies up to the Master's level. In 2002, I joined the Lao as well as the Sri Lankan Buddhist communities in the Kitchener-Waterloo area to serve them as a monk while pursuing my higher education in the religious studies field. However, ethnically I belong neither to the Lao nor to the Sinhalese ethnicities. This privileged me to move across ethnic boundaries and observe ethno-religious dynamics in these Buddhist communities across southern Ontario. I have observed that Lao and

Sri Lankan Buddhists significantly differ from each other in their socialization of children into Buddhism, although both communities are Theravāda Buddhists. The former tends to employ only informal religious education (i.e., rituals, temporary ordination for various reasons, etc.) while the latter emphasizes formal (i.e., Sunday dhamma schools) along with informal religious education. These intergenerational transmission strategies result in distinguishable modes of being Buddhist among the second-generation Buddhists in these communities. Sri Lankan Canadian young Buddhists, in comparison to their Lao Canadian counterparts, feel more comfortable in discussing Buddhist doctrine and history. They are more articulate in distinguishing Buddhism from other religions. This outstanding difference between the Lao and Sri Lankan Buddhist youths inspired me to explore the transmission strategies and their outcomes within the Sri Lankan Buddhist community in Toronto.

Being a monk in the field has shaped a set of distinct relationships with each of the three groups I interviewed. Initially, I thought that I would be able to maintain a detached researcher position in the field simply because I was not an ethnic Sinhalese. My familiarity with Sinhalese culture and being fluent in Sinhala – the ethnic language of the research community – qualified me to embark on the ethnographic research. But ironically these same competencies challenged my ability to keep the classical arm's-length distance expected in the field. With the monks, I felt a binding, intimate, and warm monastic brotherhood, which made me feel like an extremely close insider. Prior to my fieldwork, I decided to guard myself against the common pitfall of an insider ethnographer: the tendency to ignore small yet significant details. Yet I found it relatively difficult to convince the monks to take my research seriously. Some monks were reluctant to be interviewed, not simply because it looked odd, but also because they assumed that I already knew everything about the community. When I approached the monks for formal interviews, I received comments like "you know all about it, and there is nothing new to explain to you."

With the first-generation Buddhists, I experienced a typical monk-devotee relationship with a sense of spiritual hierarchy and reservation. In the eyes of the Theravāda Buddhist laity, a monk is a field of merit, a religious guide/instructor, and an example of the Buddhist way of life. These normative roles preconditioned how the first-generation Buddhists perceived me. In their eyes, I remained first and foremost a monk in the field. Some research participants considered their contributions to the research as gestures of meritorious deeds. In addition to providing interviews, some also convinced others to participate in the research. In one specific case, a woman voluntarily arranged a group interview for me at her home. Yet, I also found that the ready participation of the first generation did not necessarily mean honest responses. I suspected that sometimes they exaggerated their religious commitments to avoid disappointing me, and some shared certain information cautiously. To reduce such distortions, I constantly reminded them to be honest. I emphasized that the value of their contribution to the research would depend on accurate responses. I even called up their normative religious commitment to speak nothing but truth! I insisted that they consider me a graduate student who was there not to judge them but to study their everyday religious life. These strategies served temporarily, and they were more effective in the context of the second generation.

My interaction with youth participants was a more or less typical researcher-researched relationship. I found it relatively easy to convince youths to give honest responses. Initially, many informants – specifically those who were persuaded by their parents – expressed uncertainty and bewilderment about the interviews. Assurance such as "I am here not to judge you," "the provided information will be confidential," and "your contribution to the research will depend on honest responses" noticeably eased them. These statements seemed to effectively shift the youths' perception of me from a monk to a graduate student. My impression was that the majority of second-generation Buddhists in the field perceived me as a graduate student who happened to be a monk. Not only were they honest, they were also outspoken – even critical – about some of their parents' religious practices and cultural habits. Perhaps their preconception of a monk was not as rigid as that of their parents. In fact many of them were university students, something that probably helped them to relate to me as a graduate student. Moreover, their North American cultural upbringing normalized the researcher-researched interaction. In some cases, I had to interview female interviewees in their parents' presence, yet even in such circumstances they shared honest responses, expressed unmediated opinions, and made critical observation and remarks about Buddhist beliefs and practices. Some admitted that they enjoyed being interviewed. Some of them also mentioned that they often felt their opinions about Buddhism were taken for granted and even unheard. For them, the interviews became the means to express their views and frustrations about some of the religious services they found boring and even irrelevant. They appreciated the chance to have their voices heard and even suggested a few recommendations in regard to religious services at the temples.

How I perceived myself is as important as how I was perceived by my sources. I could not hide my explicit monastic *and* academic identities – instead I had to reconcile them. Here I repeat J.K. Gibson-Graham's (1994, 219) assertion: "I am a unique ensemble of contradictory and shifting subjectivities." As a doctoral student who happened to conduct the field research, I called myself a "monastic ethnographer" because I simultaneously wore both hats and performed both roles. These distinct roles presupposed different, even opposing, expectations and duties. The Pāli Canon emphasizes that teaching/leading a Buddhist way of life is the primary monastic duty. For example, the *Singālōwāda Sutta*, a Pāli discourse in the Dīgha Nikāya (Walshe 1996, 468), instructs monks to do the following: to prevent laity from doing evil, to exhort laity to do good, to preach to laity what they have not heard, to correct laity when they are wrong, and to show laity the path to happiness and salvation. The decision of being in the field in monastic robes alone has challenged and disrupted the classical monk-lay relationship. My role as an ethnographer in the field reversed the presumed flow of information from monk to the laity. Rather than providing the information, I was seeking out information from the laity. At times, people in the Sri Lankan Buddhist community found this discourse shift disconcerting.

My identity as a monastic ethnographer derives from how I did what I had been expected to do in the field. Gillian Rose says that researcher, researched, and research evolve in a triangular relationship where they construct each other's identities. She further asserts that the researcher is positioned "by what she *uncertainly* performs" (1997, 316, emphasis added). As I navigated the uncharted terrain of researcher and monk, I stumbled and walked across the boundaries of monk and ethnographer. For example, I requested that the monastic leadership keep me free from the religious services at the temple until I had finished conducting interviews. The request sounded untraditional and I was reminded that it contradicted monastic propriety. I explained to the monks that my dual roles (being both monastic and ethnographer simultaneously) might compromise my ability to elicit honest responses from the laity. It was hard to sell this idea, and the leadership remained unconvinced. I agreed to join other monks only at the collective services such as chanting and alms giving where I could keep a low profile.

I insisted on abstaining from preaching duties; however, such negotiations did not last for long. In times of need, I was compelled to give dhamma talks. There was simply no way around it. I felt a moral obligation to meet the requests of the faithful Buddhists. In fact, my constant presence in the community has increased the expectations around my service to that community. On one specific occasion, I was assigned to give a talk without even being consulted beforehand. This was highly confounding; whereas I had intended to sit in on the service as an observer, now I was expected to give talks, functioning in a monastic capacity. The invitations came from the first generation to address the second generation. Rather than just giving a monologue sermon, I consulted the inviters (the parents) on what they wanted me talk about.[8] At the same time, prior to the talks, I also asked the second-generation audience about their opinions on the topics that the first generation wanted me to talk about. At the end, I not only performed a monastic job (teaching/preaching Buddhism), but also engaged in the academic job (learning about the parent-child interactions and the role of monks within the research community).

Similarly, my position of monastic ethnographer required me to describe, analyze, and explain not only what others did in the field but also what I did in the field. In other words, *I was in the field* and *I was the field*. This happened as I navigated the duties and negotiated the roles of the two positions that I simultaneously held. To give an example, a couple in their early fifties whom I had previously interviewed generously arranged for me to interview their daughter. When I arrived at their home for the interview, the father greeted me with a bow. He led me to a chair covered with a customary white cloth in the living room with another chair, a couch, and a footstool. As I sat, a young woman in her early twenties came and prostrated herself before me (symbolizing monk-lay spiritual hierarchy in Theravāda Buddhism) and sat on the carpet, leaning on the couch. Immediately concerned by this, I asked her to sit on the couch. Her father also insisted that she should sit on the couch, but, being modest, she refused the offer (generally Sri Lankan Buddhists hardly sit on chairs in the presence of monks).

Then I switched my seat so that I would not have to sit on the appointed (monastic!) chair. Gesturing toward the chair with white cloth, I said to the interviewee, "The chair with white cloth is for a monk; I am not here to play a preacher's role but a researcher's role. Please consider me a researcher. I am looking for honest responses. I am not here to judge you but to seek valuable information from you about your perspectives and practices related to Buddhism. The value of this research depends on the candid responses from informants like you" (interview notes, 2008). I also asked the interviewee if she would sit on the footstool to make it convenient for the interview, which she did. Such a spatial shift was symbolically powerful to highlight my researcher's role and to make the interviewee feel more relaxed and free to share her opinions with me. However, it did not stop the interviewee from considering me a monk as well. Several times during the interview, the young woman asked for my opinions on certain things. I let her know that I would be happy to answer her questions but only after the interview, as I did not want to muddy the waters by switching into my monastic mode during the interview and possibly influence her testimony. When the interview was done, I returned to the chair with the white cloth and offered answers to her questions. It was also her parents' wish that I would explain certain issues about which their daughter was curious.

The preceding fieldwork experience illustrates that ethnographic research techniques are improvised as much as they are pre-planned. I believe that improvisation in the field is not only required but also desirable to maintain rapport with the research subjects. After all, "ethnographic research, whatever it is, is a form of human relationship" (Brown 2001, 12). In this regard, my experience indicates that ethnographic research on religion is also a form of social and religious relationship, where roles are involved and navigated. Duties are assigned, and they are negotiated. These navigations and negotiations (in other words, improvisations) enabled me to overcome the impasse derived from opposing norms and assumptions related to my monastic and ethnographic positions. If I had indiscriminately yielded to the subjects' demands, there was a great likelihood that this would have undermined the integrity of the data. Yet, if I was too intent on being an ethnographer, I risked losing their co-operation, or worse, their goodwill. The paradox of my dual identity required me to come up with an innovative ethnographic strategy: *being in the field* and *being the field*. Although I, as an ethnographer,

orchestrated the strategy in the field, it was the research community's perceptions and expectations of me as a monk that significantly
shaped the experience confirming the ethnographic reality. Lisette
Josephides (1997, 32, emphasis in original) remarks "how [we] do
fieldwork ... really depends on the local people." She also suggests
"we have to construct our theories of how to do fieldwork *in the
field*." Like all research positions, my position as a monastic ethnographer entails pros and cons.

My monastic identity gave me privileged access to the research
community and created a sort of "halo effect" that made for easy
access to the information that I sought out. Healthy and trustworthy
human relations, as Karen McCarthy Brown (2001) argues, are the
bases for successful ethnographies. I benefited tremendously from
my personal connections with many of the community leaders,
and warm relations with the Sri Lankan Buddhist laity. The monks
graciously approved my research proposal with no reservations.
They provided every possible support: introducing me to potential
research participants, distributing surveys, arranging interviews at
the temple, and sharing research materials with me. This warm rapport eased the recruitment of interviewees and data collection from
non-monastic participants. The laity's respect for the monastic institution and my role within it secured the community's cooperation
and confidence.

Being a monk in the field also had a number of practical limitations. In terms of temple attendees, I have been relatively less successful in recruiting the youths who hardly ever come to the temple.
In this context, my monastic identity seemed to work against my
intention to capture a comprehensive picture of the community. I
also noticed that my robes had a penchant for stopping gossip in
its tracks. If I were a lay insider, I would probably have had better
access to more mundane chitchat that might have given me a more
realistic picture of the community. Leaving aside community politics
and ethnic tension in my research and concentrating on dhamma
education, I wonder how much relevant information I missed by not
having access to informal conversations behind the scenes.

Overall, I felt that my research topic appealed to Sri Lankan
Buddhists, and many participants thanked me for doing the research
on the topic of Buddhist education for laity. For example, a first-generation father applauded me, saying: "you are doing a service to us
and to Buddhism by doing the research on Buddhism and youths, and

you can write a book on Buddhism for youths afterwards." Notice that he emphasized a book on Buddhism *for* youths rather than a book *about* Buddhist youths. However, this book is rather *about* Buddhist youths (and others) and their relationship to Buddhism. It analyzes the Buddhist-Buddhism relationship rather than instructing others how to be better Buddhists. That may disappoint the parent who expected me to write a book from a normative perspective. The parent's expectation also constitutes an aspect of Buddhist studies.

For the majority of Buddhists, the term "Buddhist studies" exclusively refers to the study of Buddhist texts either from a critical and objective perspective and/or a perspective of normative truth claims. The *Pāli Tipitaka* constitutes the textual foundation of Theravāda Buddhism, and the study of them is highly revered. Sinhalese monasticism holds a good reputation for Buddhist textual studies (*Ganthadhura*) in the Theravāda Buddhist world. The role of monastic ethnographer within this paradigm of Buddhist studies is not only new but also less appreciated.

In fact, I observed that some participants indirectly questioned and even ridiculed and belittled it. Interestingly, negative responses derive from the critical ethnographic research on Buddhism in Sri Lanka. Those who knew about previous ethnographic studies of Buddhism shared with me their ambivalence about it, perhaps due to the critical and analytical nature of ethnography. The ethnographic study of Buddhism in Sri Lanka (Gombrich and Obeyesekere 1988) has revealed the syncretistic nature of Buddhism, namely how Buddhists believe in spirit religion and practice deity worship. This revelation has challenged the self-perception of Sinhalese Buddhists as being the practitioners, protectors, and defenders of the "original" Theravāda Buddhist canon. The ethnographic genre has also been critical about some highly cherished institutions, like Sinhalese monasticism and religious figures such as Anagarika Dharmapala (Seneviratne 1999; Tambiah 1992). Premakumara De Silva argues that the anthropology of "Sinhala Buddhism" perpetuates essentialist assumptions about "authentic Buddhism" and "continues to address the historical and essentialist questions of who are Buddhists and who are not" (De Silva 2006, 165). The judgmental tone of these types of ethnographies has made the genre unpopular among Sri Lankan Buddhists. Susantha Goonatilake, who analyzed the research of four ethnographers,[9] comments that "post-colonial anthropology appears worse than anything colonial anthropology wrought, and, in fact, worse than the colonial writings of the 19th and early 20th centuries on Sri Lanka" (Goonatilake 2001, xiii). Given this, it is not surprising that I found that some Sri Lankan Buddhists are suspicious of ethnography on Buddhism.

The suspicion and criticism about ethnography could have contributed to the lack of monastic interest in ethnography. The objectives of ethnography – the pursuit of truth, bringing silent voices to the fore, and empowering the powerless – also relate to those of textual studies. So what hinders monastic participation in ethnography is not the objectives of ethnographic studies but rather the ethnographic research method: seeking the information from the Buddhist laity. Research contributors are not inanimate but "interactive texts" (Rose 1997, 316) that respond with a sense of creativity. The direction of ethnography often depends on both the ethnographer as well as her research contributors. In this sense, the ethnographic quest to gain knowledge about Buddhist beliefs, practices, attitudes, and religious organizations from research respondents directly contradicts the monk's traditional role as the teacher of Buddhism. Within this context, being a monastic ethnographer is an anomaly.

However, I believe that what made it possible for me to embark on the current ethnography in monastic robes was the research topic itself – dhamma education – which is intimately connected to the traditional monastic role. In other words, I would not have received the same outpouring of support and cooperation from the research community if I had chosen to study a topic that is not traditionally related to monasticism.[10] Thus both my choice of research topic (dhamma education) and my research strategy (being in the field and being the field) themselves derive from the discursive relationships in the field. Both the researcher and the researched are fellow practitioners, and active agents in the field. In this way, the current research on Buddhist education conducted by a monastic ethnographer is itself the product of internal arguments of a discursive tradition. Therefore, it sounds familiar yet strange; it relates to the Buddhist tradition, yet it does not quite fit in the monastic scholarly tradition.

Perhaps what is more important is that my research method itself embodies what it aspires to explain: the internal arguments within a community that is culturally at a crossroads between collective and individualistic cultures. Like every other immigrant community in Canada, the Sri Lankan Buddhist community is also spatially at a crossroads where the "immigrant background" itself often implies shared loyalty between the country of origin (Sri Lanka) and the country of residence (Canada). Within these cultural and spatial crossroads, Sri Lankan Buddhism, like other immigrant religions, has helped Sri Lankan Buddhists to cope with and ultimately overcome the anxieties and uncertainties of being at conjunctures. More importantly, as this book will illustrate, Buddhism has enabled the Sri Lankan Buddhists to claim those cultural and spatial crossroads and make them home. In other words, Sri Lankan Buddhists in Toronto make Canada home by combining Buddhism with Canadian multiculturalism.

The jury is still out on whether or not my "unorthodox" research method has facilitated or captured the dialogue between Buddhism and multiculturalism. I leave the judgment of my method to the readers themselves; however, I can assure the readers that the method itself attempts to accord with the advice the Buddha gave to a monk: be like a bee that collects only honey without harming the flower, its colour, or its scent.[11] Yet I also recognize that my presence as a monastic ethnographer did undoubtedly have its own impact on the discursive traditions of the community and the people who were willing to work with me.

BOOK OVERVIEW

I observe that Sri Lankan Buddhists' transmission practices and hermeneutic strategies in Toronto have derived from their experience in the late nineteenth and early twentieth century reformation. They are, however, tested, reconfigured, and appropriated to suit the local multicultural, multireligious, and secularly oriented social setting in Toronto. The Sri Lankan Buddhists in Toronto are in dialogue not only with their Buddhist tradition but also with the social realities in Toronto as they transmit Buddhist knowledge, values, and understanding to the next generation. The transmission is both transtemporal (not just from one generation to the next but involving both) and translocative (not just from Sri Lanka to Toronto, but likewise drawing on both locations as well as others). Nevertheless, it is neither disruptive (as implied in binaries such as traditional vs modern Buddhism) nor lineal (as expressed in adjectives such as "traditional," "modern," and "global" Buddhism); instead, it is dialogical – as all discursive traditions are. *Seeding Buddhism with Multiculturalism* captures Sri Lankan Buddhism's discursive formation in Toronto along with its local imperatives and translocal histories.

The next chapter focuses on how Toronto's Sri Lankan Buddhist community has evolved from a handful of families in the 1960s with no religious institution to a religious community with four independently run Buddhist temples. I will discuss three main aspects of this evolution: (a) a transition from a national solidarity to an ethnic commonality, and then to a religious solidarity; (b) a diasporic consciousness rooted in Toronto but connected to Sri Lanka and Washington, DC; and (c) a religious institutional development in three stages – namely sharing, establishing, and multiplying Buddhist resources. I emphasize the importance of Buddhist temples in the diaspora, not only as a place to congregate and practice Buddhism but also to concretize Buddhist presence in multicultural and multireligious Toronto.

Chapter 3 highlights the importance of dhamma education as an institutional practice in Sri Lankan Buddhism. I introduce it as a tradition-defining practice because it intimately relates to the contents (what constitutes the tradition) and the purpose (formation of Buddhists) of the tradition. I analyze the intellectual and institutional history of dhamma education in colonial Ceylon, postcolonial Sri Lanka, and in the diasporic setting of Toronto. Across these times and places, Buddhist educators have discursively imagined and reimagined who a Buddhist child is, so that they are capable of overcoming contemporaneous challenges and remaining Buddhist. Imagining and reimagining are intimately connected with community formation (Anderson 1983); together they enable people to lay claim to a sense of belonging to a nation, place, and culture. The Sri Lankan Canadian identity expresses and embodies Sri Lankan Buddhists' claim to belong to multicultural Canada. In that process, the redefined Buddhism in Toronto distinguishes them from their predecessors, i.e., rhetorical and Sinhala Buddhists in colonial and postcolonial Sri Lanka respectively. A spiritual discourse nevertheless enabled Buddhist educators to achieve coherence across these historical periods.

Chapter 4 exemplifies how Canada's multiculturalism policy, law, social reality has affected an immigrant religious minority, redefining who they are and what their religion is. Sri Lankan Buddhists, particularly monks, have redefined Buddhism so that its messages of harmony and inclusivity come to the fore to echo Canada's multicultural policy and social reality. In this way such monks not only demonstrate Sri Lankan Buddhists' commitment to integration into the wider Canadian society, but also extend the Buddhist mission to the Canadian public. From that point of view, the redefined Buddhism represents a hermeneutic of adaptation and integration. On the other hand, it also streamlines an early twentieth-century modernist interpretation of Buddhism that purges spirit and god worship in Sinhala religiosity. Perhaps in part in order to conform to the popular image of Buddhism as a peaceful religion, and to counter Sri Lankan Tamils' accusations of ethno-religious violence, this inclusive and harmonious redefined Buddhism generally keeps its distance from the Sinhala-Buddhist rhetoric.

Chapter 5 documents parents' role as the primary transmitters of Buddhism in Toronto, who have negotiated Buddhism interculturally in order to transmit Buddhism to their Canadian-born children. The collective culture of the parent generation is discordant with the individualistic cultural attitudes and behaviours of the second generation. This has not only triggered intercultural criticism; it has also jeopardized intergenerational transmission of Buddhism. In this cultural impasse, many parents have conceptually separated Buddhism from Sinhala ethnicity and decided to pass on at least the religious aspects of Sri Lankan Buddhism, i.e., Pāli chanting, and Buddhist beliefs and rituals. As a result, Sinhalese ethnicity markers like Sinhala language, folk music, and dance are largely omitted from transmission practices. Moreover some parents have started to act like friends with their children in order to mitigate intergenerational cultural distance. This creative move, as parents explain, is necessitated by the lack of extended family in the diaspora.

Chapter 6 describes how the Canadian-born generation perceives and practices inherited Buddhism. Monks' multicultural interpretation and parents' intercultural negotiation have facilitated the intergenerational transmission of Buddhism; nevertheless, the second generation have become Buddhists in their own right. Their Buddhist religiosity is expressed along two opposing trends: less committed, exploratory, loosely identified, and developing Buddhists vs more committed, exclusive, and self-identified Buddhists. Buddhist youths who expressed both trends have to some extent embraced "Buddhism as a way of life," a phrase borrowed from their parent generation but used with a new cultural meaning. They display attributes of what Peter Beyer and his colleagues (2013) call "Religio-culturally based seekers" who are "contributing to the construction of systematic Buddhism in Canada." (220). They are the outcome of creative Buddhist transmission practices of Toronto's Sri Lankan Buddhists whose story is about to unfold in detail in this book, starting with their community formation.

2

Community Formation of Sri Lankan
Buddhists in Toronto

This chapter focuses on how Sri Lankan Buddhists in Toronto evolved from a small cluster of immigrant families with no temple to a stable religious community with four vibrant Buddhist centres. It discusses the history of Sri Lankan Buddhists in Toronto, including their arrival in Toronto, their interaction with others, their formation as a religious community, and the establishment of Sri Lankan Buddhist temples. Currently, four Buddhist centres serve roughly 3500 Sri Lankan Buddhist families in the greater Toronto area. Their membership also extends to some Sri Lankan Buddhists who live in other small cities in southern Ontario. All four temples serve the same Sri Lankan Buddhist community, although some of them extend their service to non-Sri Lankan individuals interested in Theravāda Buddhism. The two temples that are the foci of this study, the Toronto Mahāvihāra and the Mississauga West End Buddhist Temple and Meditation Centre, regularly accommodate the religious needs of Indian and Bangladeshi Buddhists respectively. This particular openness of Sri Lankan temples is also reflected in a smaller Sri Lankan Buddhist group in the Guelph, Cambridge, and Kitchener-Waterloo region that used to gather on a regular basis at a Laotian Buddhist temple in Kitchener, Ontario. The difference was that the Sri Lankan Buddhists at the Laotian temple used to receive religious services that were given or accommodated by the Laotian Buddhist community. The dynamics of sharing and receiving religious services at all three places – the Toronto Mahavihara, the West End Buddhist Temple and Meditation Centre, and the Phommaviharam Buddhist Temple in Kitchener – resemble the earliest stage of the formation of the Theravāda Buddhist community in diaspora.

key point

Buddhism among Sri Lankans in Toronto exemplifies the function of religion in community formation.

Referring to the role of religion in community formation, Raymond Brady Williams (1988, 278) argues that religions in diaspora become crucial in inter- and intra-religious formations of immigrants. In other words, religions often group and regroup immigrants of the same religion, and they also enable immigrants to form "new relationships" among themselves as well as with "other ethnic and religious groups." Buddhism has been the communal glue that groups and regroups the Buddhists from Sri Lanka in Toronto. Moreover, Buddhism has become a catalyst to reconstruct individual and group identity, and it continues to foster relations with others, including those who are not Sri Lankan yet are still interested in Buddhism. Buddhist centres are the hubs of Buddhist practices. Religious centres not only demonstrate the dynamics of a religious community but also indicate the organizational transformation of a religious tradition within a new location. I suggest that the history of Sri Lankan Buddhist temples in Toronto relates to a general pattern of community development among religious practitioners, particularly Theravāda Asian Buddhists, in resettlement. The pattern comprises three stages of institutional progression – namely sharing, establishing, and multiplying Buddhist resources. As a precursor to the argument, let me bring in a brief history of Sri Lankans' migration to Canada.

The following discussion of the Sri Lankan immigration to Canada, particularly to Ontario, refers to the socio-political situations in Sri Lanka and Canada that resulted in the emigration and immigration respectively. The data from the Canadian immigration statistics not only correlate with the incidents in Sri Lanka that drove people out of the country, but also help us understand the community dynamics that grouped and regrouped the Sri Lankan immigrants in Toronto. Following the migration history, the middle section of the chapter lays out three stages of Sri Lankan Buddhist community formation in Toronto. It highlights the growth of the community, the tension between cultural maintenance and accommodation, and the shift in religious needs as driving forces in community development. The final section of the chapter relates Sri Lankan Buddhists' activities in Toronto to the recent pre-migration history of Buddhism in Sri Lanka. Such transtemporal (across time) and translocative (across space) analysis would help us understand the impulses and reasons behind distinct adaptive and transmission mechanisms of Sri Lankan

Table 2.1
Early immigrants from Sri Lanka to Canada

Country of citizenship	Total	Ethnic origin
		117 Ceylonese [Sinhalese?]
		10 English
		29 East Indian [Tamil?]
Ceylon	180	5 The Netherlands
		5 Portuguese
		1 German
		1 Italian
		1 Syrian
		11 Others

Note: The Canadian immigration statistics are from the following website: http://epe.lac-bac.gc.ca/100/202/301/immigration_statistics-ef/index.html. Only data from 1966 to 1996 are available. I assume that the migration trend in 1996 continued afterwards as the pulling and pushing factors of Sri Lankan migration to Canada did not change that much, except with the 2009 military defeat of the LTTE. Even then the refugee flow did not stop. In October 2009 and August 2010, two ships arrived in Vancouver with hundreds of Tamil refugee claimants from Sri Lanka.
Source: Citizenship and Immigration Statistics

Buddhists in Toronto. In other words, Buddhism in the diaspora diversely reflects the pre-migration experiences of Buddhist communities (McLellan 1999, 2008). Therefore, a historical explanation is warranted to explain why a particular Buddhist community differs from other fellow Buddhist communities.

SRI LANKAN BUDDHISTS' MIGRATION TO CANADA

For a variety of reasons, Sri Lankans (then Ceylonese) started to migrate to Canada in 1948 (Chadrasekhar 1986, 22; Boisvert 2005, 74). Their migration to Canada has been intimately connected to the events in both countries. Sri Lankans coming to Canada fall into three categories – namely students, immigrants, and refugees. In the early 1950s, there were a few students on Commonwealth scholarships at Canadian universities. Many of them eventually settled in Canada, a pattern of migration that still exists now.

The 1956 religio-cultural revival in postcolonial Sri Lanka eventually introduced Sinhala as the official language. This prompted many of the English-educated Sri Lankans to leave the country. During this time, Sri Lanka also experienced a rapid growth in population, urbanization, and internal migration. Travelling abroad to learn about and explore foreign countries also became popular to improve social status, specifically for those with money and an English education. European countries were popular destinations for many, and only 180 Sri Lankans were in Canada before the 1967 liberalization of Canadian immigration. A majority (138 or 77 per cent) of them were in Ontario, a trend that likewise continues to this day. The 1966 Canadian immigration statistics categorise them according to their ethnic background:

Not only does the above ethnic composition demonstrate the diverse ethnicities of Ceylon's citizenship, but the use of "Ceylonese" to refer to a particular ethnicity – apparently the Sinhalese – is also interesting in light of the Tamils' accusation that postcolonial Ceylon was only for the Sinhalese. In addition, the ethnic designations also indicate the complexities and confusion between national versus ethnic identities (i.e., Tamils as East Indian with Ceylon citizenship) in the formation of the modern state. Although ethnicity later played a huge role (as a selection criterion) in the Sri Lankan migration to Canada, the immigration statistics ceased to designate immigrants according to their ethnic affiliation as Canada adopted a racially neutral immigration policy in 1967.

As a part of the 1967 merit-based Canadian immigration policy, the Canadian government marketed the future prospects of Canada especially to young people in Sri Lanka. In English newspapers in Sri Lanka, "Canada was portrayed as a 'land of opportunity' that welcomed the increasing number of underemployed or unemployed but educated Sri Lankan youth" (Abrahams and Steven 1990, 31). Thus the introduction of Sinhala as the official language in 1958 and Canada's liberalization of immigration policy in 1967 encouraged English-speaking Sri Lankans to migrate to Canada. In the next seventeen years (1967–83), Sri Lankans in Canada experienced a moderate but significant growth in number every year. Although many of the migrants came directly from Sri Lanka, it is noticeable that nearly a quarter of them came to Canada as twice migrants via other countries, including Britain. Sixty-five per cent of total Sri Lankan immigrants settled in Ontario. Given that education, professional skills, and proficiency in English and/or French were the criteria for acceptance, Sri Lankan immigrants up until 1983 were more or less homogenous in terms of a social class – a Western-educated, English speaking, and urbanized population. This social homogeneity hindered religious and ethnic divergence and fostered a common Ceylonese or Sri Lankan identity.

A secularly oriented common alliance of interest, solidarity, and tradition tied the first wave of people from Ceylon together in Toronto. These pioneers founded the "Ceylonese Recreational Club" in 1968, with secular events such as cricket and cultural dances. For these families the "basement was the pivotal place for community get-to-gather ... they called them 'basement parties'" (Chandrasekere 2008, 217). The basement parties reflected closely knit communal belonging. As Ceylon became Sri Lanka in 1972, the club was renamed as the "Canada Sri Lanka Association of Toronto." It maintained a secular cultural focus with an emphasis on promoting a common Sri Lankan Canadian identity through summer camping, cricket and tennis matches, and annual Sinhala-Hindu New Year celebrations (Chandrasekere 2008, 217). Early Sri Lankans often got together on the basis of new Canadian experience and shared Sri Lankan heritage. Their English education back in Sri Lanka, a colonial legacy, mitigated the growing Tamil-Sinhala language politics in postcolonial Sri Lanka. The introduction of multiculturalism in the 1970s in Ontario also set the secular cultural tone of the association, which allowed it to foster a sense of community among the ethnically diverse (Burgher, Sinhalese, and Tamil) and religiously diverse (Christian, Buddhist, and Hindu) immigrants from Sri Lanka.

However, this sense of Sri Lankan community in Toronto was increasingly compromised as the Sinhalese-Tamil tension accelerated

Table 2.2

Classification of post-1983 immigrants from Sri Lanka to Canada

Years	Refugee	Independent	Family/ assisted relatives	Other	To Canada	To Ontario (approx. %)
1985–88	1,193	4,122	3,870	18	9,203	5,386 (58.5%)
1989–92	13,602	1,675	9,666	47	24,990	19,952 (80%)
1993–96	14,499	1,190	15,055	107	30,851	26,193 (85%)
Total	29,294	6,987	28,591	172	65,044	51,531 (80%)

Source: Citizenship and Immigration Statistics

in Sri Lanka. The 1983 ethnic riot led many Tamil-speaking Sri Lankans to flee Sri Lanka and take refuge in India as well as various Western countries, including Canada. The Canada immigration statistics report that in 1984 alone, 1,086 Sri Lankans (immigrants and refugee claimants) came to Canada. This four-digit increase of Sri Lankan migrants to Canada continued annually and even multiplied in the subsequent years. Since 1985, immigrants have been classified according to the types of visa granted to them.

With this wave of mass migration, the social homogeneity – the elite class unit – was undermined, and diverse social strata were added to the Sri Lankan population in Toronto. The "independent" and "other" categories added new dimensions to the existing social elite class. The huge influxes of refugees and so-called family/assisted relatives have outnumbered the elite class. They came from traditional villages, and they were less fluent in English and less familiar with an urban life-style. This was the case particularly with the refugees, who were predominantly Tamil. Tamil refugees were quite different from the earlier Tamil immigrants. These social differences (based on education, lifestyle, and language), Chandrasekere observes (2008, 223), created a communication gap between the Tamil old-timers and Tamil newcomers. This gap was wider particularly between

Sinhalese immigrants and Tamil refugees, because the latter's harsh experience in Sri Lanka made them suspicious of the Sinhalese in Toronto. As such, they sought out separate Tamil organizations to help them integrate into Canadian society and to support Tamils in Sri Lanka. In subsequent periods, numerous Tamil organizations have come into being with cultural, religious, and political orientations.[1] As Tamil organizations grew, the earliest Sri Lankan association – the Canada Sri Lanka Association of Toronto – suffered from the lack of Tamil participation and membership.

Stories of the Tamil exodus have to some extent overshadowed the migration stories of the Sinhalese diaspora. Economic hardship and political uncertainties in postcolonial Sri Lanka sent many Sinhalese to Canada. Sri Lanka experienced two civil unrests: the Sinhala-Tamil ethnic tension and youth unrest influenced by communist ideologies. Interestingly, both are linked to the 1958 official language policy. The policy made Tamils suspicious about the political power of the Sinhalese majority, which eventually perpetuated a civil war. On the other hand, the policy was also a "Pandora's box" with unrealistic promises and prospects of modern success. The universalization of education from the primary level to university graduation, along with making Sinhala the language of instruction, raised "peasant ambitions for white-collar and professional jobs for their children through education" (Gombrich and Obeyesekere 1988, 10). The number of candidates waiting for university education sharply increased. To accommodate them, the state introduced a number of new universities in the 1960s. Unfortunately, the university programs did not match the social and economic needs of the time.

Consequently, many of the university graduates were unemployed and frustrated with the political system, and they were directly and indirectly associated with the 1971 and 1989 youth unrest led by the Janatha Vimukthi Peramuna (JVP), a revolutionary youth movement influenced by Marxist ideologies. The 1990 *Report of the Presidential Commission on Youth* blames the quality of university education for the youth unrest. Commenting on this particular issue, Bruce Matthews (1995, 84) suggests that "the expected benefits of university education in Sri Lanka do not often appear to be realized in terms of employment." Matthews also thinks that university education in Sri Lanka has been underfunded, a factor to be blamed for so-called "brain drain," (91) which refers to the migration of educated people to other countries for better lives and career opportunities.

Echoing these factors, many respondents of the current study identified the political crises in Sri Lanka, as well as the educational and economic opportunities in Canada, as the decisive factors in their migration. The Sinhala-Tamil ethnic conflict (since 1983) and the clash between the Sri Lankan government and the JVP during 1987–90 adversely affected the quality of life in Sri Lanka. In the latter crisis alone, nearly 35,000 mainly Sinhalese youths and men went missing (De Alwis 2009, 380). Following the Tamil exodus, many Sinhalese left Sri Lanka for personal security and better opportunities. Some of them ended up being in Toronto as "refugee claimants" (Chandrasekere 2008, 228). The 1971 Canadian multicultural policy, which eventually became a law in 1988, attracted many Sri Lankans to consider Canada as their migration destination. In addition, their family ties and friendships with earlier Sri Lankan migrants to Canada prompted them to resettle in Toronto. With the later wave of migration, a mild class tension between newcomers and old-timers emerged, which eventually shaped the formation of the community.

Most Sinhalese in Toronto are immigrants. The majority of them met minimum requirements of education, language proficiency, and professional credentials to migrate to Canada as skilled workers. They represent a highly educated immigrant group with college (21.5 per cent), university (32 per cent), and graduate (32 per cent) degrees. Prior to migration, they lived in major Sri Lankan cities like Colombo, Kandy, Galle, and Matara. These personal qualifications and background factors smoothed their acculturation into Canadian society. The resulting sense of community provided further psychological and social supports for Sinhalese immigrants to succeed in resettlement.

The term community implies a common alliance of interest, solidarity, and tradition (Williams 1988, 10). It is through community organizations and institutions that the common alliances of interests, solidarity, and tradition flourish and manifest. Communal institutions and people's affiliation to them are the concrete symbols that ground the presence of a community. From that perspective, social (religious and non-religious) institutions are significant landmarks in the process of community formation. At the same time, they also reflect a set of community dynamics such as leadership, membership, and politics. Therefore, the following section discusses the formation of the Sri Lankan Buddhist community in Toronto with an emphasis on three stages of Buddhist institution development: sharing, establishing, and multiplying Buddhist resources. Bankston and Hidalgo

(2008, 70) argue that temples in diaspora provide "moral and social order" to adherents that [enable] them to conceptualize their relations to other individual adherents and to their national groups." This discussion on the Buddhist institutions captures the Toronto-based Sri Lankan Buddhists' emphasis on religion (Buddhism). It delineates how Buddhism has enabled Buddhists from Sri Lanka to differentiate themselves from other Buddhists as well as other Sri Lankans. Their self-identification as "Sri Lankan Buddhists" rather than "Sinhalese Buddhists" helps them to claim their Sri Lankan identity overshadowed by the bigger presence of Sri Lankan Tamils in Toronto. In the following section, the term "Buddhist resources" refers to anything that is essential to form a vibrant Buddhist community – including monks, temples, Buddhist artefacts, and sufficient religious membership.

SHARING BUDDHIST RESOURCES

During the 1960s and 1970s, Buddhism in Canada and the USA received unprecedented public attention due to the counter-cultural movement. Buddhism, specifically Zen, was presented in alignment with counter-cultural values such as "individualism, spontaneity, and intuition" (Seager 2002, 110). Zen *roshis*, Tibetan *lamas*, and Theravāda *bhikkhus* routinely travelled across major cities in North America. They related Buddhism to personal experience and non-violence, two particular counter-cultural themes of the time. Their audience primarily derived from the Euro-American cultural background. On the other hand, Asian Buddhist communities also increased. Tibetan refugees (since 1972) and Vietnamese, Laotian, and Cambodian refugees in the late 1970s settled in many metropolitan cities in North America, where they formed their own ethnic communities (McLellan 1999). Within this religio-cultural setting, early Sri Lankan Buddhists began forming their religious community.

Early Sri Lankan Buddhist immigrants in Toronto relied on fellow Buddhists to meet their religious needs. In the early 1970s, there were a good number of Sri Lankan Buddhists in Toronto and Montreal. They occasionally visited Chinese temples in the neighbourhood, but being Theravāda Buddhists, they found the Mahāyāna services in the Chinese language incomprehensible (Chandrasekere 2008, 226). In the Theravāda Buddhist tradition, monks are considered to be "the field of merit" (*punnakkhetta*), figures who play irreplaceable roles in merit-making rituals – a set of common practices for Buddhists. By the mid-1970s, Sri Lankan Buddhists in Toronto performed merit-making rituals with visiting monks from Sri Lanka and Washington, DC. Alloy Perera, a research respondent who came to Canada in the late 1960s, revealed that he performed *dāna* (feeding the monks) and *pirith* rituals (listening to the Pāli chanting for blessings) led by Piyadassi Thera. The latter visited Toronto and Montreal upon invitations from Vietnamese Buddhists.[2]

More importantly Buddhist aspirations and supports came from the Sri Lankan Buddhists in Washington. The relatively short distance between Toronto and Washington enabled Sri Lankan Buddhists from both cities to share resources. The Washington Buddhist Vihara established in 1966 by Sri Lankan Buddhists was the first ever Theravāda Buddhist temple in North America (Numrich 1996, xxi). Monks from Washington occasionally visited Toronto Buddhists and encouraged them to establish a Buddhist temple, a symbol of a strong Buddhist community. Dickwela Piyananda Thera, then the head of the Washington Buddhist Vihara, stated: "since 1974 we have had the great aspiration of establishing a Theravāda Buddhist Vihara in Toronto" (*Toronto Buddhist*, May 1979, 2). This aspiration was materialized by a group of eight Sri Lankan Buddhists led by Dickwela Piyananda Thera. They formed the Toronto Mahāvihāra Society, which eventually purchased a building that was consecrated as the Toronto Mahāvihāra in 1978.

The early formation of a Sri Lankan Buddhist community in Toronto underlines the "triadic relationship" that contributes to the social formation of a diasporic community. Steven Vertovec (2000, 144) theorizes that a diasporic community evolves within a web of social connections that link three distinct places: the country of current residence, the country of origin, and other countries where co-ethnic groups live. As noted earlier, the Sinhala-Tamil ethnic tension in Sri Lanka disrupted the Sinhala-Tamil unity among the early immigrants from Sri Lanka. This development signifies the effects of the country of origin in shaping the community dynamics among diasporic communities. Meanwhile, the emergence of the Toronto Sri Lankan Buddhist community with support from the co-religionists in Washington highlights the ties between co-ethnic communities that are globally dispersed. These triadic connections between Toronto, Sri Lanka, and Washington have continued to shape and foster how Buddhism is perceived and practiced in Toronto.

This initial phase of community formation could be identified as *sharing Buddhist resources.* Sri Lankan Buddhist immigrants were pioneers in the formation of a joined Buddhist organization (the Toronto Buddhist Federation) and shared Buddhist events like Vesak, the celebration of life of the Buddha (McLellan 1999, 31; Hori and McLellan 2010, 381; Shiu 2010, 94). They also shared religious/spiritual capital, like the monks with their counterparts in Washington. Sri Lankan Buddhist immigrants also occasionally shared the nearest Buddhist temples – in this case the Chinese temples in Toronto. Similar patterns took place in Ottawa. In 1981, *Toronto Buddhist* reported "the Sri Lankan Buddhists in Ottawa now have a shrine room in the premises of the Vietnamese Buddhist temple in that city and they participate in regular weekly religious observances" (*Toronto Buddhist*, May 1981, 3).

The sharing of Buddhist temple space and monks relates to an important contemporary phenomenon within the Theravāda Buddhist communities across North America (Bankston and Hindalgo 2008, 6; McLellan 2009, 91). That is, Asian Theravāda Buddhists congregate at the nearest temple as long as it caters to their sectarian form of Theravāda Buddhist practices. This particular phenomenon is quite noticeable with Sri Lankan Buddhists in southern Ontario at the time of this research (2006–11). Sri Lankan Buddhists not only share their temples with other Theravāda Buddhists of differing ethnic backgrounds, but they also used to congregate at other Theravāda temples as long as they cater to the Sri Lankan form of Buddhism.

Sharing Buddhist temples resembles Paul Numrich's (1996, 63) theorization of "parallel congregations"; the phrase, however, obscures as much as it explains. Numrich's phrase effectively explains the co-existence of two or more religious groups under the same roof who prefer two distinct religious services. The phrase however obscures the unparalleled power sharing at a sacred place, specifically where two or more ethnic groups congregate. For example, Indian and Bangladeshi Buddhists receive Buddhist services from the Toronto Mahāvihāra and the West End Buddhist Temple and Meditation Centre respectively; however, they do not hold any position on the temples' board of directors. Similarly, Sri Lankan Buddhists living in Guelph, Cambridge, and Kitchener-Waterloo used to congregate at the Laotian Buddhist Temples in Kitchener and Cambridge, but they too were excluded from the decision-making body of the temple.

In each of these cases, temple leaderships offer Buddhist services in respective ethnic forms by accommodating monks who are ethnically different from themselves. In fact, it is the presence of co-ethnic monks that attract Theravāda Buddhists to the temples that are established by different ethnic groups. The respective Sri Lankan temples in Toronto accommodate monks of Indian and Bangladeshi origin. Similarly, the Laotian temple in Kitchener sponsored a monk who is familiar with the Sri Lankan Buddhist culture. These cases exemplify how the religious services are made parallel, but this is not reflected in the human agency and institutional power sharing. In the cases of decision-making, the dynamics between the ethnic community of those who established the temple and that of the others who joined the temple often resemble a majority-minority relationship. A member of such minority community expressed: "We always feel that we are foreigners there [at the temple]. We feel that we are not wanted there, and we are not part of them. At every big function, we are participating and we are fortunate to contribute to the temple, but they [the people in power] do not acknowledge our contributions. I think it is not a good manner" (personal interview, 2008). In fact, it is this sense of marginalization that often intensifies the need for "our own temple," and it pushes an ethnic community to move from this pace of community formation, i.e., sharing religious resources, to the next phase when a separate sacred place is established.

The transition from sharing religious resources to establishing a sacred place is often determined by community membership. Williams (1988, 41) argues that the "size and length of residence" often dictate "the shape of the religious groups." In discussing Hindu immigrants, Williams states that within a smaller community, religious orientation is more "ecumenical." As the community gets larger, it tends to "splinter into regional and sectarian groups" (47). He also observes that in the early stage of resettlement, the immigrants are concerned about the economic and social stability of individual families, but as they live longer within the same region they tend to focus on the infrastructural establishment of the community, such as building religious institutions and programs related to the transmission of tradition to the future generation. I would add that as the community dwells longer and grows stronger in a particular location its expectations of the existing institution become more complex and diverse. I will discuss the implication and impact of this particular development later in this chapter.

The transition from sharing religious resources to establishing a sacred place derives from the increase in membership. Such a move could also be motivated by a desire to gain better and particular recognition and representation in multicultural Toronto (McLellan 2006, 100), where places of worship as cultural centres symbolize the tangible and concrete presence of the community. However, the move depends on "the degrees of types of social capital in a given group" (McLellan and White 2005, 237). It also requires greater economic commitment, as religious followers move from being inconsistent members to committed members. This particular shift has a greater influence on the formation and transformation of Buddhist communities in diaspora. It is the gradual increase of Sri Lankan Buddhists that enabled them to establish the Toronto Mahāvihāra.

ESTABLISHING THE TORONTO MAHĀVIHĀRA

The Toronto Mahāvihāra, inaugurated on 16 July 1978, was the first Theravāda Buddhist temple in Canada. The name "Mahāvihāra" itself symbolically invokes the introduction of the Theravāda tradition to a new location, for it refers to the first Buddhist monastery founded by the Arahat Mahinda who introduced Buddhism to Sri Lanka in the third century BCE. This invocation suggests another historic religious transmission to a new land. Dikwela Piyananda Thero, the founding abbot of the temple, wished "May the Toronto Mahavihara be able to serve Canada in the same noble way the Anuradhapura Mahavihara ... served Sri Lanka" (*Toronto Buddhist*, May 1979, 3).

The abbot's historical reference is symbolic of the introduction of Buddhism to the West, as it differs from the pattern of the introduction of Buddhism to many Asian countries including Sri Lanka. Arahat Mahinda Thero preached Buddhism first to the king of ancient Sri Lanka – King Devanampiyatissa – and his royal families and then his subjects. Similarly, Buddhism was introduced first to the elite of the royal court in China. In contrast, "Buddhist teachings and practices [in the West]" argue that Baumann and Prebish "have not been introduced from the top down, but commenced their diffusion from below, often championed by economically disadvantaged people" (2002, 3). Here, Baumann and Prebish's unspecified reference to Buddhists in the West as "economically disadvantaged people" is debatable.[3] However, they refer to an important feature of

Figure 2.1   A bird's-eye view of Canada's first Theravāda Buddhist temple –
the Toronto Mahāvihāra
Note: Located at 4698 Kingston Road, Scarborough, Ontario.
Source: Mr Ranuka Prabhashitha

Western Buddhism: people's initiatives and collective administrative
power at the Buddhist institutions in the West, which is known as
congregational polity. This initiative and administrative power from
below – plural and democratic – often determines the formation of
a Buddhist community, as expressed through establishing Buddhist
temples in North America.

In establishing temples, Buddhist leaders confront a set of economic, bureaucratic, and communal hurdles. Buddhist temples in
diaspora do not have the financial security that their counterparts
enjoy in traditional Buddhist countries. Unlike many Buddhist temples in Sri Lanka, temples in diaspora do not own property and
rarely receive state funds.[4] Instead, they depend on membership and
public donations. This has changed the Buddhist traditional practice
of dāna (voluntary contribution). Now many Sri Lankan temples in
North America rely on their pledged membership fees, which are
tax exempt. Dāna relates to sporadic and spontaneous generosity of

the faithful, where pledged membership is also voluntary but more carefully calculated.

Unlike dāna, membership fees are more predictable and reliable. To some extent, stable memberships are systematized to establish Buddhist temples, and a certain number of members are required to secure a mortgage from a financial institution to build temples. This practice further compels Buddhist organizations to change family membership to individual membership in order to meet the required membership goals. From the very beginning, the Toronto Mahāvihāra has reached out to Buddhists and non-Buddhists alike. The founders assured that the temple is open to "all sects of Buddhism and friends of Buddhism without any discrimination of colour, creed or nationality" (*Toronto Buddhist*, May 1979, 2–3). This openness derives from the inclusive nature of Buddha's teachings at the philosophical level, but it also closely ties to the Buddhist mission and its search for financial support for the costly maintenance of Buddhist temples (*Toronto Buddhist*, August 1986, 2).

Bureaucratic requirements often hinder the process of establishing a temple. According to zoning restrictions prescribed by the respective municipal authority, a place of worship is a public place that is allowed in industrial or commercial zones. A Theravāda Buddhist temple is not simply a place of worship; instead, it is also, as the Pāli term "*vihāra*" suggests, a dwelling place for monks. Traditionally, monastic residence and shrine are located on the same premise. To meet both traditional and municipal zoning restrictions, temples can only be built at an area that is residential as well as commercial. Such sites are not that common in municipal zoning.

Traditionally, temple and village are intimately connected, a reflection of the symbiotic monk-lay relationship. Monks rely on the lay community for material support, while lay people consult monastics for spiritual guidance. Many temples in Theravāda countries are located within walking distance of villages, so that monks can go seeking alms on daily basis, although this practice is rarely seen in contemporary Sri Lanka. In diaspora, it has nearly become a pattern for a temple to begin in a residential area where many of its members reside, before it moves to a more permanent location. Temples in residential areas often receive complaints from neighbours due to community gatherings, specifically during weekends. In rare cases, tensions with neighbours have resulted in legal battles (White 2006; McLellan and White 2005).

Both of the temples in this study – the Toronto Mahāvihāra and
the West End Buddhist Temple and Meditation Centre – were at
smaller locations before they moved to their current facilities. For
example, in December 2011, the West End Buddhist Temple and
Meditation Centre relocated from 1569 Cormack Crescent to 3133
Cawthra Road, Mississauga, to accommodate its growing congregation. Moreover, the locations of temples are also determined by the
residence of congregation members, who often move due to change
of jobs or children's schools. Overcoming these economic, bureaucratic, and communal hurdles, Sri Lankan Buddhists continue to
establish temples in Toronto. Temples in Toronto are not only smaller
than their counterparts in Sri Lanka, but they also lack the outdoor
atmosphere of a typical Buddhist temple in Sri Lanka. Interviewees
often nostalgically pointed out that they missed the sand floor and
soothing breeze under the *Bodhi* tree, and the sight of relic-bearing
white *stupas* – two of three salient components of a Buddhist temple
in Sri Lanka. The third component, a shrine room/hall, is now the
focal point of Buddhist temples in diaspora.

In 1978, the Toronto Mahāvihāra was started as the first Theravāda
temple in Canada. It was the only Sri Lankan temple in Toronto
until the end of 1992, when a split within the community led to
the establishment of the second Sri Lankan temple in Toronto, the
West End Buddhist Temple and Meditation Centre. Within the community, many believe that the split was caused by a disagreement
between monastic and lay leaders about the issue of overseeing the
administration of the Toronto Mahāvihāra. Chandrasekere implies
that a class tension between old-timers and newcomers caused the
split (2008, 229). In fact, the split derived from multiple causes. In
addition to the preceding causes, I argue that the 1992 split erupted
from a tension between the needs of maintenance versus accommodation of Buddhist tradition that prevailed from the very beginning
of the community formation.

From its inception, the Toronto Mahāvihāra aspired to serve three
groups: Sri Lankan expatriates, Buddhist sympathizers of Caucasian
origin and other Buddhists, specifically Theravādins with diverse
ethnic backgrounds. As the Mahāvihāra was the first public centre
related to the people from Sri Lanka, it also received support from
many Sinhalese Christians in Toronto who felt ethnic ties to the temple that they lacked within the mainstream Christian congregations
in which they participated (Chandrasekere 2008, 226). Reflecting

the common Sri Lankan ties fostered at the temple, a member of the temple's board of directors recalled that the temple had served as the "cultural centre for Sri Lankans of diverse ethnic and religious backgrounds in this adopted land" (*Toronto Buddhist*, August 1986, 10). For specifically Sri Lankan Buddhists, the Toronto Mahāvihāra conducted Buddhist rituals and festivals as they did in Sri Lanka. The rhetorical stance of openness to "all sects of Buddhism and friends of Buddhism" was often not reflected in the actual Buddhist services at the Toronto Mahāvihāra, simply because – as Williams rightly points out – "people are not 'religious-in-general,' but 'religious-in-particular'" (1988, 280).

Furthermore, some of the statements in *Toronto Buddhist*, the newsletter of Toronto Mahāvihāra, indicate a growing tension between Sri Lankan Buddhists and non-Sri Lankan Buddhists throughout the 1980s. The Toronto Mahāvihāra actively reached out to Buddhist enthusiasts. One of its pamphlets, "Mahavihara School of Buddhist Studies," declared: "We are happy to announce that the Toronto Mahavihara Society which was hitherto catering mainly to Sri Lankan Buddhist population, has opened a school of Buddhist studies, in order to extend its services even to the non-Buddhist Canadian public." It further listed twelve courses on various topics related to Buddhism.

Two of the courses were "Buddhism in Sri Lanka" and "Buddhism for Westerners."[5] One can discern a cultural tension built in the descriptions of these courses themselves. The description of "Buddhism for Westerners" says "Those who are interested in learning to really live the Buddhist life in its pristine purity, avoiding the cultural trappings that come with it, will profit greatly from this course." On the other hand, the details of "Buddhism in Sri Lanka" describes "Those who do not wish to study Buddhism as a dead theory, as a withdrawal from life or as an escape into a trance, but as a way of living, and solving problems in life would find this course very enlightening." The details of both courses provide contrasting views of what Sri Lankan Buddhism is. On the one hand, it suggests that the way Buddhism is practiced by Sri Lankan Buddhists, specifically their cultural aspects, compromises the "pristine purity" of Buddhism. On the other hand, it appreciates Sri Lankan traditions as an example of the vibrant aspects of Buddhism that address problems in life. The descriptions also demonstrate the mutual perceptions of Caucasian Buddhists and Asian Buddhists, in this case

Sri Lankan Buddhists. They could also be read as an indication of growing cultural tensions at the Toronto Mahāvihāra, which was catering to what Numrich calls "parallel congregations" (1996, 63).

Since 1981 and onwards, the Sri Lankan Buddhist community in Toronto experienced a heightened commitment to Sinhalese Buddhist culture. Reflecting this trend, *Toronto Buddhist* dedicated its editorial to "The identity crisis and the role of the Vihara" (May 1981, 3). It observed that "Sri Lankans are making steady progress towards establishing their identity as a distinct ethnic group in the country's multicultural milieu." The editorial related this trend to the psychological needs of children within the community and argued that the temple could play both roles, as a place of worship and also the "cultural haven" for the community. It likewise suggested that the temple could become a centre for socio-cultural activities so that the community could find "a truer identity." These observations and suggestions confirm that as children enter into the scene the community tends to become more culture-oriented to transmit its cultural identity to the future generation.

The aforementioned enthusiasm for Sinhalese Buddhist culture apparently tempered the temple's initial commitment to and aspiration for inclusive membership. A statement entitled "Thinking ... aloud" by the secretary of the Toronto Mahavihara reminded Sri Lankan Buddhists that: "We cannot impose our cultural values, our rules, or the generally accepted norms of our community on those from a different cultural background ... We are bound to have persons brought up in the Judeo-Christian tradition stepping into the Sri Lankan Buddhist world that exists within the temple ... we must not attempt to prejudge these friends in the Dhamma and say things that may hurt the feelings of others on mere conjecture" (*Toronto Buddhist*, May 1986, 10). The mid-1980s was the peak moment for the Toronto Mahāvihāra in terms of reaching out and offering Buddhist services to its three types of audience identified earlier. The above plea from the temple's authority hints that there was a growing cultural uneasiness between Sri Lankan Buddhists and non-Sri Lankan, specifically Westerner, Buddhists. This particular tension might have derived simply from assumed temple etiquettes within the Sri Lankan Buddhist tradition. However, the editor of the subsequent issues of the newsletter pointed out a related concern, namely the tension between cultural maintenance vs cultural adaptation. He suggested: "The Sri Lankan Buddhist, or any ethnic Buddhist for that matter, if he is really interested in propagating the Dhamma in the West, should be prepared to accept this [cultural] change ... If Buddhism is to be established in the West, it has to be able to survive within the Western cultural environment through adaptation. Adaptation is a basic and necessary principle for survival, even in the biological sphere. So it is in the psychological, sociological and religious sphere" (*Toronto Buddhist*, August 1986, 2). The debate on cultural adaptation and transformation in the context of the Sri Lankan Buddhist tradition closely ties to the lives of monks.

Since the 1960s, Buddhist monks in Sri Lanka have been a compelling theme for social scientists in search of Buddhist identity and change in the modern Sri Lankan context. Ananda Wickremaratne contends that these works more often than not conceptualize contemporary monasticism in relation to the dichotomy between "tradition and modernization." He asserts, instead, that the issue relates to a different sort of dichotomy: "It rests on a clash between two views. The lay view of what the Sangha ought to be and must necessarily be in terms of role fulfillment and the Sangha's own perception of their role and their relations with the laity" (1995, 262). These views derive from individual as well as collective (and therefore cultural) experience, and they certainly get diversified even further when more than one ethnic community shares the same place.

In the context of "parallel congregations," it is the monks who go in between the groups and play the role of cultural brokers. Bhante Punnaji was the head monk of the Toronto Mahāvihāra during the 1980s and early 1990s. He is highly respected in the community but is also known to be, as one respondent put it, "a non-conventional monk ... in his erudition, analysis and explanation." This particular characteristic made Bhante Punnaji popular among Buddhist enthusiasts from Western backgrounds, but it also attracted criticism from "conservative" lay Buddhists who wanted the monks to be, in the words of a respondent, "the paragon of virtues" (interview notes 2008).

The general reference to the need for cultural adaptation increasingly became more specific in *Toronto Buddhist*. For example, the 1992 Vesak (May) volume of the newsletter published "Sangha in the West ... Adaptation and Change: How Far Can One Go?," a speech made by the well-known Sri Lankan scholar monk Walpola Rahula at the London Buddhist Vihara England in 1974. In it, Rahula Thero generally argues that monks are paramount for the establishment of Buddhism in the West. For the survival of monks in the West, he contends:

We must understand and face the reality that *bhikkhus* living in the West cannot follow the way of life as practiced in Buddhist countries in Asia. Certain changes and modifications should be made to suit the social and economic conditions in the West, and this is quite in keeping with the tradition of Buddhist history ... Certain practices will have to be abandoned, such as the observance of *vassa* retreat which has no relevance and no sense in the West. In the Buddhist monasteries in Asia there are lay attendants to look after the needs of monks. In the West conditions are quite different. The Buddhist monk himself has to go buying provisions in the market. So he has to handle money. To go about in a market in [a] yellow robe is no respect for the robe, and it is an exotic, strange sight simply attracting the curious attention of the people. On such occasions, and also in ordinary travelling, there is nothing wrong if bhikkhus wear ordinary civil clothes, according to the custom in the West. (*Toronto Buddhist*, May 1992, 10)

Adaptation

A research respondent recalled that this particular article stirred up the community. Some people found the contents of the article to be controversial, and they expressed that adoption of such changes may eventually endanger Theravāda Buddhist identity. Nevertheless, Bhante Punnaji previously shared views very similar to those expressed in Rahula Thero's address (see Sugunasiri 2008, 101).[6] He said that such modifications would face serious objections not necessarily from the monastic authority in Sri Lanka but rather from Sri Lankan Buddhists in Toronto. In 1984–85, he predicted, "they might threaten to ... withdraw support" (Sugunasiri 2008, 101).

At the Toronto Mahāvihāra committee meeting in the end of 1992, the tension between cultural maintenance and accommodation became out of control. The lay authority of the temple took the side of cultural maintenance, resulting in the monks (including the head monk) leaving the temple. Such a voluntary or forced departure of monks is not that uncommon in the diasporic context (Numrich 2004), but it is unheard of in Sri Lanka because unlike their counterparts in diaspora (head) monks in Sri Lanka enjoy the unchallenged legal authority of the residing temples.[7] The board of directors or trustees owns the legal authority of the temples in

Toronto, with monks sharing a smaller percentage of it. In response to such abuse of lay authority over monks, some Sri Lankan monks in California reasserted monastic authority by occupying major positions (i.e., president, secretary, and director) in the board of directors, introducing bylaws preventing lay members from evicting monks (Quli 2010, 228) and holding temple deeds exclusively under monks' names (Quli 2010, 245). Within a few days of the monks leaving the Toronto Mahāvihāra, a handful of "liberal" lay Buddhists flocked together with the monks and formed another Buddhist society, which eventually established the second Buddhist temple, at the western edge of the Greater Toronto Area, known as the "West End Buddhist Centre."

Based on a similar split within the Sinhalese Buddhist community in Los Angeles in 1980, David Numrich (2004, 306–7) identifies "three key areas of tension:" *nikāya* (monastic fraternity) rivalry related to the home country, leadership struggle between "pioneers" and "newcomers," and lay-monastic disagreement over the institutional authority of Buddhist temples. In fact, it is the third of Numrich's points, namely the lay-monastic tension about maintenance and accommodation of the Buddhist tradition, which caused the split in Toronto. Janet McLellan also observes similar splits within the Vietnamese Buddhist community (1999, 114). The split was further rationalized by the growth in the number of Sri Lankan Buddhists. Mississauga was strategically chosen for the new temple; as a new suburb, it attracted many residents. During the early 1990s, many Sinhalese newcomers and old-timers alike moved to Mississauga. They were motivated primarily by better job opportunities but their move was also trigged by the increase of Tamil population in Scarborough.

The monks who left the Toronto Mahāvihāra in 1992 subsequently defined their approach to the Buddhist tradition in Toronto as "intelligent adaptation" (for a detailed discussion of this term, see chapter 3). The term, among other things, refers to equal sharing of institutional authority between monks and laity, and providing Buddhist services conducive to a contemporary cultural setting. Both means allowed the West End Buddhist Temple and Meditation Centre to establish its institutional identity as distinguished from the Toronto Mahāvihāra. The institutional authority of the West End Buddhist Temple and Meditation Centre rests with a board of trustees comprised of two monks and two laypersons. Numrich

(2004, 313) identifies two models of temple polity: "congregational" vs "episcopal." The former emphasizes lay control, while the latter highlights monastic authority in the management of the temple. The West End Buddhist Temple and Meditation Centre's board of trustees is a combination of the two models of temple polity that includes two monks and two laypersons. This arrangement allows the resident monks to adjust how they conduct Buddhist services for the community.

For a decade or so after the split, operating vehicles and an involvement in social service have distinguished monks associated with the West End Buddhist Temple and Meditation Centre from their counterparts at the Toronto Mahāvihāra. From the very beginning, the former has been offering social services, such as soup kitchens for the homeless, cultural entertaining for senior citizens at the surrounding senior homes, and assisting new immigrants in finding new apartments and jobs. The head monk is well known within the community for his sincere commitment in driving people to and from the airport and accommodating new immigrants at the temple's annexed building (when the temple was at Cormack Crescent Mississauga). The motto of the temple has been "where friendships begin and never end." With this added social dimension, the West End Buddhist Temple and Meditation Centre developed a distinct institutional identity during its formative years. Currently there is nothing except how the institutional authority is shared to distinguish the two temples from one another. All the temple services are more or less the same, and the antagonism followed by the split has since dissipated. Both temples share resources, including monks and lay membership. This reconciliation begs the question whether the split or branching off of another temple from the existing one should be conceptualized as a "schism" at all.

David Numrich (2004, 312) defines the term "schism" as referring to the "factions within a religious body [that] disagree and eventually divide over sacred understandings or practices." He describes the branching out of one Sri Lankan temple from another in Los Angeles as schism in both interpretations and practices, two leading characteristics of the term. For example, Numrich says that the schism invoked "Theravāda Buddhist texts, tenets, and traditions" (307) and a "different model of temple polity" (313). At the same time, he recalls that in Buddhism "schism" often refers to the divisions of Buddhists triggered on the basis of certain practices rather than upon Buddhist dogmatic standpoints. I argue that even this limited meaning of the term "schism" in the Theravāda context often refers to *vinaya karmas*,[8] the ecclesiastical procedures segregated along the lines of Buddhist fraternity – nikāya. The criteria upon which Numrich justifies the use of "schism" are rather what Ananda Abeysekara calls "particular shifting debates" (2002, 80) or "contingent conjunctures of debates" (107) with "their own agendas, their own stakes, and their own programs" (93). Therefore, they are not schismatic of sacred understandings or practices. As noticed earlier, the initial antagonism in Toronto gradually reconciled, and distinguishing factors faded away within a few years of the split. The split resulted in an active Buddhist institution; in that sense, the split itself is rather a "healthy" sign of a growing immigrant community that often multiplies Buddhist religious economies.

MULTIPLYING BUDDHIST RESOURCES

Religious economy, according to Rodney Stark and Roger Finke (2000, 35), refers to "all of the religious activity going on in any society." They justify the use of the term "economy" in the context of religion because religious systems reflect components of secular market economy. They argue that "religious economies consist of a market of current and potential followers (demand), a set of organizations (suppliers) seeking to serve that market, and the religious doctrines and practices (products) offered by the various organizations" (Stark and Finke 2000, 36). All of the foregoing components of Buddhist religious economies within the Sri Lankan Buddhist community in Toronto have been multiplied after a certain period of time.

The Toronto Mahāvihāra was established in 1978; after fourteen years, in 1992, the West End Buddhist Temple and Meditation Centre branched out. After a few relocations, it finally found its permanent home in December 2011 at 3133 Cowthra Road, Mississauga.

Once again after fourteen years, in 2006, two more new temples branched out from the preceding temples. They are the Mahameunawa in Markham and the Buddhist Mission Centre in Brampton. The former is a part of a new Buddhist movement started in Sri Lanka in 1999, which has more than forty centres in Sri Lanka and abroad, including the United States, England, Germany, Australia, and India (Mahamewna Asapuwa). It concentrates on meditation and emphasizes the realization of Buddhist spiritual

Figure 2.2   The West End Buddhist Temple and Meditation Centre, Mississauga
Source: The West End Buddhist Temple and Meditation Centre

achievement in this life. The Brampton Buddhist Mission Centre focuses on social and education services in Sri Lanka, to differentiate itself from other Sri Lankan temples in Toronto (*Living Buddhism*).

My survey data indicate that both generations of Sri Lankan Buddhists have developed a heightened interest in meditation and social service. The latest two temples in the community highlight those two aspects, and they cater to Sri Lankan Buddhists. The fourteen-year cycle is perhaps not a pattern, as such, but it illustrates the ramifications of unmet needs in a growing community. The cycle indicates an approximate period at which the temple leadership may need to revise the services and objectives of temples to address the evolving needs of a congregation. While the latter two temples are not part of this study, many of my research respondents look at these ramifications as "community responses" to the growth of the community, which implies greater demand for Buddhist services.

A set of merit-making rituals (*pinkam*) forms the centre of the religious lives of Theravāda Buddhists. All the rituals done in contemporary Sri Lanka are also done in Toronto, but at a smaller scale and in slightly different forms. Here, I focus only on communal rituals in which monks and lay people participate together. They could be further arranged according to their frequency or how often they are performed. *Dānapinkam*, feeding the monks, is performed on a daily basis, and is in fact the medium of symbiotic relationships between monks and lay people. Monks rely on lay people for material well-being, while lay people depend on monks to maintain spiritual guidance and aspiration. Interestingly, both parties consider the ritual to be a moral practice, and they participate in it with a sense of religious duty. A Sri Lankan monk in Toronto says: "The laymen who provide the meals are not just doing it as a kind of duty or something ... It is a part of their religious practice and they gain merit by offering food to monk[s]. And the monks accepting that food and eating the food is also part of the service" (Sugunasiri 2008, 97). In fact, there are three aspects to this practice: *buddhapūja* (offering to the Buddha), *sanghapūja* (offering to monks), and *pindima* (sharing the merits). Through the first two, the donors accumulate *pin* (merit), and in the last part, the merit is shared with deceased relatives as well as deities. Here, the monks also share their blessings with the donors.

The ritual of feeding monks has two categories that are themselves closely tied to temple membership. *Salāka dāna* refers to the monthly commitment of a family to feed the resident monks on one day of every month. This frequently takes place on weekdays, as weekends are booked for the second type of the ritual, *sānghika dāna* – feeding a group of monks (traditionally at least four) – that is often arranged at the donor's home and dedicated to specific reasons, such as marking the death anniversary of a relative, a birthday celebration, a housewarming, etc. The ritual in both forms has gone through some adaptations in Toronto. In contrast to Sri Lanka, donors cannot offer salāka dāna in the morning as they go to work. Instead, they come to the temple with food on the eve of their assigned day. For sānghika dāna, monks often drive to the donor's home. This is in contrast to what happens in Sri Lanka, where monks are given rides to and from the donor's home. Some weekends, more than one such ritual need to be performed, and in such cases, monks are divided and the ritual is done with insufficient monks. Within the community, it is a privilege to be a donor of salāka dāna, a practice often enjoyed by the founding members of the particular temple. It symbolizes a significant commitment, which makes the donor a member of the inner circle of temple membership.

The introduction of a new temple opens up new opportunities for a greater commitment. Sānghika dāna is open to anyone, even to members of peripheral communities such as Bangladeshi and Indian Buddhists who loosely associate with the Sri Lankan temples in Toronto. The volume of invitations for sānghika dana on weekends or public holidays is high, and one has to book the date months in advance. The invitation is accepted on the basis of first come first served; however, if the assigned donors of salāka dāna on weekends want to change their salāka dāna into sānghika dāna, they are given preferences.

In addition to dānapinkam (food offerings), monks are also invited for evening pirith (protective) chanting, for which people come to the temple or monks go to a devotee's home. In Toronto, whole-night pirith, a common communal ritual in Sri Lanka, is rarely done due to the lack of monks. The chanting is done to invoke blessing for a variety of individuals, including expectant mothers and their unborn children, the sick, birthday celebrators, and those who are about to undertake special tasks such as overseas travelling, new jobs, examinations, or newly married life. Marriage is a civil cere-mony, and, as in Sri Lanka, monks in Toronto hardly participate in actual wedding ceremonies and never officiate marriages.[9] However, in Toronto the bride and bridegroom more often come to the temple prior to or after marriage ceremonies. This trend is perhaps due to religion's role in weddings within the mainstream religious culture, as well as the increasing number of inter-religious marriages that are taking place among the children of Buddhist immigrants. As the community grows, more funeral services are being conducted, even for loved ones who pass away in Sri Lanka.

There are sets of weekly, monthly, and yearly programs that take place in all temples. Dhamma school for children is quite popular (the next chapter will discuss dhamma education in detail). Seniors within the community often look forward to the monthly higher precept observation, which is known as *poya* service within the com-munity. In Sri Lanka, every full-moon day is a public holiday, and Buddhists, specifically elderly people, spend the whole day at the temple engaging in various religious activities: listening to sermons, meditation, chanting, etc. In Toronto, all temples arrange the service on weekends closer to the actual full-moon day of the lunar calen-dar. Some people participate in more than one such program, indi-cating multiple memberships. Two specific poya services, *Vesak* and *Poson*, hold more significance within the community. Vesak marks the birth, enlightenment, and *parinibbāna* (experience of the final *nibbāna* or the passing away of the Buddha), while Poson marks the official introduction of Buddhism to Sri Lanka. These programs attract people of all ages, and they include more activities than other poya services.

New Year celebrations on the first of January and the thirteenth of April (the Sinhalese New Year) are annual programs centred at the temples. The former, being a public secular holiday, attracts more people to the temples to receive blessings for the New Year. The annual *kathina* ceremony in October marks the end of the Buddhist rain retreat, vassa (July–September), and it is a time of offering robes and other gifts to the resident monks. It is a time of spiritual joy expressed in a public procession. In Sri Lanka, the kathina robe is taken around the village, but here in Toronto it is ceremoniously taken around the temple.

The above-mentioned Buddhist services are common features of Sri Lankan Buddhism. When temples are multiplied, the availability of monks – service providers – in Toronto is also increased. Given the symbiotic monk-lay relationship, the religious commitments of both parties are intensified. However, the incoming resources – donations of all forms – are more or less shared or divided between the temples and monks, as the Toronto-based Sri Lankan Buddhist community remains the central service receivers. The multiplication of temples has prompted a sense of greater commitment, creativity, and even competitiveness between the temples to better serve the Buddhist community.[10] To do so often becomes a question of survival, as temples in Toronto completely rely on lay membership for their economic security.

The West End Buddhist Temple and Meditation Centre has been quite proactive and innovative in serving the community. During weekdays, it welcomes individual groups such as school children and professionals (teachers and nurses), who come to the temple to be informed on Buddhist teachings and meditation technique. People from multiethnic backgrounds come individually or with family members for counselling and spiritual advice. Upon invitation, monks may go to schools and universities to give talks on Buddhism. The annual "back to school *pūjas*" (two separate events for school and university students) are held to bless students for the new academic year, illustrating the innovative ways that the first generation can engage the second generation in the Buddhist tradition. The temple also holds a few educational programs, such as introduction to Pāli, *Sutta* classes, and meditation practice. In fact, this innovative approach was also undertaken at the Toronto Mahāvihāra during the 1980s under some of the monks who are currently residing at the West End Buddhist Temple and Meditation

Centre. With these services, the latter seems to have a greater membership with multiple ethnicities.

The Mahameunawa – one of the latest Buddhist institutions to multiply Buddhist resources – highlights contemplative orientations, which has been identified as the most inspiring issue within the community. The survey conducted for this study indicates that 96 per cent of the first-generation Sri Lankan Buddhists are interested in meditation. Some people stated that most of the time when they attend either the Toronto Mahāvihāra or the West End Buddhist Centre it does not feel much different than being at social gatherings. If this is so, the recent introduction of new temples could be understood as attempts to meet the needs that were left unmet. This also indicates that as the community grows, its religious and spiritual needs also become diverse. For example, elderly people are not overtly interested in certain programs that are designed for young families with children. Similarly, rigorous contemplative practices do not attract young parents, as they cannot leave their children behind.

What is noticeable, though, is a heightened interest in contemplative practices across all ages, i.e., youth, middle age, and the elderly. Two particular reasons could be identified behind this trend. First, the widespread public perception of Buddhism in the West that prioritizes meditation at the cost of other Buddhist practices such as rituals, interpersonal duties and, more importantly, voluntary commitment toward the betterment of a particular community, i.e., serving as a member of temple's board of directors, teaching Buddhism at the temple's dhamma school, or volunteering at the local temple. The second, and perhaps more convincing, reason for the trend is a cultural one. I suggest that the culture of individualism favours contemplative practices, which embody individualistic expression of religiosity. The increased interests in contemplative practices in Toronto have added a new temple to the community, which represents the forest-dwelling monasticism of the Theravāda Buddhist tradition.

Currently, many Sri Lankan Buddhists hold membership in more than one temple in Toronto. They go to one temple for a better dhamma education for their children; they attend another temple for intensive meditation practices; and the same people contribute to social welfare programs organized by the third temple. At the same time, many invite monks from more than one temple for Sānghika dāna in their homes. Individuals' multiple memberships indicate an important factor in the formation of Sri Lankan Buddhist communities in Toronto: voluntary membership is the initiative and sustaining power of a religious community. As it is the main source of income, Buddhist temples are more obliged than ever before to meet the needs of individual members.

Membership is unreliable not simply because it is voluntary but also because it is closely tied to individual preference. As personal interests change, so do the voluntary memberships. Personal interests are also plural. The challenge for a Buddhist temple in the diaspora is to keep up with the changing and plural interests of its members. It cannot satisfy everyone, which prompts branching out. Being one of many temples eager to serve the same community, each Buddhist temple then tends to choose a specific concentration or specialization, while still providing other basic needs. Specialization helps not only to particularize or differentiate between temples, but also to remain relevant to the community, which guarantees a shared membership. Multiple memberships also indicate the presence of multiple dimensions of Sri Lankan Buddhism in Toronto.

NOTICEABLE SHIFTS IN SRI LANKAN BUDDHISM IN TORONTO

George Bond (1988, 2004) identifies multiple Buddhist responses to modernity in twentieth century Sri Lanka. He, influenced by Robert Bellah, analyzes and categorizes these responses as reformed vs neotraditional Buddhism. These varying interpretations in Sri Lankan Buddhism, Bond argues, derive from two distinct yet overlapping sources, or what he calls the "actual or effective canon." He argues that "the Chronicles [*Mahāvamsa* and *Dīpawamsa*] constituted the effective canon of neotraditional Buddhism and the Pāli Canon has been the canon for Buddhists who have taken a reformist perspective" (2004, 238). Neotraditionalists regard "the Chronicles as the extension of the [Pāli] Canon and Commentaries" (238) while reformists "chose to follow the Pāli Canon in its 'pure' form, that is, without taking it in the context of the commentarial tradition or having mediated by monastic tradition" (246–7). Sinhalese Buddhist interpretations of these two types of canons are influenced but not determined by Western scholars' impressions and interpretations of the Buddhist canons during the mid-nineteenth century. On the one hand, neotraditionalists concentrate on the "imagined" past of the Chronicles, and they have constructed

Sinhalese Buddhist nationalism, which, according to Bond, "contributed to the ethnic conflict" (236). On the other hand, reformers seek to apply Pāli Buddhism in the present and future, and offer "the hope of calming ethnic tensions" (236). They highlight *Vipassana* (insight) meditation, Buddhism-science dialogue, and Buddhism for social development.

Sri Lankan Buddhists in Toronto inherit both neotraditional and reformist interpretations and related practices. However, it is the reformist interpretation and practices that are prevalent. Sri Lankan Buddhism in diaspora, specifically in Toronto, does not have a conducive enough socio-political environment to fully manifest its neotraditional wing. For example, the neotraditional rhetoric of symbiotic relations between Theravāda Buddhism, Sri Lanka, Sinhala people, and language does not enjoy the socio-political clout in Toronto that it enjoys elsewhere. Instead, the reformist rhetoric of Buddhism being a "scientific" religion, and its emphasis on spiritual salvation through individual contemplative practices, are quite admired by Buddhist enthusiasts in the West. Sri Lankan Buddhist temples in Toronto overtly promote the reformist interpretations. With that agenda they not only suppress the neotraditional sentiment of Sinhala Buddhist nationalism, but also withhold certain religious practices deemed as "non-Buddhist."

Anthropological studies on religion in Ceylon/Sri Lankan (Obeyesekere 1963, 1984; Ames 1964; Evers 1968; Winslow 1984) highlight the syncretic nature of the Sinhalese religiosity. Gananath Obeyesekere and Richard Gombrich (1988) theorize that Sinhala religion, the religious tradition of the Sinhalese people, is comprised of Theravāda Buddhism, which promises otherworldly salvation, and spirit religion, which addresses the worldly concerns of the people. Describing the co-existence, or rather the syncretism of these two in Sinhala religion, they say: "When one does something virtuous (*pina*), such as feeding monks, one invites the gods to empathize in the merit ... The idea – which goes as far back as the Pāli Canon – is that in gratitude to the doer for calling their attention to his good deed the local deities will protect and help him. This is the main doctrinal link between Buddhism and the spirit religion" (18). The above-mentioned doctrinal link between Buddhism and spirit religion eventually took a concrete form. Institutional forms of spirit religion, i.e., shrine (*devale*), priest of deities (*kapurala*), and rituals (*devapūja*), were accommodated within the premises of many

Buddhist temples in Sri Lanka. The deity shrines (devale), a popular point of devotion, are typically situated on either one or both sides of the Buddha's shrine in many of the Buddhist temples in Sri Lanka.

Unlike most of the temples in Sri Lanka, the temples in Toronto do not facilitate spirit religion, except in sharing merit with the deities and ancestors, a practice that itself is considered Buddhist due to canonical recommendation. In fact, sharing merit (*pindīma*) is one of ten meritorious deeds prescribed for a Buddhist way of life. The data show that the majority of the Buddhist practitioners (70 per cent) do not expect the temples to accommodate deity worship (devapūja). They believe that it has nothing to do with Buddhism. The absence of the spirit religious practices at the temples under study could be understood as a reformed practice adjudicated by a textual interpretation.

The absence of devapūja in the temple service does not necessarily mean that Sri Lankan Buddhists do not participate in or perform the ritual. Twenty-nine per cent of the research respondents somewhat agree that deity worship is a part of Buddhism, and 23 per cent believe that Hindu gods like Vishnu and Kataragama can, in fact, intervene in their everyday lives. A few of the first generation respondents revealed that on their visits to Sri Lanka they go to Kataragama, a popular destination for divine favours, even as they worship the Buddhist sites in Anuradhapura and Kandy. Moreover, in my field research I have been informed that those who felt the need for divine intervention in everyday life have sought out Hindu temples in Toronto, as well as St Joseph's Oratory in Montreal. It is obvious that Hindu deity-oriented religious impulses are still alive among the Sri Lankan Buddhists in Toronto. As Buddhist institutions do not endorse them, Sri Lankan Buddhists seek out above mentioned non-Buddhist institutions to express and channel those impulses.

CONCLUSION

I started this chapter with a brief description of the migration history of Sri Lankans to Canada, specifically to Ontario. Their migration patterns contributed to the formation and evolution of the Sri Lankan community in Toronto, from a secular association to ethnic orientation, and then to religious institutions. Then I have discussed three phases of the community formation of the Sri Lankan Buddhists in Toronto, along the lines of the origin and development of

Buddhist temples – the communal sacred place. A sense of community is not necessarily preconditioned by a specific place; nevertheless, a sacred place like a temple is a concrete symbol of the multiple resources that go into the formation of a religious community, i.e., commonly shared tradition, human resources, and a sense of commitment. The evolution of the temple closely reflects how Sri Lankan Buddhists in Toronto have evolved for the last half century.

Each phase, i.e., sharing, establishing, and multiplying Buddhist resources, is comprised of two evolving positions. Sharing Buddhist resources relates to the co-existence of two or more ethnic religious groups, or what Numrich (1996, 63) calls "parallel congregations." Unlike "parallel congregations," however, the term "sharing Buddhist resources" implies non-parallel or disproportionate human agencies involved within the co-existence of religious groups. Non-parallel human agencies are often expressed with an identification of majority and minority, or founding and joining groups. The founding group becomes the *sharers* and the joining group becomes the *receivers* of what is being shared, including temple facilities, monks, and services. From the receivers' standpoint, this becomes an evolving phase of community formation. However, I name this phase as sharing rather than receiving because the receivers are not totally free riders – they are, rather, non-parallel or unequal contributors. Two positions expressed in the second phase are the temporary and more stable establishment. Both temples in this study demonstrate that they underwent the process of location and relocation. The third phase is also comprised of two positions expressed in institutional relation: antagonism and reconciliation. The West End Buddhist Temple and Meditation Centre's branching out from the Toronto Mahavihara in 1992 resulted in uneasiness between two temples, but underlying forces were not schismatic enough to keep the two temples apart. As I discussed above, the branching out rather multiplied Buddhist resources; as such, I name it the phase of multiplication.

All three phases are closely tied to three forms of memberships: peripheral, central, and multiple. As a group joining an existing religious community, Sri Lankan Buddhists in Toronto prior to 1978 were rather peripheral members to Mahāyāna Buddhist temples. Similarly, the contemporary Indian Buddhists at the Toronto Mahāvihāra, and the Bangladeshi Buddhists at the West End Buddhist Temple and Meditation Centre only peripherally participate in the services provided by the respective founding communities. As long as the joining group remains smaller, and, more importantly, if the temple leadership creatively meets their religious needs, the impulses or momentum for establishing a new ethnic temple remain elusive. In the contemporary cases of sharing Buddhist resources, the founding communities accommodate monks who can effectively serve the joining groups. Despite such creative leadership, the members of the joining group complain that their contributions are neither acknowledged nor do they feel like they belong to the temple community. Such complaints of the joining groups allude to the lack of administrative power sharing across ethnic boundaries. It suggests that co-ethnic bonds and trust remain triumphant over lofty Buddhist teachings with universal messages. Imbalanced power relations, as well as the growth of joining groups, often lead to the next phase of community formation: establishing new institutions. Within such development, the founding groups not only lose their wider membership base but also shrink the mission field. Perhaps to prevent such economic and mission loss, two Sri Lankan Buddhist groups shared administrative power of their temples with joining non-Sri Lankan Buddhist groups (Quli 2010, 213). In such power-sharing circumstances or in the establishing phase, the peripheral members become decision makers who make greater commitments toward the establishment and maintenance of the temple.

With further growth of co-ethnic groups, new dividing impulses – such as new leadership or new orientations – start to emerge. The cultural adaptation expressed in the monk's role emerged as a diverging point. The emergence, in 1992, of a new temple where the monks and the laity shared equal power has minimized the disruption of monastic legal authority within the congregational polity in diaspora. Such institutional development refers to the third phase: the multiplication of religious resources. Temples, monks, and services are multiplied. Where more than one temple serves the same ethnic community, temples tend to develop a specific concentration in particular services, such as dhamma education, contemplative practices, and social services, in addition to the common basic services it provides. Such moves allow individual temples to distinguish themselves from other competitors and remain relevant to the community. This multiplies individual memberships, as people go to more than one temple for "better" services.

Complete reliance on membership itself distinguishes Buddhism in diaspora from its counterpart in Sri Lanka. In diaspora, temples exclusively depend on donations from its members, and monks have to share institutional power with the lay community. Both temples in this study indicate two systems of temple polity. The Toronto Mahāvihāra is congregational, where lay people exercise greater power in temple administration. The West End Buddhist Centre has managed to share the power between monks and laity equally. Both, however, differ from the temple polity in Sri Lanka that resonates with the episcopal system, where monks hold the sole legal authority. In relation to Sri Lanka, another noticeable difference is that Buddhism in Toronto overwhelmingly represents a reformist interpretation. This trend has not only marginalized neotraditional Buddhism but also suppressed the spirit religion of the Sinhalese religious system. The marginalization and suppression of those aspects of Sri Lankan Buddhism are quite explicit in the Sunday dhamma schools and dhamma education discussed in the next chapter.

3

Dhamma Education and the Historical Construction of Buddhist Identities

In Sri Lankan Buddhism, dhamma education primarily refers to the formal teaching of Buddhism to young people, and it is an integral service of Sri Lankan Buddhist temples in Sri Lanka as well as in diaspora. This chapter explores three historically situated impulses that inform the practice of dhamma education. Being an institutional practice, it relates to the identity and function of Sri Lankan Buddhism as a discursive tradition. Asad (1986, 7, 14) suggests that identity and function are two important aspects of a discursive tradition. In other words, dhamma education demonstrates that Sri Lankan Buddhism is a moral argument that seeks to form who Sri Lankan Buddhists are by inculcating Buddhist knowledge, developing Buddhist attitudes, and cultivating cultural and moral skills. In the heart of that moral formation is the ideal of the Buddhist child constructed out of canonical references yet contextualized in particular socio-political circumstances.

Exploring the questions of what the dhamma education is and who the Buddhist child is, I analyze the intellectual and institutional history of dhamma education in colonial Ceylon, postcolonial Sri Lanka, and in the diasporic setting of Toronto. I demonstrate that normative canonical Buddhist discourse is overshadowed by a set of contingent discourses that address the social, political, and cultural needs of living Buddhists in a particular matrix. As the needs have changed over time, so too have Buddhist educationists' discourses on the image of the ideal Buddhist child. The shift in discourse demonstrates the pervasive power of the socio-political system on human capability. I contend that the Sri Lankan Canadian Buddhist child imagined in dhamma education in Toronto unites the themes and values of multiculturalism with those of the Pāli canonical ideals of a Buddhist, while attenuating Buddhist rhetoric and deflating the Sinhala Buddhist nationalism of their predecessors. The preceding argument derives from my analysis of three representative published materials used in dhamma schools, namely a) *The Buddhist Catechism* (1881), the Buddhist rhetoric advocated at the origin of dhamma education; b) *Daham Pasela* (1993), the textbook series that widely disseminated the Sinhala Buddhist nationalist sentiment in independent Sri Lanka; and c) *Teaching Buddhism to Children* (2001), a manual that depicts a new type of Buddhist moral formation in the Canadian context. An image of the Buddhist child is envisioned and re-envisioned in these manuals, as dhamma education's mission is to seed the dhamma in the hearts and minds of the young.

SEEDING THE DHAMMA IN THE HEARTS AND MINDS OF THE YOUNG

The dhamma schools under discussion – the Toronto Mahavihara Dhamma School in Scarborough, started in 1978, and the West End Dhamma School in Mississauga, started in 1992 – represent the emphasis on formal Buddhist education in Sri Lankan Buddhism. Sri Lankan Buddhists in Toronto claim that they have "the largest Dhamma School in North America" (Wijesundara 2008, 16; Attygalle 2009, 8). But in comparison to Maharagama Sri Vajiragnana Dhamma School, the largest one in Sri Lanka, the dhamma schools in Toronto are simply miniatures.

The fact that dhamma schools in Toronto are small does not mean that their relevance has diminished. In fact, as this chapter demonstrates below, the opposite has been true.

Dhamma schools highlight the role of Buddhist laity, particularly women's contribution in nurturing moral children by passing the Buddhist tradition to them. Many dhamma schools in Sri Lanka are housed in local temples. Nevertheless, voluntary lay teachers comprise the whole staff, except the principal of the dhamma school. The concentration of monastic leadership and temple locations also persist in dhamma schools in the diaspora, but only where temples and monks are available. In places where no institutional Buddhism is present, the absence of temples and monks does not stop Sri Lankans from conducting dhamma schools. I interviewed a few individuals who learned and taught Buddhism in dhamma

Table 3.1

Comparison between Toronto's dhamma schools and their counterparts
in Sri Lanka

	Toronto Mahavihara Dhamma School			Mississauga West End Dhamma School			Maharagama Sri Vajiragnana Dhamma School		
	Monk	Male	Female	Monk	Male	Female	Monk	Male	Female
Teachers (including supply and assistant teachers)	2	6	17	2	6	22	10	52	188
	Total 25			Total 30			Total 250		
Students	Around 140			Around 300			Around 6,000		
Grades	11 (including junior and senior kindergarten)			5 identified with names of flowers in Sinhala (a grade is divided into few classes i.e., Sal A, B, C, D)			12 (including kindergarten and Dharmacharya)		
School calendar	27 Sundays (3–5 p.m.)			27 Sundays (3–5 p.m.)			43 Sundays (7 a.m.–12 p.m.)		
Religious observance	Once a year (only for the Vesak)			Once a year (only for the Vesak)			Once a month (every full-moon day)		
Internal management	Temple committee Teaching staff Parents' association Student leaders			Temple committee Teaching staff Parents' association Student leaders			Temple committee Teaching staff Parents' association Student leaders		
External management	Not available			Not available			YMBA (Young Members Buddhist Association) Ministry of Rel. Affairs Sasanarakshaka Manadalaya		

schools in Abu Dhabi, where neither monks nor temples were available (Dahampasela Dubai). Similarly, lay Buddhists in Guelph,
Cambridge, and London (Ontario) have initiated dhamma classes
with no temples and monks. These incidents in the diaspora amplify

the roles of laity, particularly women, in dhamma education. This, in fact, is a modern manifestation of the older generation's moral obligation, as emphasized in the Buddhist tradition.

Chandrasekera recalls that in premodern times the moral development of children took place "through the agency of the ubiquitous grandmothers and parents who for almost twenty five millennia [sic] had served as the true messengers and instructors of the Buddha Dhamma to the young ones from their infancy, side by side with the *Maha Sangha* (the monks)" (2001, 3). Here, Chandrasekera emphasizes the crucial roles of parents, specifically of mothers and grandmothers, in passing on Buddhist knowledge and practices to the successive generations. She refers to them as the "true messengers and instructors" of Buddhism, traditional epithets for monks in the Theravāda tradition. This traditional female role has been harnessed and systematized in the modern dhamma school system. Women's roles are not confined to homes, but extended to public places like temples, where women disproportionately represent dhamma school staff.

As in Sri Lanka, over 70 per cent of dhamma teachers in Toronto are female. This resembles a common phenomenon in the South Asian diaspora where "women are the primary conservators and transmitters of the South Asian family's religious heritage" (Pearson 2004, 427). Thus the dhamma school system embodies the advanced status of Buddhist laity in Sri Lankan Buddhism, particularly the female role as educator and transmitter of the Buddhist tradition.

Teachers perceive their involvement in dhamma education in a variety of ways. One young teacher explains: "Teaching Buddhism is like growing a seed. What I try to do is if I can place a seed of Buddhism in their [students'] hearts; they may not use it now, but in ten or twenty years when they have life problems they can go back to the teachings. At the Dhamma school *I am propagating the Buddhasasana* ... This is a chance to spread the Dhamma, which is what the Buddha wanted to do. The idea that I am doing something somewhat similar to what the Gautama Buddha did really got my interest up. It really inspired me. I am spreading Buddhism. My original intention was to do a service to the community. Meanwhile, I am also working hard to perfect myself in my morality and in my action" (personal interview, 2008). This testimony highlights how dhamma teachers perceive themselves and the specific type of commitment and pressure they experience as they teach dhamma. This young teacher does not expect her students to immediately practice

Figure 3.1   The West End Dhamma School staff
Note: Only four out of twenty-one lay dhamma teachers are men; the rest
are women. Such an imbalanced staff composition is very typical in dhamma
schools across Sri Lanka as well as in diaspora.
Source: The West End Buddhist Temple and Meditation Centre

what she teaches. However, she hopes that the dhamma knowledge
will be available and helpful when the students face problems later
in their lives. She perceives herself as a dhamma cultivator, who
implants the seeds of dhamma (goodness) in the fertile hearts and
minds of the young.

Many dhamma teachers, across time and space, share this perception. For example, a contemporary dhamma teacher in the
New York City public school system reveals, "No matter what,
the important thing is that we plant seeds" (Doobinin 2008, 116).
A dhamma teacher in the 1950s also expressed a similar sentiment: "When we impart Buddhism to the children, we sow the
Dhamma seed upon a field green with hope and rich in sap" (Chau
1958, xxii). Moreover, the dhamma teachers I interviewed stated
that they experience tremendous joy and satisfaction in teaching
dhamma, and they are spiritually rewarded when they see children at a tender age grow with dhamma influence and experience.
The young teacher in the preceding statement invokes a sense of
religious calling. For her, teaching dhamma is a noble endeavour,
which the Buddha himself pursued, appreciated, and encouraged
his followers to do. It is celebrated as a giving of dhamma that
excels all other giving (*Dhammadāna Sabbadānam Jināti*). She
implies that she simply follows the Buddha and his instruction as

she teaches dhamma. Here, we notice that lay dhamma teachers internalize a monastic religious calling. This sense of duty motivates her to sacrifice her time and energy. Some teachers devote their whole Sunday afternoon, as they commute from long distances for dhamma school. They also consider their commitment a service to the community and to the wider society, with the belief that dhamma schools help to produce good citizens.

Teaching and learning dhamma is the first step in the threefold formula of transforming an individual. Pannasiha M.N. There,[1] the architect of dhamma education in postcolonial Sri Lanka, reminds us that dhamma education comprises cognitive, effective, and behavioural learning (1995, 5). Similarly, Chandrasekera (2001, 6) also invokes conceptual, contemplative, and experiential knowledge: "We begin by instructing and establishing the students in ... the theoretical aspects of Buddha's entire [!] Teaching (*pariyatti*) to help them achieve that experiential understanding (*pativēdha*) of the Buddha dhamma which can only come about through individual practice [*patipatti*]." Although the claim to instruct the "Buddha's entire teaching" is unrealistic, the preceding quotation invokes a sequential development of one's spirituality in Buddhism. One starts with studying (pariyatti) what the Buddha taught; then proceeds to practise (patipatti) the teachings so that they gain experiential understanding (pativēdha) of the dhamma. This triadic connection could be dialogical as much as linear or progressive. By relating individual spiritual development to teaching dhamma, Chandrasekera invokes a Buddhist perspective on religious education, which highlights the involvement of co-responsibility, the importance of practice, and the emphasis on experiential understanding. In dhamma education, teachers and students share responsibilities. Dhamma teachers present knowledge of Buddhism to students, but students must practise what they have learned to gain the kind of experiential insight that culminates in a transformation of character. However, dhamma teachers' duty does not end with theoretical teaching; instead, they are expected to imbue their lessons with practical and experiential aspects of the dhamma.

Teaching dhamma demands spiritual commitment. Many teachers admitted that they experience a sense of moral imperative as they teach dhamma. A middle-aged female dhamma teacher states, "People have high expectations. They expect more than who I am. I take extra precaution about what I say and do." Similarly, another says, "Parents acknowledge and respect what we do and look at us differently ... sometimes they look up to us [for moral guidance]. What students learn in Buddhism, they expect us to follow." A teacher and author of a dhamma school book states that teaching dhamma is "one of the most wonderful and challenging opportunities in life" (Knight 2008, introduction). It is wonderful because children add playfulness, enthusiasm, and beautiful personalities and expressions to learning and teaching dhamma. She continues that teaching dhamma becomes most challenging simply because it requires one's commitment and dedication to the moral principles that are being taught. In other words, a dhamma teacher is expected to embody what s/he teaches. This expectation echoes the Buddha's recommendation: "Let one first establish oneself in what is proper, and then instruct others" (Narada 1993, 144). This sense of ethical expectation and commitment not only distinguishes teaching dhamma from other forms of teaching, but often also determines the success or failure of the noble effort. One dhamma teacher warns, "what we want to impart to the children, we need first to set an example." The failure to be a good example often leads to the loss of confidence, not only in the teacher but also in the dhamma. He continues "if [students] find out that their [teacher] pays merely a lip-service to the Dharma, they may lose their confidence, and their love may turn to disappointment and to dislike, and then education becomes meaningless to them" (Chau 1958, xv). Such a high expectation of moral commitment makes teaching dhamma an extraordinary voluntary service.

The dhamma schools in Toronto emulate their counterparts in Sri Lanka. As in Sri Lanka, they start with a worship that includes taking refuge in the Triple Gem, observation of the Five Precepts, chanting of the virtues of the Triple Gem, a short loving kindness meditation, the students' pledge, and a short sermon. Classes on Buddhism follow the worship. These salient aspects of a typical dhamma school continue from the very first formal dhamma school in 1895 (Susila Himi 1995, 21). In contrast to their counterparts in Sri Lanka, however, the dhamma schools in Toronto experience a dearth of resources, facilities, and official recognition, and it affects the quality of education they provide. For example, to become a dhamma teacher at the Maharagama Siri Vajiragnana Dhamma School in Sri Lanka, one has to be either a trained schoolteacher or a trained dhamma teacher with the *Dharmāchārya* certificate, the highest examination related to dhamma education. Although some of the dhamma teachers in Toronto have the same credentials, many of them have joined the teaching staff after a short training as teaching assistants. They represent an average pattern of teachers' qualifications in the diaspora, as well as in Sri Lanka – except in special cases such as the Maharagama Siri Vajiragnana Dhamma School.

In comparison, several differences stand out. First, the worship and classes are shortened in Toronto. The 2005 booklet on dhamma school management in Sri Lanka allocates one full hour for worship, and it recommends four classes with a short refreshment break in the middle (*Daham Pasal Kalamanakaranaya*, 2005, 24). In Toronto, the worship lasts only thirty minutes followed by either a long class with a refreshment break at the end or two short classes with a small refreshment break in between. The second difference is that dhamma students in Toronto, unlike their counterparts in Sri Lanka, do not sing dhamma school songs and national anthems at regular Sunday schools. The West End Dhamma School launched an anthem in 2008, but it is sung only on its annual Dhamma School Day. The third, and perhaps more substantial, difference is that no external agencies oversee and assist the dhamma schools in Toronto. As indicated in the above-mentioned table, certain governmental and non-governmental institutions – the Young Members' Buddhist Association (YMBA), the Sasanarakshaka Mandalaya, and the Ministry of Religious Affairs – oversee and assist dhamma schools in Sri Lanka. They officially register dhamma schools, distribute textbooks, provide allowances, and arrange nation-wide dhamma examinations and competitions. These overseeing measures have standardized and accredited dhamma education in Sri Lanka. In contrast, the dhamma schools in Toronto enjoy neither governmental allowances nor non-governmental assistance from Sri Lanka. On the one hand, this difference in management could be interpreted as the loss of privileges Sri Lankan Buddhists had enjoyed in Sri Lanka, as they became a minority religious community. The coordinated efforts and public recognition of dhamma education are diluted in the diaspora. On the other hand, the absence of external supervision and assistance perhaps enables Buddhists in Toronto to enjoy a sense of independence and freedom in their vision and mission. For example, Buddhist educators in Toronto differentiate themselves from their counterparts in Sri Lanka in their conceptualization of who the Buddhist child is. A comparison of dhamma schools in Sri Lanka and Toronto informs us that the practices and strategies of a religious tradition in the diaspora are rooted in the particular history of the community. That history of dhamma education is explored below by analyzing the shifting conceptualization of the Buddhist child.

HISTORICALLY ENVISIONING THE BUDDHIST CHILD

Envisioning "who the Buddhist child is" has been at the heart of Buddhist education programs in Sri Lankan Buddhism. An analysis of dhamma education textbooks demonstrates that an ideal of the Buddhist child pervades the history of dhamma education. Different Buddhist educators understand this ideal variously. One interpretation comes from Kitalagama Hemasara's lesson entitled "I am a Buddhist Child" (1992, 97). It captures both religious norms and historical imperatives that envision an ideal of the Buddhist child. Highlighting the normative discourse of the ideal, the Buddhist child declares: "I am disciplined in body, words, and mind. I do not hurt others. I do not steal. I do not misbehave my senses. I am honest. I am benevolent. I am efficient in studying and helping my parents. I am respectful, grateful, and obedient to parents, teachers and elders. I don't disturb my parents with unnecessary demands; I am content with whatever I get. I am kind to animals, sympathetic to others, and helpful to the needy. I keep myself unshaken by the eight vicissitudes of life" [author's translation from the Sinhala language].

The foregoing definition of the "Buddhist Child" invokes Buddhist concepts like the skilful one (*kusala*), and the virtuous person (*satpurusa*) of the Pāli canon. The *Metta Sutta* in *Suttanipata*,[2] a Pāli discourse memorized by many Sri Lankan Buddhists, instructs "the skilful one" to cultivate the following character traits: personal confidence, honesty, straightforwardness, obedience to elders and teachers, gentleness, humility, peacefulness, contentment, simplicity, skilfulness, prudence, satisfaction, appreciation, and morality. Skilful ones develop these virtues to awaken themselves spiritually to Buddhism. A few lessons on the *Metta Sutta* in *Daham Pasela* encourage students to improve the virtues in order to be successful in spiritual and mundane pursuits (Mahalekam 1992, 117). The fundamental nomenclature of dhamma education/school legitimates its agenda to instil the character traits of the skilful one.

We have seen in the preceding section that dhamma teachers invoke this Buddhist normative discourse to make sense of their roles in dhamma education. Similarly, students and their parents also use the same discourse to rationalize their participation in dhamma schools. This normative discourse, however, has been contextualized with historically contingent discourses of Buddhist identities derived from three distinct socio-political settings: colonial Ceylon, postcolonial Sri Lanka, and multicultural Toronto.

THE RHETORICAL BUDDHIST CHILD
IN COLONIAL CEYLON

In the late nineteenth century, dhamma education emerged as a reactionary movement against Christian evangelism, and it emulated the model of Christian Sunday schools (Bartholomeusz 1994, 61; Bond 1988, 48–52, 85–8, 111, 117–18; Gombrich and Obeyesekere 1988, 205, 211, 235; Prothero 1996, 101–6). It was a creative response to centuries-long systematic injustice ingrained in the educational system of colonial Ceylon. The Portuguese, Dutch, and British – three Western colonizers of the late medieval and modern period – ruled the island for nearly five hundred years, from 1506 to 1948. Each brought their form of Christianity and reinforced it didactically. They used religion and education to establish, and then maintain, control over Indigenous populations. Under colonial rule, the traditional temple-centred education system lost its political endorsement and financial endowment; consequently, monks lost their privileged status as educators. Instead, Christian churches became the centres of education, and Christian clergy became the agents of education. Colonization and Christianization went hand in hand, as each lent support to the other's political and religious causes, and public education was an effective way to materialize both. Thus education meant not only colonization, but also Christianization.

Referring to religious and political forces in public education, Kitsiri Malalgoda says: "The dissemination of these [political] influences and the teachings of the principles of Christianity were the primary aims of education, a task which was performed by the clergy. Instruction in schools was primarily religious, and elementary education was necessarily geared to serve the interests of conversion" (1976, 30). By the end of the nineteenth century, missionary societies felt an unprecedented freedom in establishing their monopoly in education, and the period between 1870 and 1890 was "the golden age of the missions in Ceylon" (Jayaweera 1968, 165). Yet Buddhists too felt the need for their own schools, and Piyaratana Thero founded the first Buddhist school in 1869 (Karunadasa 2004). Buddhist schools, however, lacked the rudimentary resources such as finance, institutional infrastructure, teachers, and teaching materials. They also faced political and legal hurdles. For instance, the British introduced the so-called "three-mile-rule" to prohibit founding new schools within a distance of three miles from the existing school (Corea 1969, 156). Jayaweera states that by 1880, there were 805 Christian missionary schools, and twenty-four "privately aided" Hindu schools, while there were only four Buddhist schools and one Muslim school (1968, 163). However, by the end of the nineteenth century, Buddhists had succeeded in establishing numerous Buddhist schools.

The mass movement of Buddhist education was intensified by the 1880 arrival of Colonel Henry Steel Olcott, an American civil war veteran and Theosophist who was impressed by the Buddhist victory over the Christians in the 1873 Panaduara Debate. Oppressed as they were, Indigenous Buddhists warmly welcomed Olcott and the religious and national aspirations he provided. Ananda Guruge states: "Christian-dominated English education had convinced Buddhists that, if any headway could be made in winning for the Buddhists their rightful place in society, it was achievable only through a well-knit system of Buddhist Schools" (1965, xxxii). However they lacked modern organizational skills to counter the well-orchestrated and state-funded Christian education. Being an "organizational genius," Olcott provided what was most needed, and he proceeded in organizing Buddhists for a Western-style Buddhist education. He established the Buddhist Theosophical Society and a National Education Fund to assist Buddhist public schools (Prothero 1996, 99). He mobilized Buddhist monks and laity for that cause. He imitated Christian educational institutions and employed Christian missionary tactics to raise money for Buddhist schools. With his organizational skills, the Buddhist education campaign met with immediate success. There were only four Buddhist schools when Olcott arrived in Ceylon in 1880, but in subsequent years that number increased rapidly to hundreds, with thousands of Buddhist students enrolling for education.

After a few initial efforts, during the end of nineteenth century systematic dhamma schools supplemented Buddhist education in public school. Indigenous sources confirm that C. Don Bastian, a local artist, established the first ever Buddhist Sunday school in 1872 (Nanakirti Himi 2008, 3). Nearly a decade later, in February 1881, Olcott also initiated his first dhamma school in Colombo. These efforts were experimental. Unlike Buddhist public schools, they did not succeed, as they lacked the rudimentary resources, such as dedicated trained teachers, effective educational materials, and organizational infrastructure. Nearly a quarter of a century after the first effort, Sri Vijayananda Dhamma School in Galle finally made its groundbreaking start on 3 August 1895, and it continues even today (Susila Himi 1995, 15). While the Buddhist Theosophical Society assisted with organizational skills, financial support, and effective leadership, Olcott's *The Buddhist Catechism* provided a model of a Buddhist child who could stand up to the pressure of proselytizing Christians. The ideal Buddhist child imagined in the book is skilled in Buddhist rhetoric.

From the outset, Henry Steel Olcott's (1832–1907) *The Buddhist Catechism* (1881) was a small book with a big plan. Olcott designs it as a Buddhist educational manual to facilitate imparting Buddhist knowledge to children. He divides the book into five sections: the life of the Buddha, the Dharma or doctrine, the Sangha, the origin and spread of Buddhism, and Buddhism and science. The appendix contains fourteen propositions about common Buddhist beliefs, which Olcott thought could foster a Buddhist unity. The titles of the contents and how they are arranged suggest that the book intends to educate about the past, present, and future of the Buddhist tradition. It promises to teach about the people, philosophy, and geography of that Buddhist tradition, along with its present challenges and future prospects. I suggest that *The Buddhist Catechism* imagines a Buddhist child who is united with other Buddhists and equipped with the rhetoric of universal Buddhist philosophy so that they are capable of defending Buddhism. At the core of this imagination are three themes: Buddhist unity, rhetorical skills, and philosophical knowledge of Buddhism. *The Buddhist Catechism* lays out an educational project on how to go about realizing or forming that imagined Buddhist child.

Olcott calls for a Buddhist unity. He introduces fourteen propositions as core Buddhist beliefs of Northern (Mahāyāna) and Southern (Theravāda) Buddhists. The propositions include some core teachings of the Buddha, such as the Four Noble Truths, Karma, and Nirvana. Olcott interprets these concepts in quasi-scientific terms, such as "natural truths," "a natural causation," and "highest state of peace" (128–32). Among the practices, he mentions only meditation in general and the Five Precepts, which are broad enough to be accepted by all the Buddhist traditions. It was the first endeavour geared towards a sense of Buddhist commonality in modern times. Olcott celebrates this achievement, as "the whole world can now be said to have united to the extent at least of these Fourteen Propositions" (128). He felt that Buddhist unity was a timely response to the challenges contemporaneous Buddhists faced.

Buddhists in Ceylon responded to Olcott's call for Buddhist unity variously. Anagarika Dharmapala's 1892 establishment of the *Journal of the Maha Bodhi Society and the United Buddhist World* resonated the call at an international level. The title itself expressed Dharmapala's "hopes for drawing Buddhists into a pan-Asian community linked to supporters in Europe and America" (Kemper 2015, 8). He reached out to Buddhists across Asia and raised money from Buddhists in Asia and Buddhist admirers in the West to end the Hindu ownership of the historical Buddhist pilgrimage site of Bodhgaya and reclaim it for Buddhists (Guruge 1993, 71). At a local level, many Buddhists joined united as the members of Olcott's Buddhist Theosophical Society and the Young Members Buddhist Association. The message of Buddhist unity further reverberated in later established Buddhist associations. In December 1919, Sir D.B. Jayatilaka started the All Ceylon Buddhist Congress, which functioned as an umbrella organization to connect the local and regional Buddhist organizations. Jayatilaka was "a kingpin in the Buddhist Educational Movement" (Guruge 1993, 76), and his Buddhist Congress systematized Buddhist education (Athukorala 1986, 2). In 1950, Gunapala Malalasekera, an eloquent orator and writer, founded the World Fellowship of Buddhists and put the issue of Buddhist unity in the international spotlight. These national and international organizations illustrate the legacy of the Buddhist discourse of unity in *The Buddhist Catechism*. The subtext of this discourse lay in the fact that it was responding to the non-Buddhist challenges, particularly those posed by Christian missionaries.

To counter Christian missionaries' portrayal of Buddhism, Olcott formulates a set of rhetorical devices with Buddhist information. He arranges the contents of his book as if young Buddhists were in a debate on Buddhism with Christian missionaries. He counters and then corrects the polemical portrayal of the Buddha and his teachings by Christian missionaries who delved into Buddhist scriptures "to prove the supremacy of Christianity and powerlessness of Buddhism in addressing the contemporary issues" (Guruge 1993,

23). As part of Christian proselytization, missionaries castrated the Buddha, manipulated his teachings, discredited Buddhist practices, and humiliated Buddhist followers. For example, Robert Spence Hardy, a Methodist missionary, writes in his 1874 *Christianity and Buddhism Compared*: "Sakya Muni of modern Buddhism is a creature of the imagination alone ... so that the comparison [between Jesus Christ and Gotama Buddha] is really between history and legend" (in Harris 2006, 68). Correcting such portrayals of the Buddha as a mythical figure, Olcott (1881, 27) assures:

101. Q. *What convincing proof have we that the Buddha, formerly Prince Siddhartha, was a historical personage?*
A. His existence is apparently as clearly proved as that of any other character of ancient history.

In order to convince the reader that Buddha was a historical person, he then lays out eight types of proofs, including archaeological, inscriptional, and sociological references to the Buddha (27–9).

Thomas Moscrop, a Methodist missionary teacher, writes that "Buddhism ... is too pessimistic, too cold, too antagonistic to the constitution of human nature to take the world captive" (in Harris 2006, 104). Contrasting these views, Olcott argues that the essence of Buddhism is justice, self-culture, and universal love (53–4). He defines the Buddhist path as "the preserving practice of an all-embracing altruism in conduct, development of intelligence, wisdom in thought, and destruction of desire for the lower personal pleasures" (130). This positive reorientation of the Buddhist tradition not only curbed Christian missionary attacks on Buddhism, but also trained young Buddhists to defend their religious tradition against Christian polemics.

Missionaries also accused Buddhism of being idolatrous, superstitious, and irrelevant to the world. At the Panadura Debate, both Christians and Buddhists sought out science as an "ideal weapon" to prove the supremacy of their religion over that of the rivals. Buddhists felt the need to claim science for themselves (Lopez 2008, 32). Olcott addresses that need by adding a section on "Buddhism and Science" to the manual. He relates the Buddha to a great scientist and his teaching to scientific discovery. He insists "The Buddha ... gave it [Buddhism] out as the statement of eternal truths, which his predecessors had taught like himself" (1881, 109). Referring to the previous lives of the Buddha, Olcott draws in Darwin's theory of evolution to reconcile the apparent inconsistency between Buddhist theories of rebirth and not-soul. He contends: "everything that I have found in Buddhism accords with the theory of a gradual evolution of the perfected man, namely, a Buddha, through numberless natal experiences" (75). Similarly, he also defines Buddhism not as a religion but as a "moral philosophy" (111). This statement not only distinguishes Buddhism from other religions (especially Christianity), but also underscores Buddhism's potential to advocate the freedom of thought and tolerance in the modern context. The point of the present discussion is not the accuracy or inaccuracy of Olcott's discourse on Buddhism, per se; rather, it is to show the efficacy of discourse in meeting the Buddhist needs of the late nineteenth century and to illustrate that the formation of Buddhist moral agents was motivated to defend Buddhism against Christian evangelism.

Olcott's portrayal of Buddhism in *The Buddhist Catechism* is debate-oriented. His tone and style of presentation evoke his urgent need to defend the Buddhist tradition. Olcott presents his arguments in a style of a debate. For example,

> 195. Q. *What does the Buddha call himself?*
> A. He says that he and the other Buddhas are only "preachers."
> 196. Q. *Where is this said?*
> A. In the Dhammapada, Chapter 20. (63)

The texture, tone, and style of *The Buddhist Catechism* are apologetic. As young Buddhists memorize the questions and answers of the book, they gain Buddhist knowledge, develop attitudes, and cultivate skills that enable them to counter and curb Christian missionaries' polemic against the Buddhist tradition.

Along with the preceding rhetorical formation of Buddhist children, Olcott inculcates a new form of Buddhist knowledge that simultaneously constructs and deconstructs Buddhism in late nineteenth century Ceylon. He offers a critical observation of the Buddhist tradition, followed by a new interpretation with a new voice of authority. Olcott discards some of the prevailing interpretations of Buddhist concepts that he deemed incongruous with early Pāli scriptures. For example, he states: "there is in Ceylon a popular misconception that the attainment of Arhantship is now impossible

... The Buddha taught quite the contrary idea. In the *Digha Nikaya* he said: 'Hear, Subhadra! The World will never be without Arahats if the ascetics (Bhikkhus) in my congregations *well and truly keep my precepts*" (64–5). Correcting a "misconception," Olcott emphasizes that "the nirvanic state can be attained while one is living on this earth" (81). This emphasis on an immediate experience of nirvana eventually became one of the salient features of modern Buddhism.

Similarly, Olcott's definition of the "Sangha" invokes only the spiritual meaning of the term, which allowed him to include lay people in the Sangha. He neither actively disputes nor acknowledges the Theravāda tradition's conventional use of the term to exclusively refer to monastics (45). This inclusive interpretation takes a backseat in neo-traditional Buddhism, where in practice "Sangha" refers only to monks in postcolonial Buddhism in Sri Lanka and yet, as we will see in the next chapter, it comes to the fore once again in the inclusive interpretation of Buddhism in Toronto. At a rhetoric level, one could argue that Olcott's broad interpretation of "Sangha" signifies the unprecedented rise of the Buddhist laity since the late nineteenth century; nevertheless, as Anne Blackburn's (2010) research illustrates, on a practical level the rise of laity hardly trumped monastic roles and responsibilities. Instead, both monks and laity collaborated in support of Buddhist institutions and the spread of Buddhist teachings.

Like many orientalists of the time, Olcott constantly prioritizes Buddhist scriptures over and against a living tradition, and he authorizes only those traditions that he deemed congruous with the Pāli scriptures. Olcott's interpretation of Buddhism is dubbed "Protestant Buddhism" (Obeyesekere 1970) as it redefined Buddhism to protest against Christian missionaries by employing the doctrinal and institutional principles of Protestant Christianity: an emphasis on scripture and doctrine over rituals and lay organizations. Highlighting the hybrid nature of Olcott's interpretation of Buddhism, Stephen Prothero (1996) calls it a "Creole Faith." The hybridity derives not only from Protestantism but also from Deism, Evolutionism, Theosophy, and Buddhist Universalism. Within such a wide range of hybridity, two important aspects of religious education were lost in *The Buddhist Catechism*: Theravāda particularism and practice orientation. In fact the missing aspects are the two sides of the same coin, namely the Sinhalese/Sri Lankan Buddhist culture. Later in this chapter we will see how Buddhist culture became a prominent aspect of Buddhist educational texts in postcolonial Sri Lanka; the following section briefly discusses how Olcott's own Buddhist interlocutors of the time responded to his omission.

A few important Indigenous Buddhist revivalists in late nineteenth century Ceylon expressed their dissatisfaction with Olcott's *Buddhist Catechism*. Addressing the omitted Sinhalese Buddhist culture, Ven. Mohottivatte Gunananda (1823–1890) – the famous Buddhist monk defender at the 1873 Christian-Buddhist Panadura Debate whose notoriety attracted Olcott himself to Ceylon in 1880 – published the first part of *Buaddha Prashnaya* (Buddhist Questions) in 1887 (Blackburn 2010, 136). In the preface Mohottivatte emphasized the need to re-assert the "'true' doctrines of Buddhism" in order to counter some of the "false" and "alien" aspects of Olcott's *Buddhist Catechism* (Malalgoda 1976, 252). Anagarika Dharmapala himself composed his own version of a Buddhist catechism, called *Dharma Prashna* (Dharma Questions), in 1905 (Blackburn 2010, 137). Despite his certification of the altered Sinhala version of Olcott's book as a textbook for Buddhist schools, Hikkaduwe Sumangala Thero – the regional Buddhist monastic leader of the time – assisted in composing Mohottivatte's *Bauddha Prashnaya* as well as Charles Leadbeater's *Bauddha Siksabodhaya* (Buddhist Education of Training) in 1889. He used the latter in particular to counter some of undesired interpretations of Buddhism appeared in Olcott's catechism. Sumangala Thero also supervised an English translation of Leadbeater's work as *The Smaller Buddhist Catechism* in 1902, and recommended it be used prior to Olcott's catechism in Buddhist schools (Blackburn 2010, 136). Unlike Olcott's work, Leadbeater's catechism included a lot of Pāli chanting including taking refuges in the Triple Gem and observing the Five Precepts as well as the virtues of the Buddha, Dhamma, and Sangha (Leadbeater 1902, 4–5, 25–6). The historical Buddha himself is presented as the part of the Buddhist lineage: twenty-eight past Buddhas and the future Maithriya Buddha (24). In contrast to Olcott's exclusively rhetorical formation of the Buddhist child, Leadbeater's catechism advocates an action-oriented Buddhist child who has memorized Pāli chants and obeys the prescribed individual duties to parents, monks, teachers, etc. The preceding alternate Buddhist catechisms addressed what was missing in Olcott's handbook, but they kept the Q-and-A format of the latter. A more formidable challenge to Olcott's catechism, however, came from an anonymously authored book that broke away from the catechistic Q-and-A format.

The *Bauddha Adahilla* (Buddhist Belief) was indeed an astute response to Olcott's *Buddhist Catechism*. It simultaneously appeared in both printed (first edition in 1889) and palm leaf versions in the late nineteenth century. Carol Anderson (2003, 179) attributes the book to the same author of *Bauddha Prashnaya*: Mohottivatte Thero. If that indeed was the case, the anonymity and palm leaf publication of this Sinhala book was meant to attribute a purported authority to the book in order to counter its contender – namely, Olcott's catechism. The palm leaf publication added the impression of antiquity to *Bauddha Prahsnaya* and was therefore intended to represent a greater authority than the later-developed *Buddhist Catechism*. Its second edition came out in 1894 and later became more popular, with repeated publications throughout the latter half of the twentieth century (Anderson 2003, 177). Contrasting it with its implied contender, Anderson (2003) observes: "Unlike Olcott's *Buddhist Catechism*, this book is not comprised of questions and answers about right beliefs – or even right views. It is a compilation of what to do and how to do it: it is a ritual manual, with explanation in case anyone has any doubts as to the efficacy of the practices" (173). The manual lays out, step by step and in great detail, how to take refuge in the Triple Gem (Buddha, Dhamma, and Sangha), how to request and observe the Five Precepts from monks (and what to do when monks are not available), how to sit for basic meditation, how to prepare ritual items and conduct puja (worship), and how to organize a *paritta* chanting. What makes this manual stand out from others discussed above is its detailed description of practices. According to the *Bauddha Adahilla*, neither abstract beliefs nor factual knowledge of Buddhist teaching, but rather concrete actions – like taking refuge, kneeling and bowing in front of the Buddha and monks, performing rituals, and chanting Pāli verses – make one a "true" Buddhist. Despite its action-based Buddhist formation, the handbook is entitled "Buddhist Beliefs" perhaps for a wider appeal and audience (Anderson 2003, 172). If this conflation of belief with Buddhist rituals is intentional, the move indicates creativity on the author's part. In other words, the *Bauddha Adahilla* creatively challenges the mind, thinking, and belief-oriented religious formation with an alternate one that is centred on body, feeling, and actions. The preceding discussion suggests that, beginning with Olcott's 1881 *The Buddhist Catechism*, various visions of the Buddhist child occupied Buddhists in late nineteenth century Ceylon.

The Buddhist Catechism and the *Bauddha Adahilla* represent two ends of the spectrum of Buddhist imaginings and articulations of who the Buddhist child should be. They portray two different ideals of the Buddhist child. The Buddhist child in *The Buddhist Catechism* memorizes the basic tenets of Buddhism and, in a time of need, can verbally defend these tenets. Their counterpart in the *Bauddha Adahilla* devotionally practices Buddhist rituals including taking refuge, reciting Pāli chanting, and preparing ritual paraphernalia. They certainly can explain and show *how* an ideal Buddhist child behaves but they may not intellectually rationalize and explain *what* they believe, nor *why* they behave in certain ways.

Some scholars argue that the Sinhala-speaking but English-educated elites of Ceylon internalized the rational, demythologized version of Buddhism found in Olcott's *Buddhist Catechism*, while the majority of Sinhala-speaking non-elites embodied the kind of ritual- or practice-centred Buddhism represented in the *Bauddha Adahilla* (Anderson 2003, 181). The publication records of both books[3] indicate that it was the doctrinally savvy, intellectually defendable Buddhist child, rather than their devotional and religiously behaved counterpart, who was celebrated in formal dhamma education on weekdays and in Sunday school. Olcott's belief-based rhetorical discourse dominated dhamma education in Sri Lanka throughout the first half of the twentieth century. His interpretation of Buddhism encouraged many Sri Lankan Buddhists to see Buddhism as a philosophy or a scientific religion. His rhetoric seemed more effective to meet the urgent need of Buddhists in the late nineteenth and twentieth centuries – namely, to counter and curb the Christian evangelical zeal.

Olcott's discourse has also continued in postcolonial Sri Lanka alongside the dominant discourse of Sinhala Buddhism. For example, in addition to the Buddhist spiritual development, Hemasāra (1992, 97) envisions a Buddhist child with anti-evangelical and Sinhala Buddhist sentiments. He says: "The Buddhist child is wise. He has a deep conviction in the Triple Gem. He is not misled and deceived by lies. He does not give up and betray Buddhism for material gains and for mundane benefits; instead, he admires, adores, and appreciates Buddhism more than his own lives" (author's translation from the Sinhala original). Hemasara implies that the Buddhist child learns Buddhism *correctly* and defends it against the polemics (mainly of Christian missionaries) against Buddhism. Such a rhetorical Buddhist child bears Buddhist knowledge in a way that makes them capable of defending their Buddhist beliefs, practices, and religious institutions. They are instructed not to betray the long-held Buddhist heritage for material and worldly gains.[4] While imbued with a rhetorical knowledge of Buddhism, the Buddhist child in Hemasara's lesson in *Daham Pasela* (1992, 97) also declares: "I am a Buddhist child. Disciplined by the nation's ethics (*jatika sirithata virithata hedagesunu*), I do not admire fancy dress and hairstyle. I keep myself clean, combed, and dressed in clean clothes. I go to dhamma school on Sundays and to the temple on poya (full moon) days" (author's translation). This *"Sinhala Buddhist discourse"* characterizes the contents and practices of dhamma education for laity in postcolonial Sri Lanka.

THE SINHALA BUDDHIST CHILD IN POSTCOLONIAL SRI LANKA

Sinhala Buddhist discourse asserts a symbiotic relationship between Buddhism, Sinhala ethnicity (nationality), the Sinhala language, and Sri Lanka. Although Olcott's *The Buddhist Catechism* left it out,[5] the alternate Buddhist catechistic literature discussed above suggests that the discourse was in place at least in seed form during the late nineteenth century. Anagarika Dharmapala, the well-known Indigenous Buddhist revival leader, consistently evoked this discourse in his public speeches and writing. In his "Message to the Young Men of Ceylon," he urges them "to act as patriots ... for the preservation of our nation, our literature, our land, and our most glorious religion whose source our forefathers drank deep for nearly seventy generations" (Dharmapala [1922] 1965, 501). Accordingly, the main duty of Dharmapala's "young men of Ceylon" is to love Buddhism, the Sinhala language, land and ethnicity/nation,[6] and to protect and defend themselves from foreign threats. From early on, dhamma school students were encouraged to recite a poem of aspiration[7] that invokes the Sinhala Buddhist discourse. However, the colonial socio-political system was not conducive to the mobilization of this discourse, nor was the dhamma school sufficiently systemized to effectively disseminate the discourse. Bond notices that the majority of Buddhist lay leaders rallied to Dharmapala to revive Buddhism and the Sinhala identity, but they did not share the latter's zeal to blend them (1988, 64). However, Dharmapala's Buddhist nationalism eventually gained momentum and flourished in independent Sri Lanka.

The 1950s was the most defining period in recent Buddhist history in Sri Lanka. Postcolonial Sri Lanka experienced an unprecedented political and Buddhist enthusiasm that demanded a new national identity to set it apart from its colonial past. A few highlights of the decade have had long-lasting legacies in modern Sri Lankan Buddhism. The All Ceylon Buddhist Congress established a Buddhist Commission of Inquiry in 1954 and issued a 400-page report in February 1956, just before the first parliamentary election held in April. The timing of this report signifies the growing influence of Buddhism on the politics of postcolonial Sri Lanka. The promise of political support for the report delivered a new government led by S.W.R.D. Bandaranayake. Under the newly elected government's patronage, the 1956 Buddha Jayanti – the celebration of the 2,500th anniversary of the Buddha's *parinibbāna* – was arranged on a grand scale. It was the pinnacle of Buddhist zeal that envisioned what independent Sri Lanka should look like. The 1956 Buddhist Inquiry report argued that the "restoration of Buddhism to its rightful place" would provide Indigenous national identity, along with prosperity, to the new nation (Bond 1988, 76). Dharmapala's Sinhala Buddhist discourse was resurrected as the most viable means to construct a new identity for the newly independent nation, and education was recognized as one of the main ways to instil that Buddhist national identity. The cultural practice-centred *Bauddha Adahilla* was republished in 1955, and its anonymous author was believed to live in medieval Sri Lanka (Anderson 2003, 177).

After 1956, dhamma education, like all other education sectors from primary school to national universities, worked toward the creation of an integrated national religious identity (Guruge 1993, 293). The Bandranayake government appointed a commission (the Buddha Sasana Commission) in March 1957 to study how to address the issues raised in the 1956 Inquiry.[8] The government also appointed a separate syndicate (Dhamma School Examination Syndicate) in July 1957 to look into how to deliver dhamma education widely and effectively (Madihe Pannasiha M.N. Thera 1995, 5). More than anything else this syndicate influenced the institutionalization and systemization of dhamma education throughout Sri Lanka. Its president – Madihe Pannasiha M.N. Thera – laid out a series of suggestions in the form of six reports of the syndicate in the *Sinhala Bauddhaya*, the same newspaper that was initiated by Dhammapala himself over half a century ago on 6 June 1958. The report was entitled "There is Neither the Sinhalese without Buddhism, Nor Has the Sinhalese Anything Other Than Buddhism." The report represented a new beginning for the dhamma education of the laity; it envisioned the formation of young Buddhists within Sinhalese Buddhist nationalism. Five more layers of the report followed, which laid out strategies for how to achieve that vision.[9] The sixfold report talks about the institutional form, curriculum contents, and expected outcomes of the dhamma education. The textbook *Daham Pasela* (which means Dhamma School) had thirty lessons, each to replace a few disunited books used until then.[10] The Syndicate recommended: "One of these [lessons] could be taught in the school itself, perhaps within an hour or one and a half" (Pannasiha M.N. Thera 1995, 5). The textbooks have been modified and republished in the subsequent decades, and I have used the latest version available.

The textbooks *Daham Pasela*, from grades one to ten, convey a wealth of Buddhist knowledge and teachings. Each grade contains a specially designed textbook with progressively more complex explanations of Buddhist concepts, principles, norms, values, and practices. The curriculum of the *Daham Pasela* can be classified as follows: spiritual biographies (Buddha, immediate disciples, and later practitioners), basic Buddhist teaching (including Abhidharma), meditation, Buddhist rituals (chanting and customs), history of Buddhism, and Pāli. The final dhamma school examination at the end of grade ten marks the pinnacle of dhamma education for many. It entails four topics: the biography of the Buddha (including biographies of practitioners), Buddhism and Pāli, the history of Buddhism, and Buddhist culture. The first three topics are consistent with the first four chapters of Olcott's *Buddhist Catechism*; nevertheless the texture, tone, and mode of presentation differ significantly.

Unlike *The Buddhist Catechism, Daham Pasela* includes Buddhist culture – the vibrant aspects of the Buddhist tradition – along with its history. It variously invokes Sinhala Buddhist discourse side by side with the Pāli canonical discourse of character transformation. It delves into the history of Buddhism in Sri Lanka along with special references to numerous historical figures in modern and premodern Sri Lanka. Thus *Daham Pasela* differentiates itself from its predecessor *The Buddhist Catechism* in defining the means and goals of dhamma education. Dhamma education was intended to create a distinct Buddhist child; the contents compiled under Buddhist culture have provided the ingredients to construct that identity. The emphasis on diverse customs, rituals, and ceremonies signifies the importance of action (performance) in instilling Buddhist identity. Ananda Guruge (1993, 239) observes that teaching Buddhism in independent Sri Lanka was motivated by a desire to mould a cultural identity. Seneviratne Mahalekam's *Buddhist Culture*[11] is emblematic in this respect. It classifies the subject under three themes (Buddhist customs, Buddhist artistic expression in Sri Lanka, and global Buddhist culture), which serve the formation of moral agents in three ways. The customs, rituals, and practices illustrate Buddhist decorum. The historical information of various artistic expressions generates the cultural pride, devotion, and dignity associated with Indigenous identity. The section on global Buddhist culture puts the Indigenous identity on the Buddhist world stage.

Daham Pasela celebrates the heroic actions of ancient and modern personalities, emphasizing that they are worth emulating. In fact, Sri Lankan history mentioned in *Daham Pasela* highlights a particular past that could be identified as "native authoritative discourse" (Scott 1994, xviii). It sanctifies *Mahavamsa*'s reports of the Buddha's visits to the island, and it highlights Buddhist kings' royal services for Buddhist causes. King Dutugemunu (161–137 BCE) and King Mahaparakramabahu (1153–1186 CE) receive special attention for their immense devotion and dedication to the development of Buddhism, as well as their patriotic and heroic actions in defending the Sinhala nation and Buddhism (Assaji 1993, 83–8). In addition, *Daham Pasela* pays greater attention to more recent Buddhist national heroes in the late nineteenth and twentieth century Buddhist revival.

Mahalekam (1992, 27–65) and Mahathantrige (1993, 49–59) dedicate numerous lessons on the following national heroes: Hikkaduwa Sri Sumangala Thero, Ratmalane Sri Dhammaloka Thero, Migettuwatte Sri Gunananda Thero, Variyapola Sumangala Thero, Anagarika Dharmapala, and Henry Olcott. The contribution of these figures to Buddhist education, institution, and organization are highlighted. Their conviction and courage in defending Buddhism against Christian evangelism are celebrated. At the end of the lessons on some of these biographies, students are reminded that it is their duty to contribute to the well-being of the country by supporting the Sinhala language and Buddhism. This patriotic encouragement, in fact, echoes the essence of Dharmapala's 1922 "Message to the Young Men of Ceylon." Anagarika Dharmapala, more than anybody else, has become a powerful figure through this

Sinhala-Buddhist discourse. Guruge observes, "hardly any Sinhala Buddhist young man or woman enters the cares and concerns of adult life without being reminded that precisely a hundred years ago young Dharmapala ... set for them an example which they might proudly and profitably emulate" (1993, 246). Buddhist national heroes are the means by which Buddhist nationalist discourse permeates in *Daham Pasela*.

The discourse also symbolically gets expressed in the dhamma school dress code. Dhamma schools recommend *"Arya Sinhala"* national dress (a white sarong and white collarless shirt) for boys and *"Lama Sariya"* (a white blouse with a frill around the chest and white cloth with a frill around the waist) for girls. The dress symbolizes Buddhist values of purity and simplicity, as well as nationalism. Similarly, inside the cover of every *Daham Pasela* textbook is the national anthem of Sri Lanka followed by the dhamma school anthem. This illustrates the perceived intimate connection between Buddhism and Sri Lankan nationality. Moreover, one of the five guiding principles of a prominent dhamma school in Sri Lanka is to train students "to develop correct attitudes for building a generation of religious, patriotic and national minded children" (Warusawithana 2007, i). Similarly, Madihe Pannasiha Mahanayaka Thera – the first chairperson of the Dhamma School Syndicate, which systematized and popularized dhamma education in 1950s and 1960s – later recalled that one of the main aims was to "bring up a new generation of children awakened to a new religious consciousness, glowing with a spirit of patriotism, stirred up with a deep sense of nationalism and enlivened with the commitment of their own [Sinhala] language" (1995, 5). Thus dhamma educators in independent Sri Lanka have envisioned a Sinhala Buddhist child as they responded to a postcolonial nation's call for a distinct identity. To implement their vision effectively, they also transformed the dhamma education into an institutional practice.

A few organizations take the credit for establishing dhamma education as an institutional practice in Sri Lanka. The Young Men's Buddhist Association (henceforth YMBA) established in 1889 standardized dhamma education by introducing dhamma examinations for students and teachers alike. It conducted the first ever dhamma examination classified according to grades for students in 1920, in which twenty-seven dhamma schools and 374 students participated. Similarly, in 1926 YMBA introduced *Dhammacharya* examination – but only twelve teachers from one particular dhamma school

participated (Pannasiha M.N. Thera 1995, 4; Susila Himi 1995, 23).
In 1931, the All Ceylon Buddhist Congress aspired to establish a
dhamma school in every village, but it was the Ministry of Cultural
Affairs and its Dhamma School Syndicate that ultimately carried
out that aspiration (Pannasiha M.N. Thera 1995, 5; Nanakirti Himi
2008, 5). The Syndicate's chairperson Madihe Pannasiha Maha
Nayaka Thera (1995) recalls that "in 1957 ... 172,349 students
appeared for the Dhamma examination" (4). He also reports, "by
the end of ten years [1968], the number of students ... rose up to
nine hundred thousand" (5). However, Susila Himi (1995) records
that 427,678 students affiliated to 3,427 dhamma schools sat for
the 1968 dhamma examination (1995, 23). Despite the disparity in
number of students, both writers highlight the institutionalization of
dhamma school during the 1957–68 period.

In 1981, the Ministry of Education took over the responsibility of conducting the Dhamma School Final Examination and the
Dharmacharya Examination. This systemization assured the public
recognition and accreditation of dhamma education. Those who
passed the examinations received credits recognized in the university entrance and teaching positions in schools (Nanakirti Himi
2008, 7). In recent years, the Department of Buddhist Affairs has
taken over the responsibility of conducting Dhamma School Grade
Examinations. According to the Buddhist Affair's Department, by
December 2008 nearly 10,000 (9,093) dhamma schools are in service across Sri Lanka. Over 109,000 (109,725) volunteer dhamma
teachers serve, and nearly 1.8 million (1,796,270) students learn
Buddhism in dhamma schools.

This history of dhamma education and its agendas in Sri Lanka
illustrates how it has developed from a modest start to a fully grown
institutional practice. In this development, non-governmental associations played vital roles in colonial Sri Lanka. YMBA's examinations
set an internal structure and standardized dhamma education. The
All Ceylon Buddhist Congress strived to mobilize and implement
those standards throughout Sri Lanka, but it was less successful
in accomplishing them. We notice that under the state's assistance,
dhamma education became an institutional practice with public recognition and importance. Dhamma schools proliferated during the
1950s and 1960s, and they are loosely institutionalized through official registration, annual examinations, nation-wide dhamma school
competitions, and accreditation.

From the very beginning, Sunday dhamma schools evolved as an important part of temple service to the local community. Dhamma schools reconfigured a close connection between the village and the local temple, which had been jeopardized with the introduction of church-controlled Western education. Despite lay Buddhist initiation and leadership, the local monastic leadership holds the executive power of many dhamma schools. Currently, almost every Buddhist temple (except some of the forest hermitages) in Sri Lanka runs a dhamma school. This trend is also prevalent in diaspora. For example, three of the four temples in Toronto administer dhamma schools. The fourth temple, which inclines to the forest monastic tradition, offers meditation sessions for children and youths instead of a formal dhamma school.

The image of a Buddhist child imbued with Buddhist rhetoric derived from colonial Ceylon has continued in postcolonial Sri Lanka as well as within the Sri Lankan Buddhist diaspora in Toronto. However in Toronto the image of the Sinhala Buddhist child has taken a back seat as a new conceptualization of the Buddhist child emerges in the Canadian context.

THE SRI LANKAN CANADIAN BUDDHIST CHILD IN MULTICULTURAL TORONTO

The emblem of the West End Dhamma School illustrates dhamma educationists' imagined Buddhist child in Canada. It reminds us that the history discussed above legitimates the dhamma education practice in the diaspora while the current local conditions and concerns shape it. The emblem includes a maple leaf with a white swan holding an ola or palm leaf book in its beak. The swan is collaged into the red maple leaf. The ola leaf reads the Dhamma School's motto "*Sacitta Pariyodapanam*" (purification of one's own mind) in Sinhala scripts. All of them are placed on a half-opened book. The 2008 *Dhamma School* magazine explains: "Maple leaf symbolizes Canada ... Ola leaf book symbolizes Buddha Dhamma or Buddhist Doctrine ... the swan symbolizes the student who learns the Dhamma. Swan is also a reflection of purity. It is capable of separating the 'good' from the 'bad,' a quality that a good citizen should develop. The emblem promotes the idea that the person who learns Buddhism will eventually become a good citizen in Canada and will lead a fruitful life" (Dhamma School 2008, 3). The emblem and the above interpretation capture the historical and local impulses of Sri Lankan Buddhists in Toronto. It skilfully collages the traditional symbols of swan and ola leaf with the national symbol – the maple leaf. Students wear white T-shirts marked with this emblem as the uniform of West End Dhamma School when they come to learn dhamma. Thus the symbol itself stands for a new vision of the Buddhist child who is deeply rooted in Sri Lankan Buddhist history and yet also lives in this new location – i.e., Toronto, Canada. Perhaps what is more important is the underlying assertion of the emblem: learning Buddhism makes a child a good citizen of Canada. This echoes the assertion, which we noticed in dhamma education in postcolonial Sri Lanka, that learning Buddhism makes a Sri Lankan patriotic. But this time, Buddhism coalesces with neither an ethnicity nor a language, but rather a policy, law, and social reality that stands for Canada: multiculturalism. Buddhism undergoes a hermeneutic interpretation, labelled as "intelligent adaptation" to echo multicultural values; a detailed discussion on Buddhism and multiculturalism awaits in the next chapter. Here it suffices to note how a Canadian identity comes to the fore as Buddhist educationists envision who the Buddhist child is in Canada. The Buddhist child has been reimaged as Sri Lankan Buddhists strive to teach Buddhism to a Canadian-born generation.

After four years of experimenting with the dhamma education project at the West End Dhamma School, Swarna Chandrasekera, a Sinhalese scholar specializing in the field of education, compiled *Teaching Buddhism to Children* in 2001. Chandrasekera's voluntary service in compiling the manual represents an example of Sinhalese women's dedicated contribution to dhamma education. In the process of designing the curriculum, a committee comprising monks, lay dhamma teachers, parents, and youths met to discuss the content of the prospective curriculum. The monastic leadership had the final say with respect to the contents, while Chandrasekera was responsible for the format. Chandrasekera acknowledges: "In writing this book I have benefited from the cumulative knowledge of the *Maha Sangha*, my colleagues and students; and a host of resource persons who came from diverse disciplines to make their individual contributions" (Chandrasekera 2001, 4). She gives credit to Bhante Punnaji, the most senior monk within the community, for clarifying Buddhist terms and concepts (Chandrasekera 2001, 4). Thus the book itself represents a number of diverse voices, including those of monks, men, women, teachers, parents, and youths of a Buddhist temple.

Since the book is designed as a teaching manual, Chandrasekera lays out the basics of teaching dhamma, including a list of the qualifications a dhamma teacher should possess. She also gives a ninety-minute lesson plan and practical advice on lesson preparation and presentation. A list of relevant scriptures in the Pāli canon and a redefined glossary of Pāli terms are provided for teachers' reference. Two evaluation sheets are included; one is for students and the other for teachers. The core of the book is a curriculum of Buddhism for the weekly West End Dhamma School.

Chandrasekera recommends and implements "*Anupubba Dēsana*" or "gradual preaching/teaching" of dhamma in progressive steps. She argues that "gradual teaching" intimately connects with the gradual character transformation of dhamma practitioners/students (Chandrasekera 2001, 7). This "gradual teaching" method characterizes *Teaching Buddhism to Children* in multiple ways. Chandrasekera organizes the curriculum into five steps by arranging the contents according to child growth and spiritual development in Theravāda Buddhism. Steps One (age three–six) and Two (age six–nine) are called *saddhā* (Appreciation of Goodness). Although the Pāli term saddhā is translated as "appreciation of goodness" in the curriculum, more generally it refers to a Buddhist practitioner's confidence in the Buddha, dhamma, and sangha. In Theravāda Buddhism, spiritual development starts with saddhā. Step Three (age nine–twelve) is *sīla* (self-control); Step Four (age twelve–fifteen) is *samādhi* (calm and purity); and Step Five (age fifteen–eighteen) is *paññā* (wisdom). Sīla, samādhi, and paññā are considered three learnings derived from the Eightfold Path. In Theravāda Buddhism, spiritual growth is often conceptualized as a progressive development of four qualities: confidence, morality, concentration, and wisdom. The Pāli terms for these four concepts are used to name the five steps, by classifying the first and second steps under confidence.

Each step contains twenty-three lessons. The author recommends one lesson for two Sundays and eleven lessons for the entire academic year (September–June), which means that a student is expected to spend two years at each step. Thus if a student enrolled at step one they would take ten years to graduate from the West End Dhamma School. Although students advance in progressive steps, the progression is more spiral than linear. First, the manual briefly introduces a concept or practice, and in the next step, it returns to the same issue with new information. For example, at step one the manual

introduces what Vesak is (Chandrasekera 2001, 28), in step two it
explains why Buddhists celebrate Vesak (33), and in step three it
illustrates how Buddhists celebrate Vesak (37). A similar pattern is
used in illustrating the life story of the Buddha, which runs across
steps one to four.

In terms of teaching techniques, the author suggests that storytelling is a more effective method to instil morality in everyday lives
of the students. Through steps one to four, *Jātaka* stories dominate
the content. The manual invokes the Buddha as an exemplary sto-
ryteller who imparts Buddhist knowledge, practices, and values:
"The Buddha, the great teacher, selected the popular "storytelling"
method as a teaching tool to address the masses who were lovers of
stories. This method consisted of *Dana Katha* (Stories of "Giving"),
Sila Katha (Stories of Moral Restraint), and *Sagga Katha* ([stories]
of other dimensions of existence according to *kamma* [Skt. *karma*]):
Dana Katha ... exemplify benefits of "giving" and "giving up of
self." Dana Katha ... help develop virtues of compassion, concern
for others and above all, detachment from worldly things; Sila Katha
[promote] self control and helping the practice of virtues of justice,
fairplay and equality, etc.; Sagga Katha ... exhort devotees to do
good and lead lives of purity for the purpose of evolving into higher
levels until one reaches *Nibbana*" (Chandrasekera 2001, 9).

Here, too, the author emphasizes the gradual method of teaching
in her selection of the order of stories. Sri Lankan Buddhists commonly believe that the Buddhist way of life evolves in sequence or a
logical order. One starts with giving. Through the practice of giving,
the student gradually becomes interested in ethical practices. Ethics
is considered an integral component of a successful contemplative
practice (*bhāvana*).

Teaching Buddhism to Children also educates students about
many aspects of Theravāda Buddhism, including concepts, principles,
norms, values, and practices. Sometimes they are arranged as answers
to what, why, and how questions. In lower grades, concepts like karma
are introduced casually such as "If you give love you get love" (34).
In higher grades, the term is philosophically introduced along with a
story of a monk who lost his eyes as a result of intentionally blinding
someone else in one of his previous lives (43). In the final grade, a
complete lesson is dedicated to the concept along with twelve classi-
fications of karma (51). To embody the teachings, students memorize
Pāli chants, such as the three refuges, the five precepts, the salutation

to the Triple Gem, and the discourse on loving kindness. Instructions about how to perform certain practices are provided. For example, the steps to develop mindfulness on breath and to cultivate loving kindness (*Metta*) for oneself and others are laid out in the book. Above all, what is emphasized is how people behave when the teachings are fully practiced and embodied in characters. For that, the manual discusses in detail the life of the Buddha, the Jataka stories, and the spiritual biographies of monastic and lay Sangha.

Thus although all these aspects of the Theravāda tradition (concepts, stories, and practices) are more or less included in all grades, the proportions and levels of sophistication differ. The first two grades are more about relationships, and they emphasize the appreciation of goodness in oneself, parents, teachers, friends, and others. Grade three refers to sacred Buddhist sites in Sri Lanka, and includes many spiritual biographies of monks, nuns, and lay people of the Buddha's time. In grade four, numerous celebrated virtues and values are introduced, along with some stories. In grade five, Buddhist philosophical concepts are explained with an emphasis on meditation. A few lessons are dedicated to Buddhist history, other religions, and Canadian culture. All of the lessons, regardless of grade, end with meditation or chanting. The concepts, stories, and practices in the book are presented in a way that reflects the Canadian context. Chandrasekera therefore suggests that her book contributes to the formation of Buddhists as well as to good Canadian citizens. She claims that her book fulfills a "noble responsibility of imparting an education as well as a complete formation to children so that they will be better equipped intellectually, morally and emotionally to tackle today's hurdles and face tomorrow's challenges as Buddhists and as good citizens of this great Canadian nation of ours" (Chandrasekera 2001, 6). Thus *Teaching Buddhism to Children* envisions a Buddhist child who is simultaneously Buddhist as well as Canadian. It locates this child within a web of relations that includes oneself, family and community, as well as the wider society. Accordingly, *Teaching Buddhism to Children* addresses how one relates to one's Buddhist heritage (Sri Lankan Buddhism), to others (parents, friends, etc.), and to the wider Canadian society (including both Buddhists and non-Buddhists).

Two lessons entitled "I am a Buddhist" clearly lay out what makes a person a Theravāda Buddhist. Pāli liturgical practices stand for Theravāda Buddhist identity. In subjective language, the lessons emphasize taking refuge in the Triple Gem: '"*Buddham Saranam Gacchami*' (I take refuge in the Buddha)" (Chandrasekera 2001, 26) and "Obeisance to the Triple Gem (*Ti-sarana*)" (36). These lessons relate the observance of the Five Precepts to Buddhist identity. Dhamma students are encouraged to commit to memory the relevant Pāli chanting. The worship (praising the virtues of the Buddha, Dhamma, and Sangha), rituals (offering flowers to the Buddha), and "habits" (implying that all the above practices need be turned into habits) are highlighted, and the implication is that they play significant roles in forming a religious identity. In a typical Sunday dhamma school, teachers, students, and parents take refuge in the Triple Gem and observe the Five Precepts in Pāli. They bow to the Buddha and offer flowers and other items to him. All these *actions* illustrate the traditional way to establish a Buddhist identity, preferably a lifelong one. For example, the textbook used for the lessons reads, "As long as I live, I adore the Buddha. I follow the Dhamma. I respect the Sangha" (Nanayakkara 1993, 35). The memorization of Pāli chanting and its use in liturgy particularly evoke a Theravāda Buddhist identity.

The foregoing generic Theravāda identity becomes specific as the manual relates it to certain Buddhist sacred places. The lessons on "The Vihara (Monastery)" give a Sri Lankan flavour of Theravāda Buddhism (Chandrasekera 2001, 26, 36). They highlight "*Pagoda*, Bodhi Tree, Shrine Room, [and] Monks" as the integral parts of the Sri Lankan Buddhist temple (26). The monks' presence is crucial to make a Theravāda temple, as the Pāli term "*vihara*" for temple itself means the residence. The others are honoured as symbolic presences of the Buddha. The Bodhi tree, under which the Buddha is believed to have realized awakening, stands out as a distinguishing feature of a Sri Lankan Buddhist temple. The temples in Toronto manage to maintain Bodhi plants indoors. This signifies a sense of completeness of the temple. It also reminds students that though the practice has diminished in the diaspora, *bodhipuja* – honouring a Bodhi tree as a symbol of the Buddha – is a central practice in Sri Lankan Buddhism.[12] Moreover, in these lessons, the manual introduces several Buddhist places of worship with great historical significance: Swarnamali Maha Thupa and Samadhi Buddha Statue in Anuradhapura (36). With these references, the book underscores a Sri Lankan but not Sinhala Buddhist identity. The difference is that the former is geographically located, while the latter is ethnically defined. The lessons that are related to Buddhist identity and sacred places remind the dhamma students that Sri Lankan Buddhism is an inheritance that is nurtured within their family and community.

The manual places a great deal of emphasis on how the Buddhist child relates to parents and friends, as those relationships invoke intercultural tensions deriving from collective and individualist cultures (more on this in chapter 4). It therefore highlights the hierarchical parent-child values in numerous lessons: "I Love My Parents (Honour your parents), Respect and Listen to the Elders" (26), and "My Precious Parents" (37). A dhamma teacher claims that dhamma school shapes "a generation who respect elders, specifically parents and teachers." Students in lower grades commit to memory two specific Pāli verses[13] dedicated to parents, and they are encouraged and expected to bow at the feet of the parents before going to bed. Students annually perform this ritual by bowing at the feet of their parents at the dhamma school lesson held on the Sunday closest to the traditional Sinhala New Year in April. The manual also warns students that "Peer group, friends can influence you favourably or unfavourably" (37), and it reminds them to choose friends wisely. Many youths reveal that the issues related to friendship and dating often cause disagreement with their parents. Reflecting on these concerns, the manual dedicates a few lessons to cultural tensions (41, 46). She lays out a Buddhist emphasis on mutual duties in the child-parent relationship and advises dhamma students to maintain "respect for parents and elders in the family" (41). It also puts the Buddhist concepts of "good" and "bad" friends in the context of Canadian culture (46). The discussion of who the Buddhist child is and how they relate to parents invokes numerous classical Buddhist ideals: the prospective Buddha (*Bodhisatta*) with ten progressive practices (*Dasa Pāramita*) (36), the good person (*Sat Purusa*) with sense of gratitude (34), and the devoted and duty-bound male and female householders (*Upasaka* and *Upasika*) (52).

The preceding classical Buddhist ideals comprise the normative discourse of dhamma education, and the manual employs them to envision the Buddhist child in the Canadian context. As dhamma education envisions its students as Buddhists as well as good Canadian citizens (Chandrasekera 2001, 6), we notice that Buddhism coalesces with Canadian multicultural discourse. The latter encourages Canadians to recognize, respect, and relish the cultural norms, values, practices, and goodness of others who are religiously, culturally, and ethnically different from oneself. One of the learning objectives in *Teaching Buddhism to Children* reveals that "Students will develop and demonstrate respect for other religions so that they can appreciate Buddhist values they may observe among their non-Buddhist peers ... [and] develop skills in living and sharing in a multicultural/multireligious milieu" (Chandrasekera 2001, 15). The manual implies that as students learn and practice Buddhism, they will develop the ability to care for and respect Buddhism, as well as other religions. In other words, the book not only teaches what Buddhist values are, but also encourages dhamma students to recognize, respect, and relish one's own cultural norms, values, and practices as well as those of others who are religiously, culturally, and ethnically different. In fact, this multicultural and multireligious value has been emphasized from the very beginning of dhamma education in Toronto. For example, referring to Buddhist education in Toronto, K.S. Gunaratne, a Sri Lankan Buddhist leader in the mid-80s, emphasized that "when we attempt to enlighten the child with regard to ideas and beliefs gathered by him during his association with children of other faiths, we should take the precaution not to speak in a manner derogatory of other religions. *We should advise the child to respect all religions, even though they are different from his own*" (Gunaratne 1986, 11–12, emphasis added). The preceding statement suggests that since the mid-1980s an image of a child respectful of all religions has become an overtone of dhamma education in multicultural and multireligious Toronto. It took another decade and half or so to secure its place in dhamma education curriculum in 2001. If the retention and transmission of Buddhist tradition relates to Buddhist identity, the promotion of social harmony and peaceful coexistence entails a Canadian identity derived from Canada's multiculturalism policy and law.

Teaching Buddhism to Children collages these Buddhist and multicultural discourses for the envisioned Sri Lankan Canadian Buddhist child. In lower grades, the theme of peaceful coexistence surfaces in the morals of stories. The moral of the *Swarna Hansa Jātaka* says "Live, let live and help live." In the story, the bōdhisatta (the Buddha in one of his previous lives) was born as a swan with golden feathers who helped a poor family. He gave a feather to the family every day, and the family met their everyday needs by selling the feathers. One day, the greedy head of the family caught the swan and plucked out all the feathers. Since the feathers were plucked out against the swan's will, they ceased to be golden. The moral of the story could be interpreted as the virtues of contentment and gratitude, but instead, the lesson in the curriculum highlights the importance of peaceful coexistence, which is further strengthened by insisting that "We are not living alone. Others are important. We should care for them; sharing through exchange, cooperation and team work" (Chandrasekera 2001, 32). This teaching reinforces the spirit of multiculturalism as much as that of Buddhism.

In higher grades, intercultural themes are overtly developed in full lessons, i.e., "The Value of Buddhism in Canadian Life and Cultural Conflicts" (Chandrasekera 2001, 41) and "Relevance of Buddhism in Canadian Life" (Chandrasekera 2001, 46). These lessons contextualize Buddhism in Toronto. They provide a Buddhist perspective on certain virtues related to social ethics, such as responsibility, honesty, concern for others, and the expression of love and care. The manual encourages students "to respond rationally instead of reacting emotionally and irresponsibly" (Chandrasekera 2001, 46). It also relates Buddhism to "fair exchange and trustworthy relationships with others" and highlights "charity, social service, and ... making a contribution to society" (Chandrasekera 2001, 46). These concepts remind students that Buddhism can help them enrich their social life in multicultural Canada. They are the conceptual tools used to integrate young Buddhists into the wider Canadian society. They promote multicultural values such as mutual respect, sympathetic understanding, and peaceful coexistence.

CONCLUSION: (DIS)CONTINUITY IN DHAMMA EDUCATION

We have examined how the dhamma education/school within the Sri Lankan community in Toronto derives from a specific history that traces back to late nineteenth century colonial Ceylon. Buddhist educators in Toronto, like their predecessors in colonial Ceylon and postcolonial Sri Lanka, have envisioned variously who the Buddhist child is. The Sri Lankan Canadian Buddhist child imagined in *Teaching Buddhism to Children* has inherited the Buddhist rhetorical knowledge of *The Buddhist Catechism*. They also carry forward *Daham Pasela*'s Sri Lankan Buddhist identity derived from a specific geo-historicity rather than the Sinhala ethnicity. However, it is the multicultural values of mutual respect and peaceful coexistence that characterize the imagined Sri Lankan Canadian Buddhist child.

All reimaginings of the Buddhist child have been historically contingent. They have relied on or been influenced by the socio-political system of the particular time. They are "traversed by positions constituted by varying social projects and social uses" (Scott 1994, 175). The belief-oriented rhetorical Buddhist child in *The Buddhist Catechism* superseded other images of the ideal Buddhist child simply because it effectively resisted the Christian evangelical challenges against Buddhism in colonial Ceylon. The opposing ideal, the practice-oriented and culture-based Buddhist child of the *Bauddha Adahilla*, waited for the conducive socio-political conditions to re-emerge as the dominant image of the Sinhala Buddhist child under postcolonial nationalism. Nevertheless they did not abandon their predecessor's defensive Buddhist rhetoric; instead they harnessed it alongside Sinhala Buddhist nationalism in postcolonial Sri Lanka. In multicultural Toronto, however, the Sinhala Buddhist discourse has taken backseat as the Buddhist child is reimagined as Sri Lankan Canadian. A Buddhist multicultural discourse has come to the fore in Toronto's multicultural society. Thus colonial, postcolonial, and multicultural socio-political systems have created the conditions under which the diverse reinventions of the Buddhist child took place.

The historically contingent reimagining of the Buddhist child reflects Asad's discernment of the human-social structure mutual influence. Socio-political cultural systems derived from human activities; and yet, once they are properly set up, they tend to hold certain capabilities that resemble, and in some cases even condition, those of actual human beings. He explains: "The system [modernization] ... relates to a mode of human agency ('real people doing real things'), one that conditions other people's lives. The immediate objective of *this* agency, however, is not to cause individual actors to behave in one way rather than another. It is to change aggregate human conditions ... Its systematicity lies, therefore, in probabilities, not causalities" (Asad 1993, 7). Asad asserts that the systemic agency of socio-political and cultural systems conditions human agency. It is more abstract and pervasive, so much so that one can hardly escape from it. It does not directly force individuals to act in certain ways, but it does condition where human agency is constrained or at least obliged to comply with the social structures. Social structures and systems can limit the effectiveness of human agency and autonomy. Asad (1993, 4) concludes that "people are never only active agents and subjects in their own history." People are also submissive agents who function not only as representatives but also as objects of the power of social structures and systems. In that sense, the existing socio-political systems of the time have conditioned Buddhist educators to conceptualize the Buddhist child in various ways.

As we compare and contrast the reimagined Buddhist children in dhamma education history, we can discern different sets of pressures on, and expectations of, young Buddhists. The young Buddhists in colonial Ceylon were expected to learn and defend the Buddhist tradition. Buddhism was presented to them as a universal philosophy that transcends ethnic and national boundaries. Thus Buddhist unity was the subtext of *The Buddhist Catechism*. In postcolonial Sri Lanka, Buddhism has become a cultural heritage that contributes to the identity construction of people in a postcolonial nation. The *Daham Pasela* contextualizes Buddhism in Sri Lankan history and blends it with the Sinhalese ethnic culture. The Buddhist nationalist discourse urges young Buddhists to be patriots who love Buddhism, country, and the Sinhala language and ethnicity. This Sinhalese Buddhist nationalistic discourse has been blamed as one of the contributing factors for the Sinhala-Tamil conflict in Sri Lanka (Tambiah 1992; Seneviratne 1999; Bond 2004). This discourse gradually disintegrates in Toronto, where the second-generation Sri Lankan Buddhists tend to take the Sinhala language and ethnicity at their symbolic values, and their loyalty is shared between (if not necessarily divided by) two nations: Sri Lanka and Canada. *Teaching Buddhism to Children* exclusively highlights Buddhism's connection to Sri Lanka – instead of the Sinhala ethnicity – and it emphasizes the purported multicultural values found in Buddhist teachings. By doing so, the manual has imagined who the Sri Lankan Canadian Buddhist child is.

The shift from the Sinhala Buddhist child to a Sri Lankan Canadian Buddhist child signifies the reconfiguration of Sri Lankan Buddhism's connection to nationhood. Both images invoke two distinct notions of nationhood. The Sinhala Buddhist child refers to nationhood in which locality or place, ethnicity, language, and religion are salient aspects.[14] The island of Sri Lanka was where Buddhism was introduced to its inhabitants (the Sinhala people); the Sinhala language, along with Pāli, has been instrumental in forming a distinct version of Theravāda Buddhism (Mahinda 1997, 218). From this historical perspective, for many Buddhists in Sri Lanka the Sinhala ethnicity as an organic group of people, Sri Lanka as a place or locality, and the

Sinhala language as a medium of expression are all very important to their conceptualization of Buddhist identity. The history of this particular discourse is a bone of contention (Gunawardana 1979, 1984, 1990; Dharmadasa 1992), but it flourished in independent Sri Lanka with a sense of postcolonial enthusiasm (Bond 1988, 2004).

On the other hand, the Sri Lankan Canadian child implies Canada as a multinational nation, in which the emphasis is placed on a state that embraces multiple ethnicities and nationalities. Pierre Elliott Trudeau's multicultural policy envisioned "a polyethnic state" (Kent 2008, 143). Canada was the first country to accept multiculturalism as an official policy in 1971 and subsequently as federal law in 1988. With this bold step, Cecil Foster says, Canada has claimed to be the "first postmodern nation state" in the world (2014, vii), as opposed to a modern nation state that imagines a unified national identity. Foster further reminds that "it [genuine multiculturalism] says that much joy and good can arise in the mixing of identities to produce a citizenship that is universally inclusive of all differences and diversity. These reasons alone are enough to make genuine multiculturalism postmodern" (8). Within this inclusive nationhood, immigrants and their descendants are encouraged to maintain past identities. Within this socio-political context, the imagined Sri Lankan Canadian Buddhist child is expected to uphold both Sri Lankan Buddhist heritage and Canada's multicultural values.

What made these historically contingent images Buddhist is a normative discourse of character formation that runs throughout the history of dhamma education. For example, the canonical ideals like *kusala* (the skilful one), *satpurusa* (the good person), and bodhisatta (the budding buddha) have been invoked explicitly and/or implicitly in all three Buddhist education manuals. Dhamma teachers in Sri Lanka and in the diaspora have conceptualized teaching Buddhism to children as implanting dhamma seeds into the younger generation so that they may eventually realize canonical ideals. Thus imparting conceptual, contemplative, and experiential knowledge has become the meta-narrative of dhamma education.

In practice, however, conceptual knowledge or cognitive knowing has dominated dhamma education, partly because it emerged as a formal Buddhist education for laity in modernity. Structured with curricula, textbooks, and examinations, dhamma education has widely disseminated the conceptual knowledge of Buddhism. Cognitive knowing characteristically defines the first handbook of dhamma education: *The Buddhist Catechism.*[15] It has shaped the content, tone, and purpose of the successive manuals including *Teaching Buddhism to Children*, which defines teaching dhamma as a process intended "to present a rational and coherent synthesis" of the Buddha's teaching. Consequently, all three imagined Buddhist children are expected to learn a great deal about Buddhism. The amount of Buddhist knowledge a dhamma school graduate acquires may go well beyond a layperson's standard. However, they do not practice, and certainly do not experience, everything they learn.

Dhamma students are evaluated on the basis of how much they know about the Buddha, his teachings, and Buddhist history and culture.[16] Dhamma examinations, if we consider them indicative of what is emphasized in classrooms, suggest that dhamma education prioritizes factual knowledge about the Buddhist tradition. Teachers often ask "who, what, when, where, and which" questions to evaluate and measure students' grasp of Buddhism. Integrative questions like "how, why, and in what way" are entertained to a lesser extent. Reflecting on his time at a dhamma school, a father laments: "we have memorized only some addresses related to the life of the Buddha." It sounds like exaggeration, but he insinuates that Buddhism is taught more or less like any other school subject from a historical and factual point of view. Annual dhamma examinations are used to evaluate not only the performance of students, but also that of the dhamma schools themselves. A leading dhamma school brags about its consecutive reception of "The Venerable Dr Labuduwe Siri Dhamma Nayaka Thera Commutation Shield ... It is awarded to the Dhamma School which secures the first place for best results, presenting the largest number of candidates for ... the grade tests held among the Island's entire Dhamma schools" (Maharagama Siri Vajiragnana Daham Pasela). Thus the modern formation of Sri Lankan Buddhist identity has prioritized cognitive knowledge of Buddhism. This has led to overlooking the comprehensive formation of Buddhists – with equal emphases on the cognitive, affective, and behavioural inclinations – found in premodern Buddhist literature in Sri Lanka.

Stephen Berkwitz (2004, 293) argues that the *vamsas* – the Buddhist historical narratives in Sri Lanka – not only claim truth about the past, but they also make their audience moral agents "by acting upon the ways people think, feel, and act so that they may transform themselves." The vamsas, specifically the *Sinhala Thupavamsa*, narrate the actions of past agents in such a way that they convince their audience that these past agents made it possible for current Buddhists to gain worldly and otherworldly benefit (265). In other words, the audience of the *Sinhala Thupavamsa* enjoys this life and the life after death partly because of the good actions performed by previous Buddhists. Such narratives compel the audience not only to feel joy but to also to be grateful to and dependent on the Buddhist agents of the past. They also make the audience obliged to reciprocate with their own devotional acts. Berkwitz notes, "the feelings of gratitude and dependence create obligation for a person to act and, as a result, contribute to the construction of moral agents who engage in devotional acts" (269). This phenomenon, according to Berkwitz, constitutes a "devotional subjectivity" (294). The *Sinhala Thupavamsa* demonstrates the importance of a coherent connection between knowledge, emotion, and practice in fashioning the cognitive, affective, and behavioural components of the faithful. It also illustrates how knowledge, specifically historical learning, has been harnessed for the purposes of the moral formation of Buddhists in premodern Sri Lanka.

Knowledge plays an integral role in character formation. However, I would suggest that simply knowing (knowledge for the sake of knowing) hardly contributes to the formation of moral agents. It is not all knowledge, but rather a specific type of knowledge – an *integrative knowledge* of Buddhism – that induces practices in which dhamma students evolve to be Buddhist moral agents. In other words, knowing or learning about Buddhism – education *about* Buddhism – does not necessarily make one a Buddhist. Instead, learning how to successfully integrate Buddhism into one's life – education *for* becoming Buddhists – transforms the learner. The former concentrates on the mastery of content, while the latter emphasizes the purpose of teaching and learning Buddhism. The *Sinhala Thupavamsa* exemplifies how an integrative knowledge of the past may "transform ordinary devotees into 'virtuous persons'" – but modern historiography, complains Berkwitz, has overshadowed the constructive ethical power of the vamsas with its emphasis on the importance of historical truth (2004, 287). I suggest that it is the modern historiographical emphasis on historical facts that contributes to the prioritization of factual knowledge over integrative knowledge in dhamma education.[17]

The preceding discussion illustrates the origin and development of dhamma education as an institutional practice in Sri Lankan

Buddhism. I observed that dhamma education began as a sporadic practice to address the need of living Buddhists in Sri Lanka. It took more than a half-century to evolve as an institutional practice. Among other things, governmental and non-governmental sponsorship facilitated this development. Despite the absence of such assistance in the diaspora, the practice continues to be an integral part of Sri Lankan Buddhism. I suggest that dhamma education persists, even where rudimentary resources like monks and temples are not available, simply because it is an institutional practice whose important role in the transmission of the tradition is clearly recognized. In other words, its status as an institutional practice, and the heightened need for it, are two essential conditions for a religious practice to persist and be sustained in the diaspora.

The persistence of dhamma education beyond its original time and space does not suggest that Buddhism is static. Rather the opposite is true, which illustrates the dynamic nature of Buddhism. Dhamma educators' repeated imaginings of the ideal Buddhist child illustrate what being a Buddhist means in different times and places. The three imaginations of the Buddhist child highlight that the contingent discourses of colonial, postcolonial, and diasporic settings have reconfigured the classical normative discourse of the Pāli canon to remain relevant in meeting the shifting needs of Buddhist practitioners. They display a dynamic interplay among the inherited tradition, Buddhist educationists, and the socio-political systems of three distinct times and spaces. The imagined Sri Lankan-Buddhist child in Toronto requires reinterpretation of Buddhist concepts, practices, and institutions, and that is the topic discussed in detail in the next chapter.

An Inclusive and Harmonious Buddhism: A Buddhist Response to Multiculturalism in Canada

We define our identity always in dialogue with, sometimes in struggle against, the things our significant others want to see in us.

Charles Taylor

In the previous chapter, I discussed how Buddhist educators in Toronto have reimagined the children of Sri Lankan Buddhist immigrants to be simultaneously Canadian and Sri Lankan Buddhists. The Buddhist educational manual *Teaching Buddhism to Children* provides a blueprint for how to inculcate the newly imagined Sri Lankan Canadian Buddhist identity. Its carefully crafted foreword, a statement issued by Sri Lankan monks in Toronto, encapsulates the challenges that religious leaders of an immigrant community face and how they respond to them. The monks assert: "We are not impervious to the demands of the 'religio-cultural' diversity we see around us. It is indeed the environment in which our children will have to grow up. Therefore, we believe cultural adaptation to be the regular norm" (Chandrasekera 2001, 2). So what does the religio-culturally diverse Toronto – and by extension, Canada – expect from the religious leaders of an immigrant community? According to the monks, they are expected to culturally adapt themselves and their tradition to the new environment for the sake of Canadian-born generations of Buddhists. By saying cultural adaptation is a "general norm," the monks imply that they are simply following the general pattern of cultural adaptation found in their tradition. To ground themselves in that tradition is a crucial strategy of legitimation for the monks, specifically in a new cultural setting like Toronto.

So how has Canada's expectation of cultural adaptation from immigrants been expressed, and how have Sri Lankan Buddhist leaders responded to that expectation? As I will discuss below, the 1967 liberalization of immigration intensified Canada's existing ethnic, linguistic, and religious diversities. The increased cultural diversity brought in socio-political concerns like social disintegration and national disunity by challenging Canada's policy of biculturalism (English and French). To tackle these socio-political concerns was Canada's multiculturalism policy, introduced in 1971, which eventually became a federal law in 1988. The monks state that "multi-cultural, multi-religious and cosmopolitan societies bring in their train, unforeseen situations which call for tailor made solutions. Intelligent adaptation at times is not only desirable but also necessary" (Chandrasekera 2001, 1). A contextualized reading of this statement reveals that the emergence of Canada as a cosmopolitan society defined by cultural diversity has required "tailor made solutions" from both welcoming (settled) and incoming (immigrant) communities. The multiculturalism policy has been Canada's response to growing cultural diversity. This piece of legislation, as the monks allude to, has compelled immigrant communities to initiate a "desirable" cultural adaptation. The subjective term "desirable" begs a lot of questions, including what makes a cultural adaptation desirable and for whom.

The image of cultural mosaic, the symbol of multiculturalism, suggests that what is desirable is the integration of all cultural groups into broader Canadian society. At the height of a heated debate on Ontario Muslims' effort to implement Sharia Law to settle family disputes, Lindy Hurst noted in a *Toronto Star* article that from the very beginning Canada's multiculturalism policy has insisted on a twofold message to newcomers to Canada: "You do not have to assimilate. But we [Canadians] would like you, in time, to integrate into all aspects of Canadian society" (Hurst 2007). In order to integrate into the wider Canadian society, multiculturalism policy compels immigrant communities to prove that they are socially fit and worth being integrated. Cecil Foster observes that "genuine multiculturalism calls on the historical archetypical slave, outsider, foreigner, immigrant, and asks her or him to self-identify as socially worthwhile to stake a claim to equality" (2014, 12). The Sri Lankan monks in Toronto have responded to Canada's call for cultural integration with a reinterpretation of Buddhism that they dubbed as "intelligent adaptation."

By reinterpreting Buddhism, I contend, Sri Lankan monks in Toronto engage in a hermeneutic practice to highlight the adaptability of Buddhism to Canada's multicultural social fabric. Their efforts echo what Paul Crowe (2014, 167) calls "a hermeneutic of adaptation and integration." Studying Chinese Buddhist communities in Vancouver, Crowe warns scholars against the etic application of the language of adaptation and integration in studying immigrant religious communities in Canada, as his research participants are not keen on adaptation and integration. He states, "the questions about perceptions and adaptation ... were received [by the Chinese Buddhists in Vancouver] with a mixture of puzzlement" (152–3). He further observes that the priorities of Vancouver's Chinese Buddhists have been in their institutions' "history, teachings, mission, and organization," and such priorities express "emphatic assertions that adaptation was not needed" (152–3). Crowe, therefore, concludes that the Chinese Buddhists in Vancouver "appear to be moving in a direction away from integration" (154). Rather than adaptation and integration, Crowe observes, "their main concern was the full expression of their own religio-cultural identity and solidarity with the Chinese immigrant community" (155). In contrast to Crowe's study on Chinese Buddhists in Vancouver, this study strongly suggests that adaptation and integration have been the main priorities of Sri Lankan Buddhists in Toronto. This suggests that Buddhism(s) in Canada and Buddhists in Canada are not monolithic and homogenous. More importantly, the opposing orientations of the Chinese and Sri Lankan Buddhists amplify that there is more than one way to claim belonging to multicultural Canada. In reference to that emic phenomenon in the Sri Lankan Buddhist community of Toronto, I justify my argument that Sri Lankan Buddhists in Toronto have engaged in a hermeneutic of adaptation and integration.

Warning against the etic use of the language of adaptation and integration, Crowe (2014, 167–8) asserts: "When we read the history, organization, and social dynamics of immigrant religious communities through a hermeneutic of adaptation and integration, we risk creating their stories in terms that assume a distance between 'those communities' and 'the rest of us' and contributing to the polarizing language currently affecting public discourse in this country [Canada]." I agree with Crowe that scholars should not employ the lenses of adaptation and integration in studying immigrant communities, particularly in the absence of such inclinations within the researched communities. To do so would be an imposition of the researcher's wishes onto the researched, which might fuel the fearmongering, divisive discourse that advocates assimilation. If, however, "a hermeneutic of adaption and integration" becomes an emic (as opposed to etic) language or discursively emerges within the immigrant religious community in question, then our scholarship/research becomes a venue to express the marginalized voice of immigrants. As the discussion below illustrates, immigrant religious communities such as the Sri Lankan Buddhists of Toronto themselves speak in the language of adaptation and integration. And by bringing these immigrant voices of integration to the foreground, this chapter in fact neutralizes the polarizing discourse in contemporary Canada.

Sri Lankan Buddhists – and particularly monks – in Toronto highlight the inclusivity, harmony, and secular rationality of Buddhism so that they can actively participate in Canada's secular, multicultural society. This reconfiguration of Buddhism as an inclusive and harmonious religion demonstrates the dynamic interpenetration between religion and secularism. On the one hand a secular social ethos, as expressed in multiculturalism, influences Buddhism to reconfigure itself by refurbishing its compatible elements. On the other hand, by adopting the language of multiculturalism, Buddhism pushes the private sphere boundary that secularism has imposed on religion. In redefining Buddhism to echo multiculturalism, monks emerge as cultural interpreters.

MONKS AS CULTURAL INTERPRETERS

A new cultural place and a new generation have become legitimate reasons for the Sri Lankan monks in Toronto to reinterpret key Buddhist terms. The credit for redefining Buddhist concepts, practices, and institutions goes to the Sri Lankan monks in Toronto, particularly Bhante Punnaji, the most senior and erudite monk in the community. The monks say "a Buddhist monk in essence is a teacher, a guide and a mentor to his people" (Chandrasekera 2001, 1). We will see later in this chapter that a new function is added to all these traditional roles of a monk in a new cultural setting: a function as a cultural interpreter of Buddhism. One could technically argue that

Figure 4.1   Toronto's dhamma school curriculum
Source: Author

the reinterpreted Buddhism is for a multicultural society in general. However, as the title of the book *Teaching Buddhism to Children* suggests, its more specific audience is "the children of the [Sri Lankan Buddhist] community" (2) in Toronto who, as we have seen in the previous chapter, have been reimagined as Sri Lankan Canadian Buddhists. Thus religio-culturally diverse Toronto and the Buddhist children born there have inspired a reinterpretation of Buddhism.

Reinterpretation entails adding new aspects to the tradition, and modifying and/or excising certain existing elements of the tradition;

both, however, depend on who, where, and for whom the reinterpretation is done. The existing elements are scrutinized and evaluated in relation to the contemporary social values and cultural norms. For example, Chandrasekera suggests that reinterpretation in Toronto is motivated "to avoid repeating many misconceptions and misinterpretations that had found their way into the terminology of Buddhism over the years, often conveying erroneous and un-Buddhist connotations" (2001, 4). She observes that the existing Buddhist tradition contains certain "misconceptions" and "misinterpretations," which have infiltrated the tradition and compromised "correct" Buddhist understanding. She implies that the purpose of the reinterpretation provided in her book is to shed light on the earliest form of the Buddha's teachings. This is the same strategy – going back to the foundational sources by bypassing the later interpretations – used by the nineteenth- and twentieth-century Buddhist revivalists in Sri Lanka.

The reinterpreted Buddhism has excluded certain aspects of Sri Lankan Buddhism. The monks in the community insist: "we should muster both sincerity and the courage of our convictions to even discard without regrets, those arcane, regressive customs and practices that are incompatible with the dhamma and are a hindrance to our practice" (Charadrasekera 2001, 2). What constitutes the so-called "arcane, regressive customs and practices" remains unexplained. Nevertheless, under the monks' leadership, deity worship (*devapuja*) – a significant practice that defines Sri Lankan Buddhism – is left out of Buddhist temples in Toronto. This absence of devapuja at the temples under study could be understood as a reformed practice influenced by a textual interpretation. At the same time, it is also a particular discourse derived from the reformed Vajirarama monastic tradition started at the turn of twentieth century in Colombo that spread out in Sri Lanka and abroad by the end of the same century.

Referring to the national and international glory of the Vajirarama monastic lineage, Asanga Thilakaratne (2007) asserts: "In this twentieth century, if there is a [Sri Lankan] Buddhist temple that rendered an incomparable service to both Sri Lanka and the world, it would be the Vajirarama Temple. Similarly, if there is a generation of Buddhist monks that worked tirelessly for the Buddhist culture of Sri Lanka as well as of the world, it would be the lineage of monks trained by Palene Vajiragnana Nahimi [the founder of the Vajirarama monastic tradition] [author's translation from Sinhala]" (Thilakaratne 2007,

19). In 1901, upon an invitation from a group of modern educated Buddhists, Palene Vajiragnana Nahimi (1878–1955) came to a small residence on Vajira Road at the heart of Colombo, which eventually became the Vajirarama in 1909. Until his death in 1955, he trained a group of mostly Sinhalese (but also a few foreigners including two English) monks who eventually became known as the Vajirarama monastic tradition. The Vajirarama monks embodied a reformed Buddhist mission that extended locally and internationally including North America. A leading Vajirarama monk named Madihe Pannāsīha Mahānāyaka Thero earned a reputation for establishing Buddhist temples in Sri Lanka and beyond. In 1966 he founded the Washington Buddhist Vihāra, the first Theravāda temple in North America (Cadge 2005, 25). He also had significant influence in establishing the Toronto Mahāvihāra, the first Theravāda temple in Canada. Madihe Thero served as patron of that temple, and visited a few times.

What made the Vajirarama monks effective as national and international Buddhist missionaries was Palene Nahimi's[1] hybrid monastic training that coupled tradition and modernity. Palene Nahimi emphasized inviolable traditional *vinaya* (disciplinary) codes of conduct that produced a classical monastic character with shaved head, donned in hand-dyed ochre robes and carrying a begging-bowl. This traditional monastic image was revitalized with eloquent modern language training and rhetorical skills in preaching. At a time when the English language was resisted as a sign of colonialism and imperialism, Palene Nahimi actively sought out English knowledge for his disciples. That strategy saved the English-educated, burgeoning Sinhalese middle class from converting to Christianity – and won back a few who had already been taken into the fold of Christianity. It also trained eloquent English-speaking disciples like Narada and Piyadassi Theros, who extended the Buddhist mission beyond Sri Lanka. These disciples became known as "travelling monks," and travelled internationally as captivating Buddhist preachers (Thilakaratne 2007, 21).

More importantly, Palene Nahimi's innovative, structured style of preaching made him and his disciples effective Buddhist missionaries. He introduced Buddhist sermons on public radio in 1928, so that people across the country could listen to Buddhism. As part of that task, he replaced the all-night-long, unstructured preaching tradition with an hour-long, structured sermon. Palene Nahimi also transformed Jataka story-based preaching into a thematic sermon.

He interpreted Buddhist themes alongside examples derived from the modern scientific world (Thilakaratne 2007, 22). Modernity is characterized, in part, by an emphasis on efficiency and an orientation toward results, and these values were abundantly present in the Vajirarama monastic training. Yet this training was also grounded in an ancient Buddhist image of the mendicant. The Vajirarama monks' training hybridized the traditional plus the modern. According to Thilakaratne (2007), the biggest contribution Pelane Nahimi made was "to produce a lineage of modern monks who uphold the decorum and attitudes of traditional monasticism and who are also capable of explicating Buddhism to the scientific and technologically savvy world [author's translation from Sinhala]" (Thilakaratne 2007, 20). It is from this mixed monastic tradition that the monks in Toronto who reinterpreted Buddhism are derived.

The monks in Toronto have therefore recontextualized the legacy of Vajirarama monastic tradition. The Vajirarama monks popularized the assertion that devapūja contradicts the Buddhist teaching of self-reliance; thus the Vajirarama temples in Toronto and elsewhere including in Sri Lanka do not house *devāle* (deity shrines). The monks in Toronto received training at the Vajiragnana Bhikkhu Training Centre located at Colombo suburb of Maharagama. The leading disciples of Palene Vajiragnana Nahimi – Madihe Pannasiha Nahimi and Ampitiye Rahula Himi – named the centre "Vajiragnana" to honour their beloved teacher. They extended Palene Nahimi's mission with twofold trainings. In addition to training Buddhist missionaries for national and international Buddhist mission, the Vajiragnana Centre has also focused on training young people through dhamma education. Its Sri Vajiragnana Dhamma School became the best dhamma school in Sri Lanka with the Sinhala Buddhist discourse. Its founder, Madihe Pannasiha Nahimi emphasizes that dhamma education should mould a young generation with Sinhala Buddhist nationalism (1995, 5). Accordingly, the Sri Vajiragnana Dhamma School trains students "to develop correct attitudes for building a generation of religious, patriotic and national minded children" (Warusawithana 2007, i). The monks in Toronto claim to administer the best dhamma school in North America. As we have seen in the preceding chapter, however, they have replaced the ethnically exclusive image of the Sinhala Buddhist child with its nationally inclusive Sri Lankan Canadian counterpart. In that reimagination, Buddhism becomes inclusive and harmonious. Thus monks in Toronto continue the hybrid legacy of Vajirarama monasticism with their own, recontextualized interpretation of Buddhism. And in their reinterpretation, religious inclusivity emerges as a defining feature.

RELIGIOUS INCLUSIVITY

By religious inclusivity in *Teaching Buddhism to Children*, I refer to the breadth of perspectives that reflect and include Buddhist and non-Buddhist worldviews. The manual includes definitions of the Buddha that represent different disciplines, modes of enquiry, and perspectives. For example, Buddha is defined as "A Super Human Being (*Uttari Manussa*)," and the explanation offered for his miraculous walk on seven lotuses immediately after birth is: "Seven lotuses symbolize the seven constitutions of awakening (*Sapta Bojjhanga*)" (2001, 46). This definition combines both secular humanist and religious faith-inspiring accounts of the Buddha. It simultaneously echoes as well as challenges the West's popular understanding of the Buddha.

During the nineteenth and early twentieth centuries, both Christian missionaries like Robert Spence Hardy (1803–1868) and orientalists like Thomas William Rhys Davids (1843–1922) depicted the Buddha simply as a human being. Hardy argued that Buddhism, as an ethical system with no divine intervention, exemplifies the inadequacy of European Enlightenment thought. Rhys Davids also compared the Buddha to Enlightenment philosophers, but he did so to defend Enlightenment thought. He emphasized the Buddha being agnostic but also the founder of a religion (Buddhism) with a strong ethical foundation. Similarly, he argued that the agnosticism of Enlightenment thought was neither anti-Christian nor unethical. For Rhys Davids, both an agnostic Buddha and ethical Buddhism provided "'a mirror which allowed Christians to see themselves more clearly'" (cited in Snodgrass 2007, 192). In other words, Rhys Davids used a humanist portrayal of the Buddha in order to advocate – in Judith Snodgrass's expression – "post-Enlightenment secularized Protestant Christianity" (2007, 192). Thus Hardy's humanist portrayal of the Buddha was a condemnation of not only Buddhism but also secularized Enlightenment thought, while Rhys Davids' humanist project was an approval of the Buddha in order to minimize Christian animosity toward Enlightenment philosophy. In the end, both positive and negative humanist portrayals of the Buddha were part of the "contest over the future of Christianity in an age of science" (Snodgrass 2007, 193). The humanist portrayals of the Buddha, even the positive one, disregarded how Buddhists themselves have perceived the Buddha as an incomparable teacher, the model of Buddhist teachings (dhamma), and the model for the Buddhist faithful (sangha). For example, Rhys Davids rejected faith-evoking names, i.e., Siddhartha (the one who has accomplished his aim) and Sakyamuni (the sage of the Sakyas). He used the title "Buddha" only to comparatively illustrate how Jesus became Christ in Christianity. Instead Davids favoured the family name Gautama, or Gotama, to denote the historical credibility of the actual personage, as evidenced by archaeological discoveries (Snodgrass 2007, 191).

The humanists' definition of the Buddha derived from history, archaeology, and texts, and their comparison of Gotama to European philosophers, took a new toll in the subsequent Indigenous Buddhist apologetic discourses. Buddhist modernists used humanism to highlight Buddhism's modern character. They also used historical and archaeological evidence, along with extra-canonical textual accounts, to construct a sacred biography of the Buddha. Snodgrass (2007, 199) contends: "they [Asian Buddhist modernists] tended not to discard the miraculous in the way that Rhys Davids had done, but to interpret it symbolically." In other words, modern Buddhist interpreters pushed the scientifically articulated humanist discourse to a new level, along with tradition-based, faith-inspiring accounts of the Buddha. As evidenced by the definition of the Buddha as "A Super Human Being," this trend continues in the diaspora with a new emphasis: experience. In a lesson designed for youths aged between thirteen and fifteen, the Buddha is defined as someone extraordinary "with the Super Human Experiences (*Uttari Manussa Dhamma*)" and the dhamma is "The Buddha's Experience (*Sila, Samadhi, Panna, Vimutti and Nibbana*)" (Chandrasekera 2001, 41). Here, the manual reiterates the philosophical claim that the Buddha was an experientialist, which means that everything he taught was based on his own experience. Chandrasekera also implies that one should understand the dhamma through one's own experience. This experiential discourse is not new. What is new, though, is to whom it is addressed. Historically it has rarely been used for general practitioners, let alone for a younger audience[2] (whose experience is considered to be relatively less reliable in understanding dhamma).

Only in recent times has the emphasis on experience in Buddhism become popular. Its popularization in the manual may indicate an intercultural shift from collectivism to individualism in understanding and practicing Buddhism. After all, the manual intends to teach Buddhism to a generation influenced by an increasing cultural trend towards "turn[ing] inward." Peter Berger (1979) theorizes that the forces of modernization have eroded or undermined "plausibility structures," which create a sense of a coherent, stable social order with "a very high degree of objectivity." The need for a stable social order is more pressing than ever. Nevertheless, individuals cannot rely solely on the outside world, such as society and culture (due to diverse, often contradictory interpretations). Therefore, they must turn to themselves to construct a sense of coherence. Berger (1979, 20–1) explains: "If answers are not provided objectively by ... society, [one] is compelled to turn inward, toward [one's] own subjectivity, to dredge up from there whatever certainties [one] can manage ... It should not be surprising that modern Western culture has been marked by an ever-increasing attention to subjectivity." This subjective turn informs the above-discussed experiential approach to Buddhism. It has also provided a condition where the dialogue between Buddhist meditation and Western psychology and psychotherapy has flourished.[3] Reflecting on this development, the manual defines the Buddha as "the supreme psychotherapist and healer of all times." This particular definition of the Buddha is followed by a Pāli phrase: "*Anuttaro bhisakko sallakatto*" (Chandrasekera 2001, 46). The Pāli phrase refers to the Buddha as an incomparable healer, while the interpreters' addition of "the supreme psychotherapist" captures the mood of ongoing dialogue between Buddhism and Western psychology and psychotherapy. Donald Lopez (2008, 207) suggests: "research on meditation has sought to calculate the psychological and neurological effects of Buddhist meditation ... The claim here is that Buddhist meditation works." The experiential and psychologically oriented definitions of the Buddha exemplify the wider culture's influence on Buddhist interpreters. But it is noteworthy that premodern, faith-inspiring religious definitions of the Buddha are also included side by side with their modern counterparts. That illustrates the manual's interdisciplinary inclusivity by which the redefined Buddhism in Toronto represents both traditional and modern Buddhist voices. The manual thus transcends the traditional-modern division within Buddhism. It also includes religious others as it interprets Buddhism.

Religious inclusivity refers to the consideration and inclusion of the sentiments of other religious traditions. *Teaching Buddhism to*

Children pays attention to non-Theravāda Buddhist and non-Buddhist aspects as it reinterprets who Buddha is. For instance, it says, "Buddha is a great teacher (*Sattadevamanussanam* [sic])," followed by another definition "Buddha [is] the Saviour of the worlds (*Loka Natha*)" (2001, 46). The former establishes the Theravāda emphasis on the historical Buddha and his role as a teacher, which implies that one has to rely on oneself for spiritual attainment. The latter definition is more associated with non-Theravāda Buddhism – for example the Pure Land Buddhist tradition emphasizes the reliance on the "other power" (*takiri*) of Amitabha Buddha for spiritual salvation. In general, it also mildly expresses the Mahāyāna and Vajrayāna belief in the intervention of celestial Buddhas and Boddhisattvas in one's spiritual path. Theravāda devotional literature, too, would provide countless references to "the Saviour of the worlds." Here, however, the connotation is different. The phrase invokes a this-worldly interpretation. For example, *Teaching Buddhism to Children* (Chandrasekera 2001, 46) offers this definition: "Buddha [is] seen as a competent social worker like any in modern times; he used effective social work methods in helping people: Buddha as [a] case worker (Kisa Gotami), Buddha as a group worker (started with five monks), Buddha as a community worker (resolved community conflict over the use of river water)." In this context, "the Saviour of the worlds" does not invoke a spiritual meaning. Rather, the Buddha is compared to "a competent social worker" with three related roles. Interestingly, unlike other definitions in the book these this-worldly roles of the Buddha lack Pāli equivalents. Instead, they are supported by anecdotes from the life story of the Buddha, which themselves indicate the Buddha's intervention into incidents of spiritual, social, and even political nature. In this particular definition, the interpreters in Toronto have been thoughtful, skilful, and innovative in appropriating a non-Theravāda concept of Buddha. Indeed, the "social worker" role of the Buddha was invoked in a lesson designed for senior high school students who have to do voluntary community service for their high school graduation.

Similarly, the teaching manual also addresses non-Buddhist religious views, specifically the concept of god(s). It challenges previous interpretations of Buddhism, specifically the description of Buddhism as an atheistic or god(s)-free religion. Since the late nineteenth century, Buddhism was portrayed as atheist and agnostic. This image has persisted, shaping the Western perception of Buddhism as a god(s)-free religion to the present day. This portrayal of Buddhism was carefully crafted for two paradoxical reasons. Christian polemical missionaries such as Barthelemy St Hilaire argued: "In the whole of Buddhism there is not a trace of God" (in Snodgrass 2009, 35). This portrayal of godless Buddhism was intended to highlight the "striking contrast" between Buddhism and Christianity, and to show the superiority of Christianity over Buddhism. Others described Buddhism as godless, secular religion that complemented the anti-theistic orientation of nineteenth-century Western intellectuals (Obeyesekere 2006, 71). Snodgrass (2009) notes that such "free thinkers and humanists ... saw Buddhism as proof of the possibility of an ethical system that did not depend on an interventionist god" (35). In these Christian and secular agendas, the complexity of living Buddhism was deliberately left out.

Teaching Buddhism to Children reverses the godless presentation of Buddhism. It diversifies the concept of god by including sociological (conventional), theological, and ethical definitions of divinity. Nevertheless it prioritizes the ethical definition of divinity, and asserts that the Buddha personified that concept. The lesson entitled "Buddhism and World Religions," states

There are three concepts of God (*Deva*) in Buddhism.
1 God by Convention (*Sammuti Deva*)
2 God by Birth (*Uppatti Deva*)
3 God by Purity of Mind (*Visuddhi Deva*)
All Spiritually Perfect Saints (*Arhants*) and Awake Ones (Buddhas) are Gods by Purity of Mind. They are also called God Become (*Brahma Bhuto*).

Gods by Birth are celestial beings who live in celestial spheres or heavens. The term, Gods by convention, refers to the deification of natural phenomena and of ordinary human beings. (Chandrasekera 2001, 53)

This multi-layered concept of god accomplishes a few things. First of all, it demonstrates the breadth and depth of the Buddhist treatment of the topic. The manual acknowledges and respects the beliefs in god(s) found in other religions, for example in a lesson entitled "Buddhism and World Religions." Second, the three concepts are laid out in a progressive sequence by ranking them. The Buddha and his awakened disciples, the pinnacles of Theravāda spiritual attainment, are said to be the gods become (or arisen) through the purification of the mind. They are ranked higher than the celestial beings – gods by birth, the second in the hierarchy. For example, the manual explains elsewhere: "The Buddha as seen in Buddhism is greater than *gods* because He has risen beyond not only human weaknesses, but also the weaknesses of the gods" (2001, 46). This explains that Buddha tops the Buddhist spiritual hierarchy, and he belongs to the highest category in the threefold concept of divinity. Finally, in this definition the Buddha and his awakened followers are referred to as "God Become (Brahma[4] Bhuto)" in a singular form, which echoes the West's theistic concept of God. The Buddha is compared to the ultimate focus of theistic religions, God.

The term "God Become" captures the Buddhist emphasis on spiritual attainment that distinguishes the Buddhist concept from that of other religions. It highlights that one becomes a god through spiritual attainment. This interpretation does not undermine, but rather intensifies, the importance of human agency – the integrity of Buddhism. In a follow-up interview, Bhante Punnaji explains that "Buddhism is humanistic; it is anthropocentric. It says man created god in his own image. God is a human concept. It is a concept of perfection: perfect in knowledge, perfect in power and perfect in goodness. In that sense, God is a person who is perfect in everything ... God is the ideal of religion. The person who realizes the ideal, he is called the Buddha" (personal interview, 2009). The preceding explanation echoes the Judeo-Christian concept of God in its emphasis on perfection. At the same time, it highlights a Buddhist emphasis on human agency by reversing the theistic discourse: instead of God creating humans in His image, here we have humans creating God. Or better yet, humans who have that potential. Bhante Punnaji defines Buddhism neither as theistic nor as atheistic, but as a humanistic religion where an ethical concept of god remains the ideal. He explains that the Buddha is someone who realized that ideal. Importantly, his use of the present tense, "the person who realizes the ideal ... is called the Buddha" locates that possibility in the now. These sentiments take Buddhism out of a past – of another place and another time – to highlight its relevance for this time and this place. Thus, the teaching manual suggests that Buddhism stands out from other religions not only in its breadth of the concept of god(s) but also in its efficacy in becoming god(s) or realizing the ideals of religions. Inclusivity in the curriculum also relates to community membership.

The curriculum envisions an inclusive Buddhist community. The presence of a multiethnic Buddhist demographic in Toronto provides an opportunity to form a multiethnic Buddhist congregation. This is a future possibility rather than a current reality, but the Sri Lankan Buddhist temples studied indicate the conditions that may encourage or inhibit such a future Buddhist institutional development. The use of English for services and the suppression of ethnic discourse seem to draw multiethnic Buddhist participants. For example, the West End Dhamma School teaches Buddhism to students from diverse ethnic backgrounds. Its 2009 Dhamma School Day celebration displayed the Indian and Bangladeshi flags side by side with the Sri Lankan and Canadian flags. It is not unusual to see a multiethnic audience attending Buddhist talks, meditation sessions, and sutta classes conducted in English. This sense of ethnic inclusivity is, however, less visible and less consistent in terms of temple administration and executive membership.

But at the conceptual level, gender neutrality and social equality are increasingly becoming prominent in defining Buddhist membership. For example, the curriculum defines the term "Sangha" broadly as "the community of followers of the Buddha consisting of monks (Bhikkhu), nuns (Bhikkhuni), laymen (Upasaka), lay women (Upasika)" (2001, 41). Here, the term implies that neither the practitioners' gender differentiation, nor their institutional monastic-laity distinction, determines the membership of the *Sangha*. Instead it is based upon their spiritual attainments and aspirations. We have seen the same inclusive interpretation of the term in Olcott's *Buddhist Catechism* (1881) discussed in the last chapter. Unlike its predecessor, *Teaching Buddhism to Children* qualifies the inclusive definition with the monk-laity distinction: "Monks and nuns comprise the sanctified fold of the *Sangha*," it says, implying that laymen and laywomen belong to a non-sanctified or secular fold of the Sangha (Chandrasekera 2001, 41). The latter definition marks the institutional monk-laity divide within the Buddhist community. Both perspectives, however, obscure everyday understandings and applications of the term. Data from the surveys of the community indicate that the majority of both generations (56 per cent of each) use the term "Sangha" to refer to male and female monastics only. Moreover, the gender exclusive use of the term (to refer to only monks) has significantly decreased among the second generation. Only 9 per cent of the second generation, in comparison to 19 per cent of their parents, say that monks alone belong to the Sangha.

The important issue here is that there is a conceptual/philosoph-
ical effort being made to move away from gender-biased and patri-
archal Theravāda discourse toward a more generalized or inclusive
Buddhist discourse. The simple inclusion of the broader definition in
the teaching manual itself signifies a perceptual change taking place
within the community. This change could be a response to the value
placed on gendered and social egalitarianism in North American culture.[5] This trend is nowhere as explicit as in the lesson on "Buddha's
Attitude to Women" (2001, 51). The lesson quotes a few direct statements of the Buddha from some of his earliest discourses, where
the intellectual ability, spiritual achievement, and wisdom of female
disciples were recognized and praised. It emphasizes gender equality
as a core value within Buddhism. It says, "equality is one of the basic
values enunciated in the teachings of the Buddha." It then goes on
to illustrate with an example: "The psychic wonders Gotami [the
step mother of the Buddha] displayed were equal to that of Ven.
Maha Moggallana, the Master of Psychic Powers" (2001, 51). At
the foundation of the tradition, therefore, were Gotami and Maha
Moggallana's equal spiritual attainments.

The discourse of equality has also generated much discussion in contemporary critical literature on Buddhist female renunciants. Feminist
quests for gender and social equality have often overshadowed the
religious and spiritual quests of female renunciants. Nirmala Salgado
(2014) suggests that the spiritual quests and struggle that define the
lives of many Buddhist women deserve greater scholarly attention. She
discerns that "renunciant narratives can be misinterpreted and misun-
derstood when placed, as they often have been, within a theoretical
framework of liberal feminism" (2). Therefore, she proposes to examine
the lives of female renunciants within the Buddhist soteriological paradigm so that the questions they face in everyday life would illustrate
"the meaning of key Buddhist notions such as *dukkha* and samsara
– an understanding that cannot be situated in a liberal feminist story
about feminism" (10). The manual's suggestion that there is equality
between Buddhist monks and nuns is confined to spiritual attainment.
In other words, equal spiritual attainment does not translate into gender equality. In fact the history of Buddhist monastic institution and
the protocols that govern them suggest that spiritual attainment has by
no means transcended institutional and gender hierarchies.

The reference to equal spiritual attainment between monks and
nuns in the manual does however reflect a shift in attitude about

female gender within the Sri Lankan monastic tradition. Women in Sri Lanka have striven to revive the lost bhikkhuni order since the late nineteenth century (Bartholomeusz 1994); but their triumph materialized only in 1996, with the support and encouragement of the Sakyadhita International Association of Buddhist Women (Tsomo 2009, 155, 160). The essence of the lesson in the teaching manual is that gender has nothing to do with the Buddhist spiritual path; indeed the lesson ends with the rhetorical question: "in ones [sic] journey to *Nibbana*, how can a woman's sex be a hindrance" (2001, 51). Once again, we witness a symbolic effort to foreground an inclusive Buddhist discourse, along with an emphasis on gender equality. Inclusivity also extends to secular worldviews.

SECULAR INCLUSIVITY

In search of the genealogy of and mutual connection between the secular and secularism, Talal Asad (2003, 191) argues that both concepts originated at two different historical moments; nevertheless, they eventually became interdependent in their support of each other. The early modern religio-political and economic atmosphere in Europe, specifically the Catholic-Protestant hostility, contributed to secularism's evolution as a political and governmental doctrine. With secularism's political clout, the secular eventually became a powerful alternate worldview and a way of life (as opposed to those of religion). Asad suggests that the secular "brings together certain behaviors, knowledges, and sensibilities in modern life" (25). Commenting on its impact on religious worldviews, Asad says: "the complex medieval Christian universe, with its interlinked times ... and hierarchy of spaces ... is broken down by the modern doctrine of secularism into a duality: a world of self-authenticating things in which we *really* live as social beings and a religious world that exists only in our imagination" (194). According to Asad, secularism divides this universe into two – the real and the imaginary. It prioritizes the real, as humans are able – both individually and collectively – to verify things in that real world. In contrast, the things in religion's imaginary world are beyond human (individual and collective) verification. Thus humanity is the center of the secular doctrine, which prioritizes human agency more than anything else. The ethical implications of secular worldviews challenge the heart of religious ethics: god is the ultimate source of goodness. According to secular doctrine, humans are autonomous beings; they, rather than the divine, are capable of defining what is good and evil and conducting themselves accordingly. They are, therefore, responsible individually as well as collectively for the actions they perform. This secular discourse of human agency, in fact, echoes Bhante Punnaji's Buddhist concept "God Become," and his "humanistic" and "anthropocentric" definition of Buddhism discussed above.

Teaching Buddhism to Children takes the secular atmosphere of Toronto into consideration as it interprets Buddhist ethics. Although Theravāda Buddhism highlights the importance of human agency, its worldviews go beyond verifiable parameters. Karma and rebirth are integral parts of Buddhist ethical teachings, which are not readily available for common human authentication. They remain obscured in Chandrasekera's treatment of the Five Precepts, the basic Buddhist moral guidelines: "The Five Restraints (*Panca Sila*) are the beginning of goodness. Goodness is the beginning of peace and happiness ... If you neglect moral restraint, you will be injuring or harming both yourself as well as others. Moral restraint should be based on consideration for others as well as oneself. It is based on Universal Goodwill (*Metta*), and not on the belief in punishment and reward" (2001, 47). Here, the secular sensitivity expressed in a this-worldly orientation obscures the otherworldly (religious) connotation of the Five Precepts.[6] Certainly, the context and the Pāli words maintain that the Five Precepts constitute Buddhist moral behaviour. Nevertheless, the preceding definition leaves out conventional Buddhist otherworldly language like kamma (intentional actions) and kamma-vipāka (results of actions), and it certainly values relational ethical motivation over self-centred (i.e., greed- and fear-based) moral behaviours. The term "Universal Goodwill" in the above quotation invokes a transcendent principle; however, it is not necessarily referred to as an otherworldly goal. The implication is that one should follow the Five Precepts not simply because they are prescribed by the Buddha and/or have otherworldly benefits, such as pleasant births, but because they are socially conducive to a peaceful and happy society. In other words, the Five Precepts are reworked as interpersonal ethics.

The above definition highlights social responsibility, this-worldly rationality, and self-judgment. It undermines belief-based religious ethics. The phrase "not on the belief in punishment and reward" means that both a theistic and a non-theistic religious ethics are being invoked, both divine and karmic punishments and rewards.

Here, as with secular worldviews, external authority and other-worldly motivation are put to the side while humanity is centralized. The definition locates agency in the individual self and encourages one to realize a transcendental goal: "Universal Goodwill." In so doing, the definition indicates the influence of secular worldviews on Buddhism.

The manual minimizes the otherworldly religious language of Buddhism. The multi-layered Buddhist heavens and hells are mentioned nowhere in the teaching manual except "*Sagga Katha.*" The latter literally means stories related to heavens. However, Chandrasekera defines the term as stories of "other dimensions of existence according to karma," and she highlights their ethical purpose. For example, she asserts that the heavenly stories are meant to encourage the "devotees to do good and lead lives of purity for the purpose of evolving into higher levels until one reaches *Nibbāna*" (Chandrasekera 2001, 9). Moreover, the references to religious concepts like kamma and rebirth are followed by scientific comments. In a lesson on the concept of rebirth, a phrase noting "case studies of rebirth from Sri Lanka and other countries" is added. This implies that the concepts of kamma and rebirth are not merely religious concepts. They are, rather, explanations of what is happening in society; therefore, the concepts could be and should be taught with reference to the accounts of rebirth.

The manual completely leaves out the Buddhist reference to multiple layers of heavens and hells. The survey result indicates that the majority (58 per cent) of the first generation expressed that they are "not interested" in the Buddhist interpretation of heavens and hells. They also think that those concepts are "irrelevant" in the context of North America. Such assessments of irrelevance complement the manual's wish to present Buddhism as a religion free from these otherworldly concepts. It seems to be successful in that endeavour, as a seventeen-year-old participant who graduated from dhamma school in Toronto expresses: "the Buddhist emphasis on no heaven and hell ... is fascinating." For this particular youth, Buddhism is free from the religious concepts of heaven and hell.

One may wonder if the manual's secular emphasis also underestimates a religious discourse of Buddhist ethics that entails the power of otherworldly motivations in ethical teaching, a technique the Buddha had used specifically in teaching the laity. In the discourses on conventional Buddhist morality, such as the Five Precepts and kamma, the Buddha repeatedly emphasizes the consequences of moral and immoral behaviour with specific reference to lives after death. For example in the *Anguttara Nikaya* the Buddha instructs: "There is a person who destroys life ... takes what is not given to him ... conducts himself wrongly in matters of sex ... [and] who is a liar ... As to that tainted failure in living ... issues in suffering, results in suffering – it is due to that very failure in living that with the breakup of the body, after death, beings are reborn in the plane of misery, in a bad destination, in the lower world, in hell"[7] (Thera and Bodhi 1999, 265–7). When we compare the Sri Lankan Canadian reinterpretation of the Five Precepts with its canonical counterpart, what we notice is a shift in emphasis. That is, a this-worldly interpretation supersedes an otherworldly interpretation. Certainly, both interpretations highlight different motivations and foster different commitments. Here, I do not evaluate the later interpretation over and against that canonical reference. Rather, the comparison highlights how secular sensibilities are included in the reinterpretation of the Five Precepts in Toronto. With these new emphases, the curriculum defines what Buddhism is.

REDEFINING BUDDHISM WITH THE
THEME OF HARMONY

The above-mentioned examples of religious and secular inclusivity broaden the existing definition of inclusivism. In search of Buddhist inclusivism, Kristin Kiblinger (2005, 9) defines the term "inclusivism" as "a theoretical, conscious approach to others." She argues: "a view will qualify as inclusivistic if it self-consciously recognizes a provisional, subordinate, or supplementary place within the home religious system for *some element(s) from one or more alien traditions* ... Inclusivism is a stance teaching that the thing to do in response to aliens and their religious systems is to learn about them and listen carefully to them with the hope of finding common ground and/or new resources for the home group's use." This definition of inclusivism highlights what religious practitioners do with the religions of "the other" to make them fit for their own use. However, it overlooks what practitioners do with their own tradition as they encounter "the other." The analysis of Buddhist concepts and practices found in *Teaching Buddhism to Children* suggests that one can reflexively turn to one's own tradition with a sense of inclusivity. Within this reflexive inclusivity, practitioners not only gaze at religions of the other; they also scrutinize their own tradition. For example, the teaching manual emphasizes the three concepts of god(s) and creates a religious common ground. The secular interpretation of the Five Precepts attempts to make Buddhist ethics appealing to non-Buddhists. The membership inclusivity echoes the gender equality of the ambient culture. Reflexive inclusivity not only integrates Buddhists and Buddhism into the mainstream culture, it also incorporates the religious and secular "other" into Buddhism. Above all, it redefines what Buddhism is.

In this broader scope, a Buddhist universalism supersedes a Buddhist particularism. For example, the Buddhist concept of "*Saddha*" is broadly defined as "Appreciation and worship of Goodness and Truth" (2001, 47). The term saddha is traditionally understood as having confidence and conviction in the Buddha and his teaching, which propels the person to engage in ethical and moral practices (Saddhatissa 1978, 137). Accordingly, the person with saddha reveres the Buddha and practices ethical and moral principles prescribed by the Buddha. However, the broader definition of the term also assumes a broader expectation. It argues that if we have saddha, "We are drawn towards the goal of perfection in goodness and truth" (47). The unspecified goodness and truth contextually refer to Buddhism. However, they also imply that Buddhism is all about goodness and truth, and that Buddhists appreciate goodness and truth with no discrimination.

Similarly, the concept of the Buddha is interpreted beyond Buddhism: "The Buddha is the State of Spiritual Perfection that human beings conceive, and ultimately do attain through the practice of religion (Chandrasekera 2001, 46). Here, Buddha is not a person but an abstract and impersonalized spiritual goal. This abstract and impersonalized definition emphasizes human potentiality to become Buddhas. The definition implies that one can attain the spiritual perfection represented by the Buddha not only in Buddhism, but also "through the practice of religion." Thus, it respects and even legitimates the spiritual quests found in non-Buddhist religions. This is also a good example of reflexive inclusivism, which, as opposed to Kiblinger's (2005) "inclusivism," redefines a central concept within the tradition for the use of the religious other. The definition also invokes "harmony," a celebrated virtue in the curriculum.

The teaching manual associates the virtue of harmony with Buddhism. It does so by reintroducing the recently overlooked concept of god(s) in Buddhism, as well as by replacing the self-assertive adjective "right" with "harmonious." This multilayered Buddhist concept of god(s) redefines Buddhism by undermining the widespread Western perspective of Buddhism as a gods-free religion. It centralizes the concept of god(s) in Buddhism. The manual thus minimizes possible tensions with the local theistic religious culture that could result from the concept of Buddhism as being nontheistic, or worse, atheistic. The most senior monk in the community Bhante Punnaji asserts: "it's incorrect to say that Buddhists are atheists, because when you say that Buddhists are atheists you are saying that Buddhists are bad people ... therefore I say Buddhists are neither theistic nor atheistic ... Buddhists don't believe in a creator but they believe in gods" (personal interview 2009). This indicates Bhante Punnaji's cultural sensibility to the wider Judeo-Christian culture where goodness is closely associated with the concept of divinity. The assertion that "Buddhists are neither theistic nor atheistic" reveals, perhaps, Buddhism's ideal – the "middle way" – in dealing with its ambient religious "other," which is treading in between two extremes: fierce confrontation or traceless assimilation with the ambient non-Buddhist culture. Both options could be detrimental for a minority religion's survival. The broadly defined Buddhist concept of god(s) tends to avoid both extremes, and it maintains Buddhist integrity. It suggests that Buddhism is a religion of harmony – a claim that follows from the reinterpretation of the core teaching related to the Buddhist way of life.

Teaching Buddhism to Children (Chandrasekera 2001, 50) illustrates the theme of harmony in its following reinterpretation of the Buddhist Eightfold Path:

1 Harmonious Perspective (*Samma Ditthi*)
2 Harmonious Visualization (of goal) (*Samma Samkappa*)
3 Harmonious Speech (*Samma Vaca*)
4 Harmonious Action (*Samma Kammanta*)
5 Harmonious Lifestyle (*Samma Ajiva*)
6 Harmonious Practice (*Samma Vayama*)
7 Harmonious Attention (*Samma Sati*)
8 Harmonious Equilibrium (*Samma Samadhi*).

Here, the term samma is translated as harmonious instead of right, the common English translation. The word right carries a spiritual arrogance along with a truth claim. That is, if one says that the Buddhist lifestyle or perspective is right, it implies that other lifestyles or perspectives are wrong. The statement carries a self-asserting assumption and other-denying rhetoric that may induce religious intolerance and interpersonal tension and impede inter-religious enquiry, respect, and understanding. From a broader perspective, the term "harmonious" embodies the comprehensive meaning of the "Middle Path," a synonym for the Eightfold Path. Generally, the term "Middle Path" envisions a life of balance that transcends two extreme modes of living, namely extreme sensual gratification and self-torture or self-denial. The term "harmonious" demonstrates Sri Lankan Buddhists' sensitivity to the pluralistic society of Toronto. It endorses a Buddhist way of life in a pluralistic society, but it does not necessarily nullify other ways. This context-sensitive interpretation begs the question of the hermeneutic authority. For that, I will now turn to the criteria in Theravāda Buddhism that legitimate the appropriation and interpretation of tradition.

The *Mahaparinibbāna Sutta*[8] (Walshe 1995, 255) lays out how to assess the authority and authenticity of interpretations. This Pāli Sutta instructs that the authority of sutta (doctrinal discourses) and vinaya (disciplinary collections) surpasses all individual and communal authorities. In this particular Sutta, the Buddha states that one may claim that "this is the Dhamma, this is the discipline, this is the Master's teachings," and the claim could be justified by saying it was heard from "the Lord's own lips ... a community of elders and distinguished teachers ... many elders who are learned, bearers of the tradition ... [or] one elder who is learned" (Walshe 1995, 255). The Buddha instructs monks that such claims should be compared to and scrutinized side by side with the Buddha's doctrine and discipline. The claims should be accepted as "the words of the Buddha" if only they accord with the doctrine and discipline. If the claims contradict or do not conform to the doctrine and discipline, the monks should conclude that "assuredly this is not the word of the Buddha" (1995, 225). Here, the authority of doctrinal and disciplinary guidelines is equal to the authority of the Buddha himself. Thus the discourse shapes the traditional understanding of who holds the authority in interpreting the words of the Buddha, and it explains how to assess the authenticity of any given interpretation. The sequence of criteria mentioned in the *Mahaparinibbāna Sutta* recalls that, after the Buddha, the Sangha holds the highest authority, followed by a few senior learned monks. A single senior learned monk holds the least authority; nevertheless, he remains authoritative within the tradition. Regardless of who authorizes the interpretation, the Pāli sutta indicates that the authenticity of the interpretation ultimately depends on its accordance with doctrinal discourses (sutta) and disciplinary collection (vinaya).

The themes of harmony and interpreters' authority do meet the interpretative criteria discussed above. As previously mentioned, Bhante Punnaji bears the responsibility of reinterpreting the terms under discussion. The joint forward statement of *Teaching Buddhism to Children* (discussed at the beginning of this chapter) also indicates that Bhante Punnaji's interpretation received the collective consent of his monastic colleagues. More importantly, the interpretation provided – particularly the theme of harmony – does accord with the early Pāli doctrinal discourse (sutta), the supreme authority in Theravāda Buddhism. By adopting the term "harmonious" as an adjective to describe the Buddhist perspective (i.e., harmonious Perspective), Buddhist lifestyle (i.e., harmonious Lifestyle), and other components of the Eightfold Path, Bhante Punnaji represents Buddhism as a positive force. One may argue that the term "harmonious" invokes the popular Western vision of Buddhism as a religion of peace, of non-violence, and of non-confrontation (Shiu 2010, 108), and therefore perpetuates a stereotyped image of positive Buddhism. It may. The advocates, however, refer to the *Madhupindika Sutta* in the *Majjhima Nikaya*,[9] one of the early middle-length doctrinal discourses in the Pāli canon to defend the theme of harmony. In that particular discourse, answering the questions "What does the recluse [the Buddha] assert, what does he proclaim?" the Buddha utters: "Friend, I assert and proclaim such [a teaching] that one does not quarrel with anyone in the world with its gods, its Maras, and its Brahmas, in this generation with its recluses and brahmins, its princes and its people; such [a teaching] that perceptions no more underlie that brahmin who abides detached from sensual pleasures, without perplexity, shorn of worry, free from craving for any kind of being" (Nanamoli and Bodhi 1995, 201). The Buddha's reply illustrates that what the Buddha taught promotes external and internal harmony. The words like "gods," "princes," and "people" imply that the Buddha's teaching advocates harmony at all religious, political, and social levels. In the second section of the answer, the Buddha highlights that his teaching also brings harmony at psychological and spiritual levels. This internal harmony derives from the detachment of sensual pleasure, mental worries, and latent craving.

Elucidating his choice of the term "harmonious" to replace the more commonly used translation of "right" for the Pāli term "sammā," Bhante Punnaji states, "*Sammā* has nothing to do with right or wrong. It refers to harmony. It is the opposite of conflict ... The Buddha was looking at the same world with a different way; that is a harmonious perspective. If you look at it [the world] in a harmonious way, you will not come into conflict with anyone in the world, and you won't come into conflict with reality. When I use the word 'harmonious perspective,' what it means is that you are not in conflict ... not only with reality, but also with other religions and other people and even with yourself" (personal interview, 2009). What we see here is a definition of Buddhism: Buddhism is a particular perspective that brings harmony into diverse relationships as one relates to oneself, to fellow humans, to nature and, in sum, to the internal, social, and natural realities in the world. This theme of harmony is one of the core aspects of the inclusive interpretation, and according to Bhante Punnaji it derives from the Pāli canon. This canonical definition of Buddhism resurfaces in a Buddhist educational curriculum guide to teach Buddhism to those who are born and/or raised in multicultural Toronto. Janet McLellan (2009, 165) identifies the need for "a shared interpretative discourse" that would facilitate the intergenerational transmission of the Buddhist tradition in Toronto. I would suggest that the inclusive interpretation of Buddhism, along with the theme of harmony, addresses this need within the Sri Lankan Buddhist community. We should not forget that such an interpretation has emerged as a response to "the demands of the 'religio-cultural' diversity" in Toronto (Chandrasekera 2001, 2). By connecting their reinterpretation to the Pāli canon, Bhante Punnaji and his colleagues claim that they are in accordance with the "original" teachings of the Buddha. This stance gives them liberty and legitimacy in making Buddhism viable to a new location epitomized by the secular ethos expressed in multiculturalism.

MULTICULTURALISM AS A COMMON LANGUAGE: "TO WIN THE HEARTS AND MINDS OF CANADIANS"

The monks suggest that *Teaching Buddhism to Children* goes "a long way in fulfilling our own vision about the propagation of Dhamma in the Canadian context" (Chandrasekera 2001, 2). This reminds us that Buddhism is a missionary religion. Historically, it is indeed the first of all missionary religions. When we put the reinterpreted Buddhism within that long historical context of Buddhism, it reveals the missionary character of Buddhism. Its mission is not limited to the Canadian-born children of Sri Lankan immigrants; instead, as the preceding statement suggests, Canadian society at large can benefit from the reinterpretation. The teaching manual reiterates that Buddhism is good for many (if not all), and it promotes harmony and supports common social values. It describes "Buddhism as a Way to Common Weal and Happiness (*Bahujana hitaya, Bahujana sukhaya*)" (Chandrasekera 2001, 46). That means that Buddhism is not restricted only to those who call themselves Buddhists. Rather, it contributes to the well-being and happiness of the many, including Canadians.

That broader mission and vision stand out in a statement issued by the leading Sri Lankan monk for the 2013 inter-Buddhist Vesak, the Buddha's birthday celebration, at the Mississauga Celebration Square. He said: "It's gratifying to note thousands in the West and in this our own country, Canada, are being attracted to the message of Buddha, the Enlightened, the Awakened. This fact alone throws a heavy burden on us as Buddhist monks and nuns to re-examine our mission and find out how best we can disseminate the Words of Buddha and values that Buddhism stands for" (K. Dhammawasa Nayaka Thera 2013). For the monk, Canada is an open, fertile, and certainly also a challenging field for the Buddhist mission. He acknowledges the wider public interest in Buddhism and is energized to deliver the dhamma to those attracted to it. Nevertheless, he says, it is "a heavy burden" – one that requires creative means to accomplish a mission. This head monk laid out his strategy: "In my opinion, the first thing to do is *to recognize the liberal and humanistic goals and practices prevalent in the Canadian society which highlight the same values we Buddhists adhere to.* It's not uncommon to find Canadians practicing or contributing to the same Buddhist values and virtues" (K. Dhammawasa Nayaka Thera 2013, emphasis added). Notice the connection the monk makes between Buddhism and secularism.

Liberal and humanistic values and practices are the common ground where Buddhism and Canadian society meet each other. The monk hopes that to build on these secular values and share them with "Canadians in general," is "going to be mutually beneficial."

The implied mutual partners are Buddhist immigrants and the wider Canadian public. That hope derives from immigrants' desire to be equal, beneficial, and contributing members of the society that they have chosen to be part of. Forster (2014) reminds that "they [immigrants] want to become full and active members of the new grouping they have joined" (9). The monk refers to an example of how his hope and strategy to contribute to the Canadian society at large has been implemented within his congregation: "In our own Sunday School we teach our children to observe goodness where and when they see it and appreciate the same." He implies that no one, including Buddhists, has a monopoly over the definition of goodness. Goodness may come from a variety of sources. To appreciate goodness for the sake of its own merits requires broad attitudes and skills; that is what his Sunday school program claims to deliver. In brief, Buddhists with such dhamma education would not have a parochial view of goodness and would therefore pose no threat to Canadian diversity. Within this broader context, the inclusive interpretation and the theme of harmony that we have discussed above relate to a cultural configuration of Buddhism as it seeks roots in Canada – a country increasingly defined by its official promise of commitment to multiculturalism.

Multiculturalism is one of three features that define Canada (Stevenson 2014, 206).[10] Canada's image of a cultural mosaic helps to distinguish it from its southern neighbour, with their cultural melting pot (Hansen 2014, 84). In fact, the term "multiculturalism" was coined (ironically, by an American academic) in 1963 to distinguish Canada from the United States.[11] Eventually, it became a Canadian signature term to refer to the country, its people, and their way of life. For example, Foster (2014, 32) asserts that "multiculturalism in Canada is more than [an] ideology and theory – it is a way of being, an existence, that has to be the point of departure in any analysis of who we are as a people, what we want, why we act the way we do, and how we happen to be the way we are." Therefore, it is no wonder that the Sri Lankan monks in Toronto reflect and incorporate Canada's multicultural vision and values as they reinterpret Buddhism in Canada.

Multiculturalism in Canada emerges out of anti-dominance resistance posed by the marginalized "third element" of Canada's population. From the late 1950s, the Ukrainian Canadian Committee and the Canadian Ethnic Press Federation in the Prairies opposed the notion of a "bicultural Canada" on the basis that such a designation would ignore the ethnic cultural identities of Canadians who were of neither British nor French extraction. In 1964 in the Upper House the senator Paul Yuzyk from Saskatchewan, a man of Ukrainian descent who competes with Pierre Elliott Trudeau for the designation of "father of multiculturalism," argued: "In reality Canada never was bicultural; the Indians and Eskimos have been with us throughout our history ... Furthermore, the projecting of the idea that Canada is bicultural not only excludes the non-British and non-French groups, but denies the multicultural character of the British group, which can only lead to disunity" (in Stevenson 2014, 216). Similar arguments for multicultural (opposed to bicultural) Canada continued in the subsequent years. For example the Ukrainian-Canadian William Skoreyko, a Progressive Conservative MP from Alberta, argued in the House of Commence: "Mr Speaker ... I do not think that you can build a united Canada by recognizing one or two races as the only races in this country. They must all be recognized as they have been in the past" (in Stevenson 2014, 218). Such resistance to biculturalism at Canada's high political institutions conditioned the British and French to give due recognition to minority ethnic groups. In 1968, the Royal Commission entitled the final volume of its report *The Cultural Contribution of the Other Ethnic Groups* (Stevenson 2014, 218). Upon the report's recommendation, Trudeau's liberal government introduced the policy of multiculturalism in 1971, which subsequently was transformed into a federal law in 1988 by Mulroney's conservative government. Thereafter, multiculturalism has characterized Canada – i.e., the first postmodern country in the world that fostered a multiethnic nationalism (Foster 2014, 8), "a world leader in diversity management" (Winter 2014, 54), an immigrant-friendly country (Reitz 2014, 121), and a land of economic opportunity for multinational investors (Abu-Laban and Gabriel 2002; Kymlicka 2004). This brief history of multiculturalism reminds us that the multicultural social reality of Canada resulted in a policy that eventually became the symbol of Canada. Thus multiculturalism evolves from a social reality, to a state policy, to a national identity.

Multiculturalism emerged as a governing ideology and a state policy to manage Canada's "3M" reality: multicultural, multilinguistic, and multireligious diversities, particularly those of immigrants. The Harper government's (2006–15) Ministry of

Citizenship, Immigration and Multiculturalism accurately captured whom multiculturalism was meant to serve. Its minister, Jason Kenney, issued a statement in 2012 that reminds us that the multiculturalism program "promotes our core democratic values, history and institutions," and in turn the government expects all Canadians to embrace them. In particular, according to Kenney, "new Canadians work hard to learn our languages, our values, and our traditions, and in turn are welcomed as equal members of the Canadian family" (Kenney 2012). In theory, multiculturalism assures the existence of multiple practices, worldviews, ethos, and rationalities. It does not, however, treat them as equal. Multiculturalism neither espouses all cultures nor does it indiscriminately set them free beyond limitations. It is not an all-embracing and value-neutral philosophy. Instead, it has fundamental norms that scrutinize incoming cultural norms and practices. According to Phil Ryan (2014, 99), core democratic principles such as freedom of conscience, equality, and human rights are the fundamental norms of multiculturalism. Embrace those inviolable secular values, and learn the official language(s), and equal Canadian citizenship is promised. This message seems to find a receptive audience in the statement of the Sri Lankan monk that we discussed above.

The reinterpretation of Buddhism as inclusive and harmonious reflects the evolving multiculturalism policy. Since its 1971 inception, the policy has evolved to reflect and address emerging issues with Canada's integration of immigrant communities. This evolution has added different dimensions to the policy. A 2007 Canadian government report on the policy identifies four stages of multiculturalism policy, and correlates a specific decade to each stage: ethnicity (1970s), equity (1980s), civic (1990s), and integrative (2000s)[12] (Kunz and Sykes 2007, 21).[13] Its description of the last two decades is worth quoting, as all points (except the problem source row) are echoed in the reinterpretation of Buddhism.

Table 4.1
The evolution of multiculturalism policy in the 1990s and 2000s

	Civic multiculturalism (1990s)	Integrative multiculturalism (2000s)
Focus	Constructive engagement	Inclusive citizenship
Reference point	Society building	Canadian identity
Mandate	Citizenship	Integration
Magnitude	Participation	Rights and responsibilities
Problem source	Exclusion	Unequal access, "clash" of cultures
Solution	Inclusiveness	Dialogue/mutual understanding
Key metaphor	"Belonging"	"Harmony/jazz"

As the table above shows, the government discourses of multiculturalism in the 1990s identified exclusion as a problem that has compromised immigrants' participation in the Canadian citizenship. "Inclusiveness" has therefore been suggested as a solution to that problem. The theme of inclusivity in *Teaching Buddhism to Children* (2001) in fact reflects back on the 1990s issue of exclusion, offering solutions that complement the Canadian policy of multiculturalism. Moreover, the reimagined Sri Lankan Canadian Buddhist child also echoes the "inclusive citizenship" that became the focus of the next decade's multiculturalism. Note how closely the policy's key metaphors – i.e., belonging (in the 1990s) and harmony (in the 2000s) – echo the reinterpreted Buddhism with its emphasis on inclusivity and harmony. This multiculturalism-Buddhism correlation indicates Sri Lankan Buddhist interpreters' sensibilities to Canada's multicultural reality in everyday life. It also has been their response to Canada's call for integration of immigrant communities into the Canadian society. Such sophisticated religious responses may surprise many, because religious diversity never received as much attention in Canada's multiculturalism policy as did ethnic and linguistic diversity (Biles and Ibrahim 2005, 164). The final report of the Policy Research Initiative (PRI) acknowledges that a secular conceptualization of multiculturalism prevents Canadians from fully addressing the enduring religious diversity in Canadian society. To rectify this critical flaw in Canadian multiculturalism, the PRI recommends that religious diversity deserves serious policy attention in order to realize the overall goals of multiculturalism (Final Report of PRI 2009, 1, 12). So what does Sri Lankan Buddhism's engagement with multiculturalism refer to?

I suggest that the redefined inclusive and harmonious Buddhism illustrates its participatory role in a secular world. Multiculturalism policy encourages minority communities to participate in Canadian public life (Bramadat 2005, 10). In a modern, cosmopolitan, and pluralistic society, secularism seems to override religious worldviews. John Biles and Humera Ibrahim (2005, 166) argue that contemporary Canadian public discourses, such as immigration and multiculturalism, refer to religion with extreme caution. They identify a few reasons for such caution, including the "fear that religion is inherently intolerant and therefore a threat to the 'Canadian diversity model' itself." This fear derives from early modern Christian denominational rivalry; secularism perpetuates it to separate religion from politics, by legitimating itself as a political and governmental doctrine. In other words, secularism as a political doctrine dictates where religion should be: in the private sphere. This is privatization of religion marks a loss of the power that religion used to enjoy in shaping the public sphere. The public role of religion is now replaced with a secularism that determines the contents and methods worthy of the public sphere. It is the secular ideologies that decide who and what are worthy of this public sphere, as well as how one should claim to access to that sphere.

Religion has responded to secularism variously. José Casanova's (1994, 211) thesis of "de-privatization of modern religion" details how religion has resisted being in the private sphere. Talal Asad (2001, 2) likewise contends that secularism not only separates religion from politics, but it also "presupposes new concepts of 'religion,' 'ethics,' and 'politics,' and new imperatives associated with them." Asad implies that if a religion wants to influence the public, it has to speak in a secular tone/language. Accordingly, secularism assumes that religion needs to tone down its exclusive, self-assertive, and other-denying aspects if the latter wishes to play a role in the wider society. Does then multiculturalism, a secular ideology intended to manage diversity (including religious diversity), become instrumental for religion to access the public at large? This case study suggests that it is a possibility. The redefined inclusive and harmonious

Buddhism intimately echoes the values and ethos of multicultural-ism. This then signals that Buddhism does not endanger multicul-tural Canada, and it implies that it certainly can engage with and contribute to the wider Canadian public. Nevertheless Buddhism's implied claim for public engagement differs from other incidents of religions' efforts to have access to the public sphere through rights and privileges enshrined in multiculturalism.

The emergence of Buddhism as an inclusive and harmonious reli-gion demonstrates that multiculturalism has enabled Buddhist monks to reimagine their religion. Solange Lefebvre and Lori Beaman (2014, 11) observe: "multiculturalism as an ideology acts as a filter through which religion is imagined and shaped in the public sphere." By appro-priating the multiculturalism discourse, Sri Lankan Buddhist monks in Toronto have made Buddhism palatable to the Canadian public at large. Ironically, multiculturalism – a diversity managing tool of sec-ularism – itself has become Buddhism's tool/language to engage the secular public. One could put the argument the other way around: Sri Lankan monks in Toronto have positively responded to the pluralistic, yet secularly oriented Canadian society with an inclusive interpreta-tion of Buddhism. Canadian multiculturalism provides them with her-meneutic tools to take their Buddhist mission to the wider Canadian public. As the pertinent reinterpretation of Buddhism emerges within dhamma education in Toronto, it directly contributes to the ongoing debates on religion and education in Ontario.

RELIGION AND EDUCATION IN ONTARIO

From the very beginning, public education in Canada evolved as part of Christian missions by Anglican, Catholic, and Protestant denominations. By the mid-nineteenth century, schools in Ontario evolved into two parallel systems. Public schools were Anglican and Protestant, and separate schools were mainly Roman Catholic. Sec-tion 93 in *The British North American Act* (1867) guaranteed public funding for both public and separate schools as an essential step in the federation of Canada (Johns 1985, 96). During the 1960s, how-ever, the provisions for confessional Christian religious education in Ontario public schools were challenged by the emergence of secular-ism as a viable worldview. At the same time, the increase of religious diversity through immigration in the 1970s and 1980s also effected a change to the role of religion in public schools.

In response to the preceding social trends, the public school board in Ontario has implemented some changes in teaching religion. Under Keiller Mackay's recommendation in 1966, confessional religious education was replaced with a more religiously neutral moral and values education. In 1971, a course on world religions was introduced. The 1982 adoption of *The Canadian Charter of Rights and Freedoms* brought further changes in teaching religion in public schools. The charter replaced "the imaginary of the Christian nation" with a "secular social imaginary" that envisioned Canadian citizenry beyond the Christian faith (Bowlby 2014, 33). Secularism's constitutional triumph over Christianity guaranteed individual freedom to believe or not believe in religion. Therefore, religion-based moral education contradicts the individual freedom of conscience and religion guaranteed in the charter. Accordingly, in 1991 the Ministry of Education in Ontario adopted a policy that referred only to "education about religion"; it allowed instruction and study of religion, but not indoctrination and practice of religion.[14] Consequently, religion has become just another secular subject in public schools, but the secular turn had no impact on the constitutional right of Catholic schools in receiving public funds. This pseudo-secularization of public education has been challenged by minority religious communities in Toronto, as they have demanded public funds to maintain their own religious schools.[15]

Minorities' demands for parochial schools represent one end of the spectrum of religious responses to secularized public education. An alternative response has been to call for equal and better representation of all religions in public schools. Generally, Buddhists in Ontario fall on the latter end of this spectrum. They have neither established Buddhist schools, nor have they lobbied for public funding for independent religious schools.[16] As such, in relation to Buddhism in Canada Bruce Matthews states: "it is fair to conclude that Buddhism is a religion free of dogmatic fundamentalism, esoteric restrictions or unusual demands for parochial schooling" (Matthews 2006, xxi). Buddhists do, however, ask for better representation of all religions in public school curricula. Lois Sweet (1997) notes that, in the mid-1990s, fifty Buddhist temples in Toronto lobbied the World Interfaith Education Association of Ontario for better representations of all religions in public schools (251). These observations show the Buddhist reluctance to accept religiously segregated schools, albeit they do not explain the reasons behind this reluctance. They also tend to give the impression that Buddhists in Toronto share a general consensus on this issue, which may not be the case.

I observe that Sri Lankan Buddhists in Toronto fall into three categories, namely those who support, oppose, or remain undecided on the issue of parochial schools. Many Sri Lankan Buddhists tend to favour the idea of a Buddhist day school. Seventy per cent of them say "yes" to the survey question: "If you had a choice, would you send your child(ren) to a Buddhist day school similar to a Catholic school?" Similarly, a group interview with ten parents provides the same expression (seven yes, one no, and two undecided). However, as the discussion unfolded, many of them withdrew their support for Buddhist day schools for economic, social, and philosophical reasons. Many cannot and/or do not want to bear additional high costs for their children's basic education while they pay taxes for public education.

Many dhamma teachers and some parents oppose parochial day schools for social reasons. They insist that a parochial school system is socially detrimental. They believe that, in the long run, it would threaten the social and religious harmony of a multicultural society by segregating younger generations on religious lines. A fifty-year-old father of two children says: "What I feel is that when multi-religious and multicultural people fall into one category they start respecting [each other] more ... it makes the ground to co-exist; the public school is a better choice." The underlying assumption is that parochial schools would segregate Buddhist children and hinder their integration into the mainstream society. Expressing her opinion about the absence of Buddhist day schools, a middle-aged mother and dhamma teacher says: "Actually, I do not mind that because I do not need it; if we come to this country ... we need our children [to] move with [the] wider culture ... we do not [want to] lock them [up]." Some also refer to the cultural disparity among the contemporary Buddhists in Toronto as a reason not to have a Buddhist day school. Linguistic and ethno-cultural diversity among Buddhists in Toronto often overshadows a shared religious philosophy, and thereby obstruct the formation of a collective Buddhist identity (McLellan 1999, 209). Without an effective Buddhist co-religiosity in Toronto, the implementation of Buddhist schools is unlikely.

A few respondents highlight that Buddhism differs from other religions; as such, they argue that there is no need for Buddhist day schools. One father states: "Since Buddhism is not a religion, but it is a way of life, we should not fall into that category [of those who demand for parochial religious day schools]." This reluctance derives from a philosophical or epistemological conceptualization. Buddhist leaders whom I spoke with find the Western education system scarcely contradicts their religious and educational values. The above-discussed financial, socio-cultural, and epistemological reasons explain the absence of independent Buddhist schools in Ontario.[17] I would say that these reasons do indeed justify the Buddhist reluctance for parochial schools. At the same time, the inclusive interpretation of Buddhism goes with a Buddhist call for better representation of all religions in public schools. Suwanda Sugunasiri, a well-known Sri Lankan Buddhist lay leader in Toronto, suggests that spirituality[18] derived from the religious and secular traditions "should be taught compulsorily at all grades, beginning with the kindergarten and continued through high school" (2001, 160). The inclusive and harmonious Buddhism discussed above is not meant for public school; nevertheless, it illustrates how a religion could or should be adopted for general education in a multicultural and multireligious society like Canada.

By reinterpreting Buddhism to echo the themes of multiculturalism, Sri Lankan Buddhists have demonstrated their commitment to adaptation and integration into the Canadian society. I have agued that *Teaching Buddhism to Children* exemplifies what Paul Crowe (2014) calls "a hermeneutic of adaptation and integration" (167). Despite Crowe's warning against the etic use of the phrase, I have employed the phrase with two justifications. First, this study highlights that the hermeneutic of adaptation and integration has become an emic (opposed to etic) language that has emerged discursively within the Sri Lankan Buddhist community in Toronto. In other words, Sri Lankan Buddhists in Toronto speak in the language of adaptation and integration. Second, I suggest that this study in fact resists the polarizing discourse of us (citizens) vs them (immigrants) by bringing the immigrant voices of adaptation and integration front and centre. In the debates and discourses on immigrant communities, the language of adaptation and integration – particularly from immigrants themselves – often gets marginalized. Within that context, Sri Lankan Buddhists' inclusive interpretation of Buddhism has emerged as what Peter Grant calls "an integration strategy" of immigrants who wish to "participate fully as citizens of their new country" (2007, 92).

Sri Lankan Buddhists' reinterpretation of Buddhism also echoes Alasdair MacIntyre's concept of a "tradition of enquiry" (2000, x). MacIntyre says a tradition of enquiry is rooted in historical conditions, as shaped by the beliefs, institutions, texts, and practices of a particular community. As the founding context, time, and place change, the tradition and its adherents face an "epistemological crisis," which requires an intellectual as well as a practical response. As "the inhabitants of a particular community" respond to the particular epistemological crisis, traditional beliefs are reformulated and practices are remade. MacIntyre says that such a change in tradition takes place for not only intellectual reasons, but also because of practical concerns – such as human relations with fellow beings, with wider society, and with nature in general (2000, 209). If the tradition represents a culture that is significantly different from the ambient and dominant culture, then it undergoes a cultural reconfiguration. David McMahan (2008) identifies two specific ways in which Buddhism as a tradition reconfigures itself in its dialogue with Western culture. He contends: "I underline the fact that a tradition that is introduced into a new cultural context ... must re-create itself in terms of the prevalent intellectual discourse, as well as the tacit background understanding of a society. The former are important especially for a tradition that, like Buddhism, has appealed mostly to educated cultural elites in the West and has therefore had to make a distinctive intellectual case for itself. But perhaps more important for success is that the tradition be able to engage with a culture's lived world" (15). The pertinent inclusive interpretation relates to Buddhist interpreters' "tacit background understanding" of Canadian society. The lived world in Toronto is comprised of religious diversity, secular ethos, and the public policy of multiculturalism. The inclusive interpretation engages with all of them at a collective level. It also echoes a similar discussion at an individual level within the same community.

AN INDIVIDUAL ENGAGEMENT WITH MULTICULTURALISM

In the late 1970s and early 80s, the Sri Lankan Buddhist Suwanda H.J. Sugunasiri emerged as "the Buddhist spokesman" (McLellan and Hori 2010, 388) who claimed "to be the voice of the Buddhists in Toronto" (386). His social activism took two expressions: Buddhism and citizenship in multicultural Canada (390). These two expressions were often intertwined in his professional life, voluntary service, and writings. Influenced by Buddhist teachings and practices, Sugunasiri has passionately engaged with Canada's multiculturalism. He wrote *Towards Multicultural Growth* (2001) as his "deep critical reflection as a participant-observer" of the multiculturalism policy since its inception. He perceives that the 1971 policy grew out of the 1967 point-system immigration that officially ended the race- (European) and religion- (Christianity) based immigration to Canada. From that perspective, it intended to end racism expressed in white supremacy against non-white people and culture, so that all people regardless of their skin colours, religions, cultures, and languages could live in harmony, justice, and equality. Outlining the three-decade long history (1971–2001) of the policy, Sugunasiri argues that it evolved from a formative stage to a chaotic multiculturalism as both white and non-white communities in Canada forgot the original purpose of the policy itself. Sugunasiri also intervenes with a set of recommendations that he thinks would transform the policy into "integrative multicultural-ism" so that the ideal of multicultural Canada could be truly realized.

Sugunasiri admires the introduction and implementation of the policy during the 1970s and 80s – what he calls "formative multicul-turalism." At this early stage, the policy slowly addressed the systemic racial discrimination that impeded the living standards of immigrant communities. Multicultural programs diminished the systemic bar-riers so that immigrants could have access to basic needs – namely, decent housing, suitable employment, proper healthcare, and better education. He praises Canada's two foundational national groups – the Anglophone and francophone communities – for their economic prudence, liberal attitudes, and political wisdom, which brought multiculturalism to the fore. He suggests: "To the White folks of Canada ... we [the post-1967 immigrants] need to bow with deep respect" (29). He also explains how the members of immigrant cul-tural groups rose to the occasion by taking part in various govern-ment and non-government multicultural organizations. Sugunasiri reveals that upon invitation he served as a member of the Ontario Advisory Council on Multiculturalism and Citizenship. Such invita-tion, according to Sugunasiri, meant recognition that the newcom-ers have something to contribute to Canada. More importantly, the opportunities to contribute to multicultural programs also made them felt that they are a "part of Canada" (2001, 23). Describing the ethno-cultural leaders of the 1980s as "change agents," Sugunasiri writes: "They went about facilitating change in a *systematic* fashion ... working with the system. While they valued their own cultural heritage, they were respectful of Canadian society, its institutions and values. They worked *interculturally*" (2001, 26, emphasis in original). He implies that multicultural programs enabled the immigrant leaders to address the systemic discriminations that were affecting the everyday lives of fellow immigrants. They also formed the bridges between the ruling English/French cultural groups and incoming various ethno-cultural immigrant minorities.

The above slow progress in race relations was hijacked by what Sugunasiri calls "systemic abuses" of state resources by immigrant themselves. In the name of multiculturalism, many distinct cultural groups mushroomed with "ethnic brokers" (32) who exploited the policy loopholes for themselves and their parochial groups. They also lobbied for family and refugee sponsorship for their clients. In addition to genuine family members and refugees, many economic refugees arrived in Canada. These newcomers or "multicultural boomers" (34) lacked the professional and language skills of their predecessors. Therefore, they started to strain Canada's welfare, healthcare, and legal-care systems (35). Sugunasiri highlights that the demands of immigrant groups emboldened the racist tendencies in Canada's majority (non-immigrant) society; consequently the minority-majority race relations deteriorated in the 1990s (69). Communal relations among minorities (immigrant groups) themselves also took a disturbing turn. Various ethno-cultural immigrant groups competed among themselves for multicultural program funding, and more importantly the ethnic and religious tensions in immigrants' countries of origin started to dictate communal relations in Canada. In this "chaotic multiculturalism" as Sugunasiri states "What we ... have is an ironic twist. Even though the intent of multiculturalism was to overcome classical racism, we ended up in a situation in which *racism had overcome multiculturalism*" (74, emphasis in original). He thinks that the misconceived multiculturalism has multiplied and dispersed racism in the form of ethnocentricism. This ethnocentrism has intra-grouped members of ethnocultural minorities and given them a sense of ethnocultural superiority over others who are ethnoculturally different. Thus ethnocentricism has undermined the kind of inter-grouping expected from the multiculturalism policy. In other words, ethnoculturalism has bonded members of discrete ethnocultural communities rather than bridging diverse cultural groups so that a multicultural mosaic of Canada might emerge. Sugunasiri blames immigrant communities for impeding the realization of the just and equal Canada envisioned in multiculturalism. He also criticizes Canada's majority communities (English and French speakers) for holding onto racist views and attitudes that have challenged multicultural Canada.

Challenging the view that multiculturalism is meant only for immigrant groups, Sugunasiri argues that the policy was meant for both hosting cultural majorities and incoming cultural minorities, and therefore he invites Canada's founding nations and immigrant groups alike to contribute to Canada's multicultural project (116–17). Although Sugunasiri's recommendations for "integrative multiculturalism" lack clarity, he seems to suggest that multiculturalism is a mechanism with political, social, and legal dimensions that facilitates the interactions between non-dominant and dominant cultures (119). He expects both immigrant and non-immigrant communities of Canada to develop a take-and-give attitude so that multicultural Canada becomes a reality. He states: "By this [integrative multiculturalism] we simply mean taking the best of *all* our cultures and integrating them towards an emerging Canadian 'neo-culture'" (125, emphasis in original). Once again, he encourages Canada's immigrant communities to adapt themselves to Canada's work ethics, cultural ethos, and traditional values. He also reminds them "to make their own *contribution* to the host culture" by "sharing one's own culture" (122, emphasis in original). From an immigrant's perspective, Sugunasiri lays out his opinions on eight dimensions (law, polity, economy, education, media, arts, family, and spirituality) of Canadian society that together, he suggests, form integrative multiculturalism (128–98). He ends his book by defining who a Canadian is. Among other things, he highlights cultural sensibility and flexibility as important characteristics of Canadians. He claims: "A Canadian ... respects with critical compassion the culture[s] of other Canadians; [and also] contributes the very best of one's own culture towards building an ever-changing Canadian culture" (208). The reinterpretation of Buddhism discussed in this chapter illustrates both characteristics. On the one hand, the inclusive interpretation of Buddhism reflects the secular and religious cultural diversity of multicultural Canada. On the other hand, it also brings forth the best of Sri Lankan Buddhism so that it can contribute to multicultural

Canada. Thus the above discussion indicates that multiculturalism has been at work within Toronto's Sri Lankan Buddhist community at individual and collective levels.

CONCLUSION

Throughout this chapter, I have contended that the contents of *Teaching Buddhism to Children* demonstrate a hermeneutic effort by Sri Lankan Buddhists in Toronto to express their commitment to adapting and integrating into the Canadian multicultural society. Monks in particular, imbued with twentieth-century Buddhist missionary training, reinterpret Buddhism inclusively so that it echoes the themes of multiculturalism. The Buddhism that emerges in their inclusive interpretation is a religion of harmony that acknowledges and respects both the religious and the secular "other." As discussed above, the source of this positive image lies within one of the earliest Pāli discourses (the *Madhupindika Sutta*).[19] It means that the inclusive interpretation neither originates in Toronto, nor is it an invention of the monks in Toronto. Not being original, however, does not diminish the creativity of the monks. Rather, the textual inspiration (if not reliance) in fact legitimates their interpretation. None of these issues, however, eclipse the importance of enquiring why the harmonious discourse has come to the fore now, and in Toronto. As I have discussed earlier, the inclusive interpretation signifies a cultural configuration and participatory role of a minority religion. As Buddhism intends to participate in and contribute to the wider Canadian public, it finds multicultural themes instrumental in mitigating its limitation in secular society. Canada's multiculturalism provides the social, political, and cultural conditions for an inclusive interpretation of Buddhism to come to the fore.

Ironically, the act of omission is also an integral part of an inclusive interpretation. For example, the Sinhalese Buddhist nationalistic discourse has been excised in Toronto. In addition to the discourse's irrelevance to the Canadian context, the Western preconception of Buddhism may also contribute to the omission. Phra Kantipalo, a Theravāda monk of Western origin, vividly notes: "the nationalist mixture in Asian Buddhism is unattractive to Westerners, much of it being merely exotic while some features of it are repulsive and actually anti-Buddhist" (Khantipalo 1990, 30). Such anti-nationalist perspectives on Asian Buddhism, which are expressed by many Western

Buddhists, also shape, in part, the emerging Sri Lankan Buddhism in Toronto that distances itself from the Sinhalese Buddhist nationalist discourse (discussed in the last chapter). In fact many Western Buddhists regularly attend the weekly meditation sessions at both the temples discussed here. Then the question is: does the positive image of Buddhism as a religion of harmony, as implied in the inclusive interpretation, also relate to the Western perception of Buddhism? The connection seems too obvious to miss.

Referring to the public projection of Buddhism in the West, Henry Shiu (2010, 108) observes: "almost always Buddhism is depicted as gentle, non-violent, 'nice,' so much so that there is a danger that an overly positive stereotype is being created." This positive image could be a double-edged sword for two reasons. First, it can impose a certain mode of being Buddhist or a Buddhist identity that may obscure and control the real-life experience of Buddhists. For example, McLellan and White (2005, 244) observe that some residents in the Caledon area in Toronto resisted the Wat Lao Veluwanaram on the basis of their "popular notions of Buddhist practice." The residents complained that collective Buddhist rituals performed at the Lao Buddhist temple did not conform to the individualistic Buddhist contemplative practices. Second, the positive image represents a significant power of religion in a secular world, where diverse religions compete with each other to attract new adherents. The first generation's "intelligent adaption" in its total spectra – the omission, addition, and reinterpretation – exemplifies how Sri Lankan Buddhists have capitalized on the positive image of Buddhism to define who they are.

Referring to identity construction in the private sphere, Charles Taylor observes that "we define our identity always in dialogue with, sometimes in struggle against, the things our significant others want to see in us" (1992, 32–3). Taylor defines the term "significant others" as "others who matter to us" (32). Questions such as who matters to us and why they matter are worth exploring because they make us understand the intricacies of individual and group identity formation. At the same time, the questions may lead us to various, even contradictory answers. However, the causal connections between them may convince us of the existence of power relations. In other words, defining our identity with or against the others who matter to us often results in certain complements or consequences. The outcomes manifest in binary forms, namely approval or condemnation, consideration or indifference, exclusion or inclusion, marginalization or integration, etc. These corresponding actions embody the vibrant yet volatile struggle over recognition.

If we can extend Taylor's insight into the dialogical principle of identity formation in the public sphere, we may decipher how immigrant religious groups also reconstruct their communal identities through a redefinition of their religious traditions, because religion has become a salient individual and group identity marker in resettlement (Williams 1988; McLellan 1999; Kurien 2007). If the process of identity formation is truly dialogical, the wider society or the majority also undergoes an identity change. However, the positive and negative outcomes within the dialogical process matter more to the minorities than to the majorities. Accordingly, the positive image – Buddhism as a religion of harmony – expressed in the inclusive interpretation encapsulates the first generation's response to "the demands of the 'religio-cultural' diversity" in Toronto (Chandrasekera 2001, 2). In other words, the image of harmony resonates with what the majority of others (whose opinions do matter) expect an immigrant religion and its faithful to be. In the reinterpreted Buddhism of *Teaching Buddhism to Children*, Sri Lankan Buddhists in Toronto emerge as an adaptive and integrative community. Multiculturalism paved the way for them to hermeneutically or philosophically project themselves as such. In everyday reality, however, they negotiate between two (individualistic and collective) cultures. That intercultural negotiation is the subject of the next chapter.

5

The Intergenerational and Intercultural
Negotiation of Buddhism

The Pāli canonical Sigāla Sutta in the *Dighanikaya* prescribes that it is a parental obligation to restrain their children from evil (*pāpānivāranti*) and establish them in good (*kalyānenivesanti*). The same Pāli discourse suggests that a good child promises: "I will keep up the family tradition" (*kulavamsamthapessāmi*) (Walshe 1996, 468).[1] Although the term "family tradition" does not specify a religious tradition, one can argue that in the context of parental duties related to good and evil, the term refers to a religious tradition; at least, that is how Sri Lankan Buddhists interpret the canonical reference. This scriptural reference explicitly authorizes the intergenerational transmission of the inherited (Buddhist) tradition. Sri Lankan Buddhists (monks, dhamma teachers, parents, and grandparents alike) invoke this discourse repeatedly. As such, the intergenerational transmission of the Buddhist tradition marks one of the significant aspects of Sri Lankan Buddhism in Sri Lanka as well as in diaspora, including Toronto.

In relation to the intergenerational transmission of Buddhism in Canada, Peter Beyer (2013, 211), suggests that "immigrant Buddhists may not be overly successful at passing on this [Buddhist] identity to their Canadian-born or raised children, and indeed, statistically, Buddhist parents in Canada are the least likely [of all immigrant parents] to pass their religious identity on to their children." Beyer's observation of the failure of Buddhist transmission in Canada does not accurately characterize Sri Lankan Buddhist parents in Toronto. Instead, this chapter demonstrates that Sri Lankan Buddhist parents as primary transmitters of Buddhism in Toronto have adopted a process of intercultural negotiation that has facilitated the passing of

Buddhism to the Canadian-born generation. By intercultural negotiation I refer to a dialogical relationship between two generations
influenced by two cultures: Sri Lankan Buddhist parents shaped by
the collective Sinhalese Buddhist culture and their Canadian-born
children who are inclined to the individualistic North American
culture. As such it is both intergenerational and intercultural. The
dialogic process has evolved in the form of the intercultural and
intergenerational criticism that led to an effort to delink Buddhism
from Sinhalese ethnicity. The rhetoric of the Buddhism-ethnicity
(or dhamma-culture) distinction subsequently paved the way for a
new cultural construction of Buddhism in Toronto that integrates
elements from both collective Sinhalese culture and individualistic
North American culture in a form akin to friendship.

The following discussion on the threefold (cultural criticism, dhamma-culture distinction, and friendship) intercultural negotiation of
Buddhism will explain that disagreements between generations are
not new. What is new in diaspora, though, is how they are expressed.
With the cultural dimension heightened, the parent-child discrepan-
cies have come to the fore as intercultural criticism that often alarms
immigrant parents. In response to this diaspora-specific intergenerational issue, Sri Lankan Buddhist parents in Toronto have employed
the dhamma-culture distinction and adopted a friendly role to keep
intergenerational communication channels open. These strategies are
formed at a communal setting where Buddhist temples, discussed in
chapter 2, function as mediating grounds between the first and second
generations as well as collective and individualist cultures. The resident monks at these temples – who function as "cultural interpreters"
(see chapter 4) and "intermediaries" (more on this below) – have variously facilitated the intergenerational and intercultural negotiation.
The transmission strategies below have emerged within the web of
the monk-laity, family-community, and parent-child dynamic connections, and they highlight immigrant parents' sensibility and role as the
primary transmitters of Buddhism in the diaspora.

IMMIGRANT PARENTS AS THE PRIMARY
TRANSMITTERS OF BUDDHISM

Parents have become the primary transmitters of the Buddhist
tradition in Toronto. The first-generation respondents reveal that
their religious socialization as Buddhist children in Sri Lanka was

more of a "cumulative project." What they learned at public and dhamma schools in Sri Lanka was fortified in the family setting, at the community level, and in the wider culture. Therefore, their religious mentors came from a variety of walks of life and through multiple relations with monks, schoolteachers, parents, grandparents, extended family members, community members, and so forth. Within this wider support system in Sri Lanka, parents were not necessarily the primary influential figures in terms of religious socialization. Parents in Toronto lament that these multi-faceted cultural enforcements are not only missing in Toronto, but sometimes their children also become confused by contradictory or opposing cultural messages. Many parents feel overwhelmed, specifically in the absence of grandparents, with the sense of responsibility in transmitting Buddhist and Sinhalese cultural values to their children. Ninety per cent of the first generation, and 68 per cent of the second generation, report that parents and grandparents are "extremely responsible" for passing the Buddhist tradition to the future generation. When it comes to who is actually influential in leading a Buddhist way of life, 60 per cent of the second-generation survey respondents state that their parents play the "extremely influential" role. Only 15 per cent say so in relation to grandparents. More than 70 per cent of the second generation lives in a nuclear family setting, which means the important role of grandparents in passing religious traditions on to the future generation is noticeably absent in Toronto. Within such a context, immigrant parents bear the heavy responsibility in transmitting Buddhism to their Canadian-born children. For them, monks are the biggest allies in realizing this obligation.

After parents, monks have been identified as the second most responsible, as well as influential, figures in the process of transmitting the tradition. This implies that the community understands the transmission of the Buddhist tradition as first and foremost a family matter, with religious professionals there to facilitate the process. Parents often accompany children to the temple and encourage them to participate in arranging the offerings to the Buddha (buddhapūja) and then ceremonially bringing them to the altar. At religious services at home, such as food offering (dāna) and protective chanting (paritta/pirith), younger people are encouraged to take active roles in serving food and beverages to the monks. The presence of young people often requires an explanation of the service, along with Buddhist teaching in English. Parents ask the monks in advance for such English services. The monks at both temples surveyed in this study can communicate in English, but only a few of them give talks in English. Sermons in English differ significantly from their Sinhala counterparts in content, emphasis, and nuances. Sinhala sermons often invoke Sinhalese cultural values, such as taking care of elderly parents, being grateful to them, and performing religious duties. One also hears these concerns in sermons in English, but often more emphasis is placed on meditation, emotional balance, self-control, and temperance. Experience-based anecdotes are more prevalent in English Buddhist talks than in those given in the Sinhala language, and this appeals to youthful audiences. Referring to Ajahn Brahm – a British-Australian monk who is regularly invited by the community to give dhamma talks – one Buddhist youth says, "I like him. He is so direct, he does not go around, and he is straight to the point ... He relates back to his life experiences. It shows that he is learning from them, and you try to apply your experience to it."

English-speaking monks within the community often become intermediaries between Sri Lankan Buddhist parents and their descendants in Toronto. Pressing concerns for parents are their children's excellence in education, association with "unworthy" companions, peer pressure to engage in substance abuse, and premature sex. In addition to their own advice and guidance to their children, Buddhist parents sometimes consider the monks as their allies to get these parental concerns across to their teenagers. They send their children to monks for moral guidance on these issues. In addition, they come to the temple or invite monks to their homes on specific occasions of children's lives, such as birthdays, university entrance, and pre-wedding celebrations. Sometimes monks are directly or indirectly requested to provide their children with Buddhist perspectives on pressing concerns. For example, I witnessed that after numerous dānapinkam, Bhikkhu Saranapala of the Mississauga Buddhist Cultural Centre gives talks in English on the importance of higher education and Buddhist virtues[2] that promise success in life. He is, in fact, well known to the youths within the community and is often consulted for Buddhist perspectives on pressing issues.

A Sri Lankan Canadian youth interviewed in *Growing up Canadian* praises the monks at the Mississauga temple: "the priests are very open with the kids, like the youth, and they're able to get across to the youth much better than the priests here, in Scarborough" (Carriere 2013, 276). Commenting on the youth's reference to the creative roles of monks in Toronto, Kathryn Carrière rightly observes: "Serving as a bridge between older, more conservative generations and their often-times Canada-born children, her temple priests used faith as a common tool to close generational gaps" (Carriere 2013, 276). In addition to communication skills in English, the monks' North American cultural understandings and willingness to integrate them in their interactions (more on this in the section on "Being Like Friends") with congregations enable the monks to serve as a bridge between first- and second-generation Buddhists. The following statement of a prominent lay practitioner sums it up: "The people [to] whom we are catering today are [a] dying generation. They would die and what [would] the younger people do? The new generation will not follow 100 per cent all the Buddhist tradition and the rituals that were followed by their parents in Sri Lanka and here in Canada. So we do not need monks who cannot speak in English; who cannot communicate in English. We need monks who can not only deliver sermons in English but who would think [in English], who would able to reflect and convey dhamma to our children in a manner that they will preserve certain aspects of both cultures suitable to this time and era as well as inculcate the knowledge of dhamma to them [children]" (personal interview, 2009). English speaking and interculturally versatile monastics are a crucial resource in immigrant Buddhist communities. They reduce intergenerational tensions and also pass Buddhism to the next generation. Sri Lankan monks in Toronto engage Buddhist youths in programs like Buddhist Soup Kitchen, Meditation in the Park, and inviting popular Buddhist preachers like Ajahn Brahm.

At the 2008 youth forum, Ajahn Brahm addressed issues pertinent to youths: sex, drugs, education, and relationships. Young people asked questions about Buddhist perspectives on abortion, homosexuality, karma, and relationships with individuals from different cultures and faiths. While answering those questions from a Buddhist perspective, Ajahn Brahm also reminded the Buddhist parents to "respect your kids," and, in the context of marriages of their children, he also asked the parents to "think for the happiness of your child, but not for your status." This reference to the status of parents in relation to their children's accomplishments or lack of them echoes one of the second generation's complaints about their parents (more on this in the next section). The powerful intergenerational role the English-speaking monks play within the community is illustrated on the one hand by Ajahn Brahm's advice to the parents to prioritize "the happiness of your child" over status, and on the other by Bhikkhu Saranapala's youth talks on life success (mentioned earlier). The presence of such capable monks is crucial in transmitting the integrity of the Theravāda Buddhist tradition to a new generation born and/or raised in North America.[3]

Buddhism in North America often echoes the concept of self-preference. In the context of religion, self-preference means freedom of thought in practicing or not practicing religion(s). Buddhist scriptures celebrate individual freedom, and they invite (*ehi passika* or come and see) but do not seek to impose Buddhism on people. They promote self-reliance in spiritual development. Specifically in modern Sri Lankan Buddhism, the Buddha's role as a spiritual teacher (*akkhātāro*) is emphasized more than any other role. Buddhist monastics are encouraged to spread the words of the Buddha, but not doing so is not a violation of monastic rules. Lay people are instructed to practice Buddhist teachings in everyday living, but proselytization is not a part of the Buddhist calling. Despite the influence of Protestant Christianity on modern Sri Lankan Buddhism, Steven Kemper (2005, 27) observes: "one thing [that] 'Buddhist missionizing' did not borrow from Protestantism was its emphasis on conversion proper." In the long Buddhist history, the Buddhist self-reliance discourse has, perhaps, not met a culture as individualist as contemporary North America.

The North American individualistic culture perfectly embodies the discourse of Buddhist self-agency. However, it has become a double-edged sword in establishing Buddhist communities across North America. Wendy Cadge (2005, 196) identifies "the 'come and see' attitude and flexibility in teachings and practices" as one of the adaptive strategies employed by both Asian and non-Asian Theravāda Buddhists. She says that this strategy contributes to the growth of Buddhist organizations, as it "favors loosely bound organizations that enable a range of people to be involved in different ways." Similarly, the first-generation Korean Buddhists in Los Angeles have used the Buddhist self-agency discourse to combat Korean Christian pressure and to construct their Buddhist identity in resettlement. They negotiate their identity and develop their self-esteem in relation to their views on "the other" – the Korean Christians in Los Angeles. Sharon Suh (2004, 203) observes that Korean Buddhists perceive themselves to be "more authentic

Koreans and better Americans" by associating the Buddhist virtue of self-reliance to "the cardinal virtues of American culture itself – independence, self-rule, and democratic values."

However, this effective use of the discourse by the first-generation Buddhists has played out differently in the context of the second generation within the Korean Buddhist community in Los Angeles. Suh (2004, 170) argues that the "emphasis on Buddhist karma and self-agency has had the unintended consequences of an increasing Christianization of many second-generation Buddhist children." She suggests that the Buddhist discourse of self-agency has led Korean Buddhist parents to leave their children themselves to decide if the latter want to inherit the parents' Buddhist religion or leave it altogether and convert to Christianity. This lack of parental guidance in intergenerational transmission of Buddhism has been exploited by Christian missionaries to convert young Koreans from Buddhist families. Thus the Buddhist emphasis on self-reliance, the same virtue credited for making Korean immigrants better Americans, has become an ineffective means of, or even an obstacle to, transmitting their Buddhist tradition to successive generations. In other words, Korean Buddhists' beliefs in karma and self-agency have deflated parental energy, urgency, and responsibility in transmitting Buddhism to their children. The agency of children has overridden the parental agency and authority. Beyer (2013, 221) too identifies that "the flexible, even optional character of the Buddhist belief and practice" contributes to the failure to transmit Buddhist intergenerationally.

Due to the long history of Buddhist educational programs for laity in modern Sri Lankan Buddhism, and creative efforts in making the program more effective – as discussed in chapters 3 and 4 – the Buddhist discourse of self-agency has not disrupted intergenerational transmission in the Sri Lankan Buddhist community in Toronto. Sri Lankan Buddhists are well aware of the discourse, and they in fact often employ it to define Buddhism as a philosophy in order to distinguish Buddhism from other religions. They, however, rarely invoke the discourse of self-agency in the context of the religious identity of their children. The survey data highlight that the first generation ranks the self-agency of the second generation as the third in importance, preceded by the guidance of parents and monks. Eighty-five to 90 per cent of the first generation respondents consider parents and monks "extremely responsible" for passing Buddhism on to the Canadian-born generation. In comparison, only

64 per cent of them associate such responsibility with the second generation. That means, in relation to the transmission of Buddhist tradition, the first-generation Sri Lankan Buddhists hold their children relatively less responsible. There is no doubt that they recognize children's preference, but they place it under the moral guidance of parents and monks. Consequently the majority (62 per cent) of Sri Lankan Buddhists in Toronto do not think that youths should enjoy their own discretion in following or not following any religion.

At the same time, they do not think parents have the right to "impose" Buddhism on their Canadian-born youths. For example, 84 per cent of the first generation agree, "parents should not impose ... [instead they should] educate their religion to youth." The survey data consistently indicate that parents consider themselves as primary transmitters of Buddhism; monks are the great allies in materializing that moral obligation. As illustrated earlier, formal Buddhist education has become the primary means through which that intergenerational Buddhist transmission takes place. Within this context of education, many parents acknowledge that their religion requires modification to suit the needs of their youths. For instance, over 50 per cent of parents disagree with the following survey statement: "Youth should follow their parents' religion as it is." This suggests that parents acknowledge that their form of Buddhism requires tweaking to address the needs of their Canadian-born youths. This acknowledgement combined with their heightened role as the primary transmitters of Buddhism encourages the first generation Sri Lankan Buddhists in Toronto to culturally negotiate Buddhism. Intercultural criticisms between the first and second generation instigate that negotiation.

INTERGENERATIONAL AND INTERCULTURAL CRITICISM

Intercultural criticism between the first and second generations is the first of three components of intercultural negotiation. It illustrates that generational issues tend to become cultural tensions in immigrant communities. Disagreements between first- and second-generation Buddhists are often perceived to be intercultural, as each generation is influenced by a distinct culture – the first generation by the Sinhalese ethnic culture and the second generation by North American culture. Generally, the former orients toward collectivism, in which group concerns, values, and communal expectations are prioritized. The latter, however, centres on individualism that prioritizes personal interest, feeling, and reason as the driving forces (Triandis 1995). Unresolved issues deriving from such two opposing cultures can disrupt the intergenerational transmission process, unless they are systematically addressed at a community level.

The first generation finds a lot of good things in the ambient dominant culture in Toronto. Some of them went so far as to say, "it is here [in Canada that] real Buddhism is practiced; people practice Buddhism even though they are not Buddhists. In principle, there are more Buddhists here than in Sri Lanka; there are more Buddhist values here than in Sri Lanka." The Buddhist values and principles they find expressed in the ambient culture in Toronto include social ethics such as equality, mutual respect, fairness, human and animal rights, and so forth. Rather than taking the preceding statements at face value, I read them as the expressions of the immigrants' justification of leaving their country of origin, as well as their appreciation of their country of current residence and its culture. But, though the Sri Lankan Buddhists appreciate the things they consider to be positive in the surrounding culture, they are also acutely aware of the less positive sides of the culture, which become significant concerns in raising their children in Toronto.

The first generation complains about the influence of individualism in the lives of their children. Many of them consider themselves to be liberal, and, as such, they appreciate the individualistic ideology that one is capable of knowing or deciding what is good and bad for oneself in leading a good life. But they believe such a liberal outlook should be gradually incorporated into life as one matures with age, knowledge, and understanding. They conceptually understand the importance of individual independence, but this understanding is not culturally materialized. They prefer their children, even when the latter reached adulthood, to live under their moral guidance, and they would like to contribute to adult children's significant life decisions in areas such as higher education, career choices, interpersonal relationships, and marriage.

Parental interventions (or moral guidance, as the first generation understands it) in youths' lives trigger intergenerational misunderstanding and cross-cultural criticism. Parents justify their behaviour as "tough love" for the betterment of their offspring. Many youths understand that, but some believe that the parental pressure is also motivated to increase the family fame, to increase reputation within the community, and to maintain social face through the achievements of the children. Referring to his parents, one university undergraduate student notes, "parents are very much concerned about [the] social perception of their children ... they are very influenced by social perception and stereotypes within the community." The effects of youth culture on the lives of their children generate conversations. Children's behaviours and achievements sometimes become the basis to measure and pass judgment on the success or failure of different parents. A young female interviewee observes: "When I go to the socio-cultural events, I notice people are talking nonsense. To sit in between and hear all of it, it is so frustrating ... since I was born and grew up here my mentality is different and I get frustrated. I don't like the narrow-mindedness of people who are making judgment on others. There are a lot of judgments on others ... It is the gossiping about things in the older community that really bothers me. It seems that parents are so curious about what [someone] else's child is doing, but first they should have to see what their child is doing" (personal interview, 2009). The interviewee describes her parents' generation as being judgmental, narrow-minded, and intrusive. Some other second-generation research respondents also echoed her sentiment about the first generation. At time they find their parents conservative, controlling, and stereotypical. Youths relate these characteristics to their parents' culture as much as to specific personal traits.[4] Similar characterizations of parents and their culture by immigrant youths are also noted elsewhere (Smith-Hefner 1999; Ong 2003; Zhou 2006). The preceding testimony furthermore indicates youths' depreciation of parental cultural traits, and they often express their frustration in front of the parents and elders.

Youths' unguarded criticism of parental behaviour stirs up intergenerational cultural tension. Parents complain that the expressiveness of the North American culture is increasingly influencing the hierarchical parent-child relationship in the Sinhalese culture. I notice that many of the first-generation respondents refer, with almost a sense of nostalgia, to how obedient they were to their parents, teachers, and elders. They say that such celebrated virtues are missing in the second generation due to opposing cultural values in North America. One young woman who migrated to Canada as an adolescent compares both cultures:

There are a lot of conflicts between the Sinhalese culture and the North American culture. We were growing up in a culture where you are supposed to respect at all times anybody who is older than you. Sometimes it is not always possible to do. Sometimes, you do not agree with the view of the older person, but you are not supposed to go against them. In our culture you are supposed to act like you agree with them. But then in the North American culture, if you do not agree with something you just speak up and stand up. You don't have to agree with everything ... I remember when I was small growing up I was known [as] one of the quietest person, for sure studious but very quiet. In Sri Lanka that was good. It is good thing to be a quiet student. But here [Canada] it is not. Here in North America you are supposed to raise your hand up, and you are supposed to ask questions. (Personal interview, 2009)

Raising one's voice against parents, teachers, and elders is considered a sign of disrespect in the Sinhalese culture. Specifically, talking back to parents is understood as undermining the sacredness associated with parenthood.

In Sinhalese Buddhist culture, a religious language is often invoked in child-parent relationship. Parents are referred to as *gedara budun* (Buddhas at home). As such, children are culturally expected to venerate and obey to their parents. To do so is understood as children's duties toward one's parents. Such traditional language of duty sounds foreign to children born in Toronto. The Buddhist parents I interviewed complain that children in North America are better informed about their rights than their mutual duties. They are influenced by social egalitarianism rather than vertical relationships. A middle-aged mother says: "they [children] do not want any lecture from us." Parents associate such youth rebellion with North American popular culture, which for them is characterized by self-indulgence and the lack of religious underpinnings. As such, they perceive that their children are often victimized by materialism and secular worldviews that may diminish the Sinhala Buddhist cultural emphasis on honouring, respecting, and more importantly taking care of parents at their old age. A father asserts: "in the Sinhalese culture we are attached to our parents; my parents were attached to their parents. We do not send our parents to senior homes when they are old. We look after our parents and they look after our kids. We

stay together. Whatever property you have, you give it to your kids."
He finds that this sense of intergenerational bonding is missing in
the North American culture, and he worries that his children will be
affected by it.

The possibility of being ignored in old age by their children is
one of the biggest concerns of the parents who grew up in a collective culture and raise their children in an individualistic culture.
A young woman comments: "parental expectations are keeping up
with culture, taking care of parents when they become older. My
mom worries that I am not going to take care of them and [will be]
putting them in a senior home when they get older." This particular
statement captures the first generation's anxiety about having their
children grow up in a new cultural setting. These concerns make the
immigrant parents emotionally more vulnerable because they rationalize the sacrifices they have made and the hardships they have
been through in resettlement for a better future of their children. To
minimize these legitimate fears and worries, immigrant parents with
teenage children seek out co-ethnic organizations and institutions,
which tend to become "mediating grounds" between the ethnic and
wider cultures (Zhou 2006, 328). The Sri Lankan Buddhist temples,
particularly their dhamma education programs, play a crucial role in
connecting two generations influenced by two cultures. One noticeable strategy that has emerged in response to intercultural and intergenerational tension is to distinguish dhamma from culture.

DHAMMA-CULTURE DISTINCTION AS
A PEDAGOGIC STRATEGY

Language as a medium of transmission shapes the nuances of what is
being transmitted; its efficacy shines when transmitters and receivers
alike claim proficiency in that language. The Canadian-born children
of Sri Lankan Buddhist immigrants in Toronto hardly demonstrate a
sophisticated knowledge of the Sinhala language. They can manage
to get by with their little Sinhala at home, the epicentre of ethnic
language within the Sri Lankan Buddhist diaspora. Even at home
they tend to respond in English rather than in Sinhala, even if their
parents communicate in Sinhala. Perhaps what prevents them from
speaking in Sinhala is their "funny" accent, which often amuses the
first generation. A young woman explains: "I can speak in Sinhala,
but I don't. I can communicate with my friends, and I do. But at

home I don't. I can understand it perfectly fine. I guess I am shy with my accent. I do not have a Sri Lankan accent, I have a very Canadianized accent. When I talk in Sinhala, it sounds very funny." Ethnic language is the ubiquitous identifier of a particular ethnicity. The decreasing application and knowledge of Sinhala language among the second generation signifies that the latter's connection to the Sinhala ethnicity is increasingly becoming symbolic at best. This however does not impede the transmission of Buddhism to the Canadian-born generation, as Buddhist programs designed for children and youth are conducted mainly in English. The transition from Sinhala to English as the medium of instruction has practical reasons, and Buddhism's relaxed attitude to language certainly has helped ease the transition.

Buddhism from the very beginning downplayed the *santa langua* claim in understanding truth/dhamma. Theravāda Buddhists believe that the Buddha taught in a non-elite vernacular that was eventually named the Pāli language, as opposed to the elite language of Vedic Sanskrit. The Buddha's preference for Pāli – a language of commoners – over Sanskrit was perhaps motivated by a practical reason: making his teaching accessible to a wider audience. It also led to developing a Buddhist philosophy of language that suggested that language does not inherently relate to truth. Language is nonetheless an important tool, second to one's direct experience in realizing nibbāna, the ultimate reality as understood in Buddhism. Neither the Buddha's rejection of Sanskrit nor the sophisticated Buddhist philosophy of language, however, prevented Theravāda Buddhists from transforming Pāli as the santa langua. Consequently, Pāli became the ubiquitous pan-Theravāda identity (Collins 2010).[5] Such linguistic religiosity has always been tempered by the use of vernaculars for practical reasons in religious life, i.e., chanting scriptures as ritual acts; reinterpreting the contents of scriptures; and preaching and practicing dhamma. All these activities simultaneously contributed to passing on Theravāda identity as well as re-contextualizing Theravāda. Sri Lankan Buddhists in Toronto repeat the same Theravāda history by replacing one vernacular (i.e., Sinhalese) with another one (i.e., English) while keeping Pāli as the language of Theravāda liturgy or ritual.

After a few experiments back and forth using Sinhala, English, or both, Sri Lankan Buddhist leaders in Toronto decided to teach Buddhism to children in English. That decision evolved organically from the late 1980s to early 1990s. It has not been free of resistance, and there are a small number of parents who still argue that Buddhism should be taught in Sinhala. This number, however, is increasingly shrinking. Dharmadasa [fictitious name], a dhamma school teacher explains:

> The first thing I was wondering was that, is it the right thing to teach dhamma in English to Sri Lankan students who mostly belong to Sinhalese families. When I have discussed this matter with other friends, their explanation was that the children cannot speak in Sinhalese and that's why we have to teach Buddhism in English. I was in a denial state initially ... My belief was that we should make attempts to teach dhamma in Sinhalese [because then] it is not only the dhamma we are providing to them, but we are also providing their mother tongue to them. But then I understand that it would be practically difficult to make them understand Buddhism ... I find that some of our parents speak in English at home, so that the children are exposed to English culture at home ... So I could understand the explanation that is given to me by my friends and others that it is difficult to teach Buddhism in Sinhalese to the students who do not understand Sinhalese. So if you try to teach dhamma to them in Sinhalese, they would understand neither dhamma nor the language. (Personal interview, 2009)

The preceding interviewee alludes to a few important issues related to the salience of Sinhala language in the context of dhamma education. He expresses the dilemma of separating Buddhism from ethnic culture. With his reference to the importance of a mother tongue – a key feature of an ethnic culture – in the context of dhamma education, he invokes the relationship between Buddhism, Sinhalese culture, and language. But practical reality, such as the Canadian-born generation's lack of the Sinhala language, makes Dharmadasa realize the difficulty in passing on that ethno-religious identity. Parental experience supports separating Buddhism from Sinhalese culture. The interviewee implies that the main priority of dhamma education is not language but "dhamma" – a term that is traditionally used to refer to the Buddha's knowledge and wisdom, which transcends specific ethnic and cultural boundaries.

Moreover, Dharmadasa laments how some Sri Lankan Buddhists in Toronto prioritize English over Sinhala when they communicate with their children. In fact, Chandrasekere (2008) observes that only 66 per cent of Sinhalese parents in Toronto are interested in teaching the Sinhala language to their children (179), and some converse in English with their children (172). On the other hand some parents are quite committed to the notion that their children must learn Sinhala. Those commitments are expressed in numerous ways, such as a strict rule of "Sinhala only at home," the regular visits and presence of grandparents in Toronto, the second generation's long visits to Sri Lanka, regular attendance to the heritage language program funded by the regional school board, and in rare cases even moving back to Sri Lanka to expose children to the Sinhala culture. All these sacrifices involve extra costs, commitments, and compromises that only a few can afford. I notice that only a few, in fact, have made one or more of the above sacrifices to pass their language and culture to the second generation. Above all, the second generation resist their parents' pressure to learn Sinhala by highlighting the lack of pragmatic application of Sinhala in their everyday life, such as in school, in entertainment youth culture (TV, music, internet, etc.), and also with their peers, many of whom come from non-Sinhalese ethnic backgrounds.

Although both English and Sinhala languages are interchangeably used in Buddhist services where both generations participate, English has become a preferred medium in the context of Buddhism. Disapproving of this trend, a prominent member of the community says: "there are a lot of people in our community who surprisingly think that they have heard a really good sermon if it is only delivered in English." The survey data also indicate that both generations prefer English to Sinhala. Indeed 83 per cent of the first generation emphasizes the importance of English while only 53 per cent say the same about Sinhala. Understandably, preference for English increases in the context of the second generation. This indicates that the Sinhala language is increasingly becoming symbolic rather than practical in Toronto.

Moreover, both generations relate temples to religious identity rather than ethnic identity. In the survey conducted, they consistently emphasized that the role of temple is to help them uphold and deepen their commitments to Buddhist learning and practices. Echoing that sentiment, temples hardly provide services dedicated to specifically ethnic elements of the Sinhala culture such as Sinhala language teaching, traditional music and dance classes, and arts and crafts events. Temples do organize events like a Sinhala music show and traditional dance performance in order to raise funds to support the temple management costs. It is the first generation rather than the second generation who attend those events. To appreciate and enjoy the rhythms and lyrics of traditional Sinhala music requires considerable pre-exposure to them, a condition missing in the second generation's Canadian upbringing. Thus, Sri Lankan Buddhists' preference of English over Sinhala, relating temples to religious identity rather than ethnic identity, and their diminished enthusiasm for ethnicity-oriented temple services consequently determines what is passed on to the Canadian-born generation. In that intergenerational process, ethnicity indicators like the Sinhala language, music and dance, arts and crafts are not passed on to the second generation as much as are Buddhism and associated religious aspects. Consequently, the second generation can recite the basic Pāli chanting, refer to the Sakyamuni Buddha's life story, and identify what the basic Buddhist doctrines are. More importantly, they can also perform basic merit-making ceremonies (pinkam) like offerings to the Buddha (buddhapuja) and to the monks (sānghika dāna).

The foregoing analysis of what is transmitted (and what is not), and the means of that intergenerational transmission, highlights Toronto's Sri Lankan Buddhists' tendency to distinguish ethnicity from Buddhism. A middle-aged mother of two youths and a dhamma teacher says: "As parents [who are] bringing Buddhism from the Eastern part of the world to the Western part of the world, we also grab Western values. Having said that, are we practicing Buddhism totally the same way we practiced Buddhism in Sri Lanka? I'd say no! *The practices are different, but has the essence changed? Or has the dhamma changed? No!* In a different cultural setting we adapt to that cultural situation, and we practice dhamma. One can say it is a modified way; maybe it is a modified way. Through that modification what we do is not anything other than dhamma" (personal interview, 2009). The preceding testimony relates to an important aspect of the psyche of the faithful. Although social scientists tend to conceptualize religion as (or even to reduce it to) an expression of psychological, social, and cultural processes, the faithful have a different understanding. The interviewee, perhaps due to migration experience, is quite sophisticated in separating Buddhism from culture. She understands perfectly that religious practices are culturally bound, but for her there is something more than culture – that is what she calls the dhamma. Dhamma, for her, is the "essence" of Buddhism and it does not change. Such essentialization of Buddhism contradicts not only the Buddhist teaching of impermanence (*anicca*) but also an academic understanding of Buddhism. However, one should not ignore Buddhist practitioners' impulses to essentialize or reify Buddhism. Instead, historical and empirical analysis of Buddhism in practice should discern how essentializing rhetorics are formed and why. Such analysis not only dis-essentializes Buddhism but also explains why essentialization of Buddhism is important for the Buddhist faithful. For example, we notice that the preceding interviewee simultaneously locates Buddhism within as well as outside of history. She historicizes culture, locating it in a particular time and space. She however refuses to do the same with what she calls dhamma. For her, dhamma transcends time and space. What is important for scholars is to discern the purpose of her essentialization of dhamma. I argue that the rhetoric of dhamma as essence enables her to validate novel Buddhist practices and to justify the intercultural integration discussed below. More importantly, it facilitates the intergenerational transmission of Buddhism.

The dhamma-culture rhetoric has a long history within Sri Lankan Buddhism in Sri Lanka. The recent Buddhist history in Sri Lanka indicates that the dhamma-culture distinction enabled Buddhists to particularize as well as universalize Buddhist tradition, depending on their agendas. For example, a caste-free monastic tradition, reintroduced from Thailand and Burma during the eighteenth and nineteenth centuries respectively, took a new form as a caste-oriented tradition with the influence of the Sinhala ethnic culture (Blackburn 2001, 65). In contrast, the Buddhist reformism of the late nineteenth and early twentieth century in Sri Lanka separated Buddhist abstract concepts from their ambient culture and interpreted them along with modern universal values: freedom of thought, individual rights, and social equality. Anagarika Dharmapala particularized and universalized Buddhism simultaneously, depending on his audience. To a Sinhalese audience he asserted that Sinhala and Buddhism are inherently connected – as such, for him "giving up on Buddhism" meant "giving up on being Sinhala" (Kemper 2005, 28). In contrast, for Western audiences Dharmapala presented "the universalistic Buddhism" that can liberate people from "priestcraft, materialism, and sheer theology" (Kemper 2005, 29, 32). Dharmapala's universalistic Buddhism was the heart of a new interpretation that is eventually called *The Making of Modern Buddhism* (McMahan 2008).

What made that Buddhist modernization project possible was the emic argument that dhamma is different from culture.

The same argument has emerged in other Sri Lankan and non-Sri Lankan Buddhist diasporas. For example, Stewart Chandler (2005, 175) observes that Master Xingyun, the founder of Foguan Shan transnational Chinese Buddhist organization, urges practitioners to "localize" Buddhism in diaspora. Chandler states that by "localization of Buddhism" Master Xingyun "means that customs which have been generated by Buddhists in China and other cultures over the centuries may be replaced by other customs more appropriate to each new region into which the Dharma is introduced. The essential teachings remain the same, while culture-specific practices can vary." This call for replacing Chinese culture with North American culture is labelled as "de-ethnification process" (Verchery 2010, 213). It is the same dhamma-culture distinction that emerged within the Sri Lankan Buddhist community in Toronto. The difference is that Foguan Shan uses the distinction to attract more non-Chinese Buddhist converts than the children of Buddhist immigrants. A closer reference to the phenomenon is noticed among Sri Lankan Buddhists in the United Kingdom and the United States. Mahinda Deegalle (2008, 19) observes the religious-cultural distinction at the Sri Saddhatissa International Buddhist Center in London, UK. Paul David Numrich (1996), who studied Buddhists from Sri Lanka in Los Angeles, observes that "Dharma Vijaya's [the Sri Lankan Buddhist temple in Los Angeles] leaders made a comprehensive programming decision to divorce Sinhalese culture from Buddhist religion" (102), and notes further that "Sinhalese parents there do not ... stress the inculcation of Sinhalese cultural identity in America" (107). Numrich interprets the leaders' decision and parental concern as an "ethnic isolation" (107). He concludes that "this divorce has not been fully successful" (102), nor has it facilitated the transmission. Instead, Numrich argues, the decision impedes the transmission of the Buddhist tradition to the second generation (97). My observation of the dhamma-culture separation in Toronto echoes Numrich's; nevertheless, I interpret and explain the trend differently. I suggest that the dhamma-culture distinction derives from the motivation to distance Buddhism from the ethnic conflict in Sri Lanka and to transmit Buddhism to the Canadian-born generation.

The Sri Lankan civil war (1983–2009) that ravaged both Sinhalese and Tamil in Sri Lanka for nearly four decades influenced the ways in which Sri Lankan Buddhism has been presented in Toronto. In the height of that war, William McGowan wrote an article entitled "Buddhist Backlash Hobbles Sri Lanka" in the *Globe and Mail* on 27 August 1987. He linked the violence to Buddhism, calling it "more fetish than philosophy, more ideology than religion, Sinhala Buddhism is less a path of piety than a way of ostentatiously displaying tribal solidarity." This harsh criticism of Sri Lankan Buddhism in a leading newspaper must have been a major blow to Toronto's Sri Lankan Buddhist community. As a religious minority, they could not be oblivious to such an unsympathetic characterization of their cherished religious tradition. The following statement by the editor of the community's magazine, *Toronto Buddhist*, expresses the Sri Lankan Buddhist community's reaction to the *Globe and Mail* piece. It separates Buddhism from Sinhalese ethnicity: "He [McGowan] is so ignorant as to think that there is a special variety of Buddhism, namely Sinhala Buddhism. He should have known that Buddhism in Sri Lanka is Theravāda, prevalent also in India and in South-east Asia. There is, therefore, no special branch of Buddhism named Sinhala Buddhism. The writer displays gross ignorance of even the basics of Buddhism" (*Toronto Buddhist* 9 (1987): 4). This is a prime example of Toronto Sri Lankan Buddhists' resistance to the ethnic characterization of their religion. The etic application of the term "Sinhala Buddhism" emerges within the context of the Tamil-Sinhalese ethnic tension. The emic rejection and denial of that term is intended to shield Buddhism from the ethnic violence. What then is Sinhala Buddhism? What does it have to do with the Sinhala-Tamil tension?

Defining the term, Deegalle Mahinda (1997, 218) states: "Sinhala Buddhism has two meanings – Buddhism in the Sinhala language and Buddhism practiced by the Sinhala people." Thus it invokes a long historical symbiotic relationship between Buddhism, the Sinhala people, and the Sinhala language. Its synonym, "Sinhalese Buddhism," has figured in the titles of numerous books and articles about Buddhism in Sri Lanka since 1970s (Bechert 1978; Norman 1978; Reynolds 1972; Saram 1976; Southwold 1983). Buddhism's (dis)association with the ethnic tension in Sri Lanka has generated many lively scholarly discussions (Abeysekara 2001; Bartholomeusz 2002; Deegalle 2006; Grant 2009; Spencer 1990; Tambiah 1992). These critical studies reveal that the claim of inherent connection between Buddhism and Sinhala ethnicity was first made in the early twentieth century to oppose colonialism and Christianization, and was reutilized in 1950s and 1960s for political ends (Obeyesekere 1975, 251). This "Sinhala Buddhist" discourse makes it harder for Buddhism to escape the accusation, unless the inherence of Sinhala Buddhist identity is deemphasized, deconstructed, and ultimately denied. To do so seems to be political suicide in postcolonial Sri Lanka.

McGowan's *Globe and Mail* piece suggests that Sri Lankan Buddhist migrants to Western democracies, particularly those who coexist with Sri Lankan Tamils as in Toronto, had to confront the ramifications of the Sinhala Buddhist claim for dominance in post-colonial Sri Lanka. That includes not only the bad press discussed above but also a fire attack on Scarborough's Sri Lankan Buddhist temple. As a result, they have to neutralize the Sinhala ethnic connection to Buddhism. As noted in chapter 1 on community formation, the Sinhala-Tamil tension in Sri Lanka intensified in the 1970s, as the common Ceylonese/Sri Lankan national identity was replaced by new formations of identities along ethnic and religious lines. Unlike Sri Lankan Tamils in Toronto (Amarasingam 2015), the Sinhalese in Toronto have highlighted their religious/Buddhist identity over ethnic identity. The *Toronto Buddhist*'s outright rejection of the ethno-religious term – i.e., Sinhala Buddhism – in favour of a trans-ethnic identity – i.e., Theravāda Buddhist – could be read as a means of vindicating Buddhism from an association with ethnic violence. It also signifies Toronto Sri Lankan Buddhists' effort to downplay the claim of an inherent connection between Buddhism and Sinhala ethnicity. This effort has become a pedagogic strategy in the dhamma education program.

As the first-generation Sri Lankan Buddhists are motivated to pass at least their religion on to their Canadian-born children,[6] the dhamma-culture distinction has emerged as an intergenerational transmission strategy to pass Buddhism on to the Canadian-born generation. It has mainly advanced the Buddhist aspects of Sri Lankan worldviews and practices while leaving behind aspects that are perceived to be exclusively associated with the Sinhala ethnic culture. Its impact is, however, felt beyond the dhamma education program. The section on the child-parent and monk-laity relationships lays out how the dhamma-culture distinction has encouraged and enabled Sri Lankan Buddhists to integrate Buddhism into the North American culture. Thus the outcome of the transmission strategy is not necessarily "ethnic isolation," as Numrich suggests; it is rather an intercultural integration of two worldviews and ethos that oppose each other in constructing social relations.

BEING LIKE FRIENDS:
AN INTERCULTURAL INTEGRATION

The past two sections have discussed how intergenerational dis-agreements have expressed themselves as intercultural conflicts that tend to widen the generational gap and challenge the intergen-erational transmission of Buddhism. To mitigate the latter, some first-generation Buddhists highlighted the Buddhism-culture dis-tinction. They have also responded to the growing cultural gap by incorporating an egalitarian friendship model. An integration of egalitarian and hierarchical values is noticeable within Buddhist practices, specifically in the context of the monk-laity relationship, as well as in the parent-child interaction. In traditional Sinhala society, these relationships are layered with social and religious connotations. For example, parents are not simply progenitors – they are also called creators, gods, and even the two Buddhas at home who deserve veneration, respect, and material support in their senior age from their children. On the other hand, monks are considered to be spiritually superior to laity, though they are bound by social obligations and responsibilities such as provid-ing leadership in social issues. Monks are expected to take action whenever the Buddhist public, nation, and country are under threat from internal and external influences.[7] What we notice in Toronto is that Buddhist parents and monks juxtapose the religious and social connotations associated with their roles, and they maintain hierarchical relations in religious contexts while integrating egali-tarian values in social contexts.

Many Buddhist parents whom I interviewed state that they are becoming more like friends with their children. In the Sinhala cul-ture, the parent-child relationship significantly differs from that between friends, as the former is vertical while the latter is horizon-tal. These contrasting relationship models are marked not only by how individuals behave in relation to each other, but also by the top-ics and issues they discuss with each other. In the Sinhala Buddhist culture, sex and drugs are taboo topics in parent-child discussions. However, some parents in Toronto are becoming open to discussing those issues with their teenaged children for the purpose of moral guidance. A father of a teenage boy and a pre-teen girl in Toronto compares his experience with his son to his experience he had with his own father in Sri Lanka:

As children we had a lot of respect. We would not even communicate with our parents often. That was due to respect, it was more hierarchical. We would do whatever is asked to do. We would not question. We had a huge gap. But *here we are like friends*. We discuss things. I should say that there are good things that I have brought from Sri Lanka, and there are good things I have learned from this culture as well. One of the good things is that we tell even a nine-year-old child that 'you have [the] right to ask and to question,' so that we can discuss anything ... And, it is that constant communication here [in Toronto] that I lacked with my father [in Sri Lanka]. There was no need for that because ... we had the societal bond. We had the relatives; the whole village knew each other. Therefore, there is no way to go into the wrong path like getting to drugs and so on. Here those chances are in abundance, smoking, drugs, underage sex ... I have told my teenage son that "you can ask anything you want. I would explain all to you." I have made that shift because of that fear or risks of not having constant communication with children would misguide them. (Personal interview, 2009, emphasis added)

The respondent explains that he has learnt to play a less hierarchical role with his children as a part of cultural adaptation in Toronto. He observes that the top-to-bottom interaction that he had with his father in Sri Lanka lacked direct communication. His aunts and uncles in the collective and extended family setting in Sri Lanka mitigated the parent-child generational gap by keeping checks and balances in the moral upbringing of the young generation. The interviewee realizes that the traditional parent-child dynamic has become less effective in Toronto as the intermediary aunts and uncles are not readily available to fill the generational gap. Within this nuclear family setting in Toronto, many Sri Lankan Buddhist parents are adopting a friendship model of interaction with their children in order to become more effective parents. For them, *being like friends with children is a part and parcel of being effective parents.*[8] The parents have adopted an egalitarian cultural means to achieve the hierarchically defined goals of parenting.

Nevertheless, some parents resist such egalitarian adaptation. They try to maintain an exclusive hierarchical parent-child relationship. They lament that teens in the community are losing touch with Sinhala Buddhist culture because parents are not strict enough in raising them. A dhamma teacher criticizes the trend: "the teens are too Westernized. In a way, a lot of things have to do with the parents ... I notice that the parents are not parents anymore. They are trying to be friends." While parents try to be friends with their children in order to keep the channel of communication open, they also try to maintain the religious connotation and practices related to parent-hood. In this regard, the parents heavily rely on temple services like dhamma schools, where teachers often emphasize the Buddhist perspective on the parent-child relationship. They encourage dhamma students to be grateful to their parents and respect them by bowing at their feet. I have seen parents summoned – especially during the Sinhala New Year – at the dhamma schools, where students kneel down and bow in front of their parents as Buddhists do in front of Buddha statues. Similarly, monks highlight the parent-child reciprocity in their talks during the memorial services (pinkam) dedicated to departed parents or grandparents. Thus we witness that both North American social egalitarian and Buddhist hierarchical values are integrated in the parent-child relationship. This intercultural integration is also noticeable in the context of monk-laity interaction.

In the Theravāda Buddhist tradition, lay people greet monks with bows, which are reciprocated with silent or expressed blessing, but never with a similar bow. This symbolizes the religious hierarchy between them. This sense of hierarchy shapes other everyday interactions, such as addressing, giving and taking, sitting, and conversing. These vertical interactions are still firmly in place within Toronto's Sri Lankan Buddhist community. However, one can also discern that the North American egalitarian values are encroaching into the monk-laity relationship.

Once again, we notice that the language of friendliness is visibly present in the interactions between monks and laity. The motto of the West End Buddhist Temple and Meditation Centre, one of two main Sri Lankan Buddhist Temples of this study, reads: "where friendships begin and never end." Traditionally, the concept of friendship has been prevalent between laity to laity and monastics to monastics, but it is hardly invoked in the context of the monk-laity relationship. Even in the rare instances it does appear, it is more of a religious or spiritual friendship (kalyānamittatā). Answering an interview question, "In comparison to Sri Lanka, what has been changed in Toronto?," people repeatedly referred to ways in which they relate to the monks in Toronto. They find the monks are more approachable, understanding, open, and friendly compared to their counterparts in Sri Lanka. A middle-aged woman expresses: "I find the priests [monks] here are friendly with us ... *we talk to them like our friends*. I feel very comfortable and feel very much at ease sitting face to face to discuss things with monks." The interviewee says that she did not feel the same in Sri Lanka because "priests [monks] in Sri Lanka are elevated."

Similarly, another informant suggests that the openness, expressiveness, and social equality of the North American culture is influencing the interaction between monastics and laity in Toronto. She says that "you can go and sit down and talk to the monks, and they won't look down upon you. *You feel that you are treated as equals*." These testimonies refer to monks' conscious or unconscious integration of social egalitarian values in their interactions with the laity. For example, it is very common that when people visit the temples in Toronto, the resident monks, as a gesture of hospitality, serve the visitors with Sri Lankan tea and snacks. I have also seen many occasions in which monks gave rides, as a friendly gesture, to temple visitors who rely on public transportation. These services are unthinkable from fully ordained monks in Sri Lanka, but monks in Toronto treat the laity as their personal visitors. One could argue that these adaptations are conditioned by the absence of temple boys (*abittaya*) in Toronto, but I suggest that they also symbolize the monks' integration of social egalitarianism in their interactions with the laity. A similar trend is noticeable in London, UK where a leading Sri Lankan monk has been officially recognized for his "viable and friendly" relationship with Sri Lankan lay Buddhists (Deegalle 2008, 13–14).

Kathryn Carrière (2013) observes: "Unlike the majority of Buddhist temples in the Toronto region, the Sri Lankan temples have Sinhalese monks who are able to relate [to] their congregations *on a very personal level* because of ethno-cultural similarities" (276, emphasis added). This is an important observation on the specificity of how the monks at Toronto's Sri Lankan temples relate to their congregations; however, Carrière misses the point by relating it to the monks' ethno-cultural similarities of their congregations. Studies on Buddhists in Toronto (McLellan 1999, 2009) suggest that Buddhist service providers like monastics, ritual specialists, and dhamma teachers belong to the same ethno-cultural demographics of those whom they serve. If Sri Lankan monks' very personal relations with their congregations derive from their "ethno-cultural similarities" of those served, studies could have documented the same with the Buddhist service providers in Chinese, Burmese, Cambodian, and Laotian Buddhist communities in Toronto. Then there is no speci-ficity of the monks at the Sri Lankan temples in Toronto as Carrière suggests. Yes, co-ethnicity and cultural familiarity can forge better communications in any interpersonal relations, including monk-la-ity interaction. In addition to that, I connect the personal relations at the Sri Lankan Temples in Toronto, as illustrated in the comments of Sri Lankan Buddhists cited above, to the monks' integration of a friendship model of interaction with the laity.

These integrations, however, do not compromise the traditional hierarchical monk-laity relationship. Even a casual observer would notice that the first thing that a Sri Lankan Buddhist (first and sec-ond generation alike) does upon their arrival to the temple is to hon-our the monk (sometimes even before the Buddha) with a bow. The appeal for the top-to-bottom monk-laity relationship is decreased in the context of the second generation, but the majority of both generations still find it relevant in Toronto. The survey indicates that 83 per cent of the first generation and 70 per cent of the second gen-eration state that "the hierarchically defined lay and monastic roles within the North American context" are relevant. As a response to the egalitarian social setting, the monk-laity hierarchy is diminished in social interactions, but it is still well maintained in the religious context. This echoes the intercultural integration in the parent-child relationship discussed above.

CONCLUSION

We have witnessed that intergenerational tensions within the Sri Lankan Buddhist community in Toronto have taken cultural forms. The disagreements between the first- and second-generation Bud-dhists have been interpreted as cultural mismatches between the collective Sinhala culture and the individualistic North American culture. In particular, the hierarchical social interactions in the Sin-halese culture turned out to be inadequate in building interpersonal rapport in a Canadian society defined by egalitarian social values and interactions. As such, an egalitarian friendship model of inter-action has emerged not to replace but to supplement the roles of monks and parents. It appears to be a paradox as being friends is quite different from the hierarchically defined roles of monks and parents, but we should not miss the nuances expressed in a father's statement cited above: "here we are *like* friends." If we contextualize the phrase in relation to ubiquitous hierarchical practices like bowing to monks and parents, it becomes obvious that *being like friends* has become a strategy of monks and parents to achieve what they themselves desire: passing Buddhism on to a new generation, albeit one influenced by an egalitarian culture.

So what to make of this intercultural negotiation in multicultural Toronto? It demonstrates that despite the rhetoric of multiculturalism discussed in the preceding chapter, what is happening on the ground is more interculturalism/biculturalism. The particular ethnic culture of Sri Lankan immigrants is in dialogue with the dominant culture of North America. Cultural negotiation and integration have taken place between those two cultures. Sri Lankan Buddhists' intercultural negotiation echoes the following definition of immigrants: "Traditionally immigrants struggle to maintain as much as possible of their previous personal culture and traits. They do not see themselves as arriving in a new land and culture without prior socialization of value. Neither do they dismiss all their prior socialization as meaningless in the new society. Indeed, they often argue that cultural hybridization can enrich the new society by allowing them to contribute the best of their primary socialization. As social actors on a new stage, they perform differently from the script society hands them; they act as if they are actually and authentically one of *us* – citizens aspiring to remake to their likeness themselves and the world around them, just as, they perceive, any other citizen would" (Foster 2014, 9). Cecil Foster's "cultural hybridization" of immigrants echoes the intercultural negotiation and integration of the first-generation Sri Lankan Buddhists in Toronto. John Berry (2014, 231) theorizes that cultural integration emerges as a natural response of ethnocultural groups to the larger society's commitment to multiculturalism. Accordingly, the bicultural/intercultural integration discussed above is Sri Lankan Buddhists' response to Canada's multiculturalism. It more importantly highlights the role of religion, in this case Buddhism, in the integration process.

Buddhism among Sri Lankan Buddhists in Toronto has become the medium that facilitates intercultural negotiation and adaptation. In the previous chapters, we have seen that the Buddhist educational manual in Toronto has foregrounded a Buddhist multicultural discourse. Buddhist temples in Toronto have become the intercultural mediating grounds. In this chapter, I have argued that an intercultural negotiation has developed in three folds: intercultural and intergenerational criticism, dhamma-culture distinction, and hierarchical-egalitarian interactions. The last two have emerged as transmission strategies of the first-generation Buddhists in response to intercultural criticism that challenged the intergenerational trans- mission of Buddhism. Therefore, they illustrate the creativity of the first-generation Sri Lankan Buddhists who strive to pass Buddhism to their second generation born in Canada. How the latter have responded to and received what is passed on to them is a different story. For that story of Sri Lankan Canadian Buddhists in Toronto, let us turn to the next chapter.

6

Growing up as Sri Lankan Canadian
Buddhists in Toronto

The preceding chapter discussed the ways in which Sri Lankan Buddhist parents in Toronto have culturally negotiated Buddhism so that their Canadian-born and/or -raised children receive it. This chapter is going to investigate how the Sri Lankan Canadian Buddhists have received what is being passed on to them. Rather than being passive receivers, young Buddhists of the Sri Lankan community in Toronto actively appropriate the Buddhist beliefs and practices of their parents' generation to suit their lives, having been influenced by an individualistic culture. In doing so, Toronto's Sri Lankan Canadian Buddhists themselves have become creative actors in their own right. The key concept discussed in this chapter is youths' individualistic and egalitarian cultural appropriation of an inherited Buddhist tradition that is generally characterized by collective and hierarchical cultural traits. I suggest that it is an intercultural appropriation, as both parent and youth generations live in an intercultural domain overlapped by both collective/hierarchical and individualistic/egalitarian cultures. Their intergenerational dynamic interactions often display aspects from both distinct cultures in various degrees. In other words, immigrant parents and their children embody both cultural features, and they actively integrate values and practices from both cultures. As discussed in the last chapter, the parent generation has adopted some individualistic cultural modes; in this chapter, we are going to witness how the youth generation has retained some of the collective values and practices of their parents' generation. This collective-individualistic cultural blend defines the intergenerational dynamic of the immigrant community.

As the youth generation has received the Buddhism of their parents, I argue that Buddhism emerges as a way of life that highlights personal conviction and integration in everyday life. This individualistic orientation of Buddhism differs from the first-generation Buddhists' social convention and community orientation expressed in the same phrase: "Buddhism as a way of life." As such, the phrase illustrates intergenerational continuity and divergence. In the ways in which Sri Lankan Canadian Buddhists have received, reconstructed, and reclaimed inherited Buddhism, they demonstrate the characteristics of the "religio-culturally based seekers" used in the study of *Growing up Canadian* to define its one segment of multiethnic Buddhist youths born to Asian Buddhist immigrant parents in Canada (Martel-Reny and Beyer 2013, 215). Paradoxically, though, Sri Lankan Canadians' reception of inherited Buddhism challenges the general conclusion in *Growing up Canadian* that the intergenerational transmission of Buddhism in Canada has failed.

SRI LANKAN CANADIAN BUDDHISTS AS "RELIGIO-CULTURALLY BASED SEEKERS"

Peter Beyer and his research team for *Growing up Canadian* (2013) have made a tremendous contribution to our understanding of the second-generation Buddhists, Hindus, and Muslims in Canada. To map out the religious identities of young Canadian Buddhists alone is an ambitious project. It is a herculean task for many reasons: young Canadian Buddhists have belonged to diverse ethnicities and Buddhist traditions; they have come from various socio-economic family standards; and more importantly, they have grown up with various degrees of religious socialization that range from zero activities to numerous well-established formal Buddhist educational programs for children and youths. For example, the Laotian Buddhists in Southern Ontario who arrived in Canada as refugees in the late 1970s still struggle to establish formal Buddhist educational programs. On the other hand, as this study has shown, Sri Lankan Buddhists in the same region who migrated to Canada as immigrants have set up Buddhist educational and social programs for their Canada-born children early on, in some cases even prior to establishing Buddhist temples. Therefore the young Buddhists of these two Theravāda Buddhist communities alone would highlight the importance of specificity in understanding their religious identities.

Among others, *Growing up Canadian* interviewed forty-seven Buddhist youths (twenty-eight women and nineteen men). The book provides a general view of how Canadian-born and/or raised Buddhists with multiple ethno-Buddhist backgrounds are doing with their respective inherited Buddhist traditions. The research does reveal that in general young Canadian Buddhists do not receive effective Buddhist religious socialization that would inculcate a strong Buddhist identity. This general observation is a good start in understanding the next generation of Buddhists in Canada, and more importantly, it invites in-depth studies focusing on specific communities so that more nuanced understanding and insight about the young Canadian Buddhists may emerge. This is such a study. With a deeper look at the Sri Lankan Buddhist community in Toronto, this book has laid out a success story of the intergenerational transmission of Buddhism in Canada. It rather amplifies what has been already implied in *Growing up Canadian* itself.

Only five Sri Lankans (four women and one man) were included in the forty-seven Buddhist youth participants of *Growing up Canadian* (i.e., just above 10 per cent). They stand out from fellow non-Sri Lankan young Buddhists interviewed. Three women belonged to the category of "religio-culturally based seekers," while the fourth woman belonged to the "a little bit Buddhist" category. Which category the sole Sri Lankan Buddhist male participant fits in remains unclear in the book. What is worth noticing is the fact that the majority (60 per cent)[1] of Sri Lankan participants belong to an important segment of young Canadian Buddhists – i.e., religio-culturally based seekers, who are shaping the emerging Buddhism in Canada. Therefore, their long definition below is worth quoting:

'Seekers' are those who take religious or spiritual questions seriously in their own lives, whether they actually consider themselves Buddhist or not ... We call them religio-culturally based seekers, because the way that they take these questions seriously bears in each case a clear relation to the religion of their families, Buddhism, but sometimes with an admixture of another religion like Christianity, Shinto, or Hinduism, to the culture of their families, or both. The category of course includes a fair amount of internal variety. [1] There were *those who had a modest connection* in their seeking to the religion and culture of their families and [2] *those who understood Buddhism primarily in diffuse moral* as opposed to specific belief or practice terms. But [3] there were also *a few who were in their own terms practicing Buddhists* and had undertaken to appropriate Buddhism for themselves – who had … set about to carry on the Buddhism of their parents but in such a way as to reconstruct that Buddhism with relation to their own religio-spiritual searches, their own experiences, and their different lives in Canada. These few could be seen as contributing to the construction of systematic Buddhism in Canada; Buddhism was an integral part of their lived religious lives" (215–16). [The researchers also observe that] the religio-culturally based seekers … actively constructed their own Buddhism, based on their own experience, inclinations, and research. (Martel-Reny and Beyer 2013, 220, emphasis and numbers added)

The category of "religio-culturally based seekers" (hereafter seekers) is broad enough to include the majority of Sri Lankan Canadian Buddhist youths discussed in this study.

In the above long quotation, at least, three internal variations (see the added numbers in the above quotation) of the category emerge. In particular, types two and three respectively resonate with the developing and self-claiming Buddhists of this study (more on this below). Young Buddhists' "seekership" in *Growing Up Canadian* has also emerged in this study as expressed in one young woman's self-description: "I might call myself Buddhist, but I would rather say I am seeking truth." This language of seekership implies the same ambiguity, circumspection, self-judgment, flexibility, and progression implied in the term "developing Buddhist" (see the section on developing vs self-claiming Buddhists). What is more important is the affinity between the self-claiming Buddhists of this study and the third type of seeker mentioned in *Growing Up Canadian*. For both groups, Buddhism has been an "integral part of their lived religious lives" (Martel-Reny and Beyer 2013, 216) and they have "actively constructed their own Buddhism, based on their own experience, inclinations, and research" (Martel-Reny and Beyer 2013, 220). The researchers of *Growing up Canadian* highlight the importance of the seekers, particularly the third type, in the reconstruction of Buddhism in Canada. However, their voice and contribution become insignificant in the study's overall conclusion as they represent a very small minority of the study's total Buddhist sample.

Growing up Canadian concludes that the majority of second-generation Canadian Buddhists do not retain the Buddhism of their parents. Commenting on nineteen young male Buddhists interviewed for the research, Peter Beyer (2013, 211), the principal researcher, concludes: "they were not adopting a Buddhist religious identity, let alone being engaged in Buddhist practice, to any great degree." On the other hand, young Buddhist women take Buddhism seriously not in terms of "religious beliefs and practices," but in terms of "religious questions" (Martel-Reny and Beyer 2013, 233). Their engagement with Buddhism, although better than that of male counterparts, remains occasional and peripheral compared to their engagement with their respective ethnic culture (Chinese, Vietnamese, Thai, etc.). The researchers put it thus: "Buddhist religion" in the lives of young Buddhist women "was more optional than that culture" (234). They also conclude that young Buddhists perceive Buddhism to be a "good, tolerant, flexible, and not a 'pushy' religion" but their knowledge of "what exactly Buddhism was in concrete terms often appeared to be very vague" (234). Thus Buddhist young women score higher in terms of questioning, researching, and thinking about the role of religion in their lives when compared to their male counterparts; however, these women neither have critical knowledge of Buddhism and nor do they creatively engage with Buddhist practices. In that sense, they too, similar to their brothers, hardly contribute to the ongoing "global reconstruction" of Buddhism in the contemporary world.

Overall, *Growing up Canadian* suggests a substantial failure in the intergenerational transmission of Buddhism in Canada. This is partly because the young adults interviewed did not grow up with "explicitly religious socialization," which according to Beyer (2013, 220) is a necessary condition to uphold a strong religious identity. Marie-Paule Martel-Reny and Peter Beyer (2013, 221) explain: "Among the reasons for this [lack of knowledge of Buddhism among the Buddhist participants], as we have seen, was the lack of an explicit Buddhist socialization, the failure of the parents to effectively pass on their Buddhism, and the flexible, even optional character of the Buddhist belief and practice that was passed on."[2] In addition to the lack of children-oriented Buddhist programs, the researchers identify two more reasons for the gap – namely, the ineffectiveness of Buddhist parents in transmission and Buddhism's liberal attitude toward (dis)engaging in Buddhist beliefs and practices. Thus, according to *Growing up Canadian*, the Buddhist community, individual Buddhist families, and the Buddhist tradition itself all contribute to the failed intergenerational transmission of Buddhism in Canada. It is commonsensical that without communal and family efforts in intergenerational transmission, children's knowledge and understanding of parents' religion will remain minimal and nominal at their best. On the other hand, when Buddhist socialization activities are in place at family and community levels, we could expect a young generation with a strong Buddhist identity.

The past chapters of this book have illustrated that Buddhist education for young boys and girls has been an integral part of modern Sri Lankan Buddhism, and that religious socialization has persisted in Toronto with the themes of multiculturalism and creative intergenerational transmission strategies. The Sri Lankan-Torontonian Buddhist youths studied here suggest that the general conclusion of failed Buddhist transmission in *Growing up Canadian* does not apply to the Sri Lankan Buddhist community in Toronto. If the statements of participants with Sri Lankan Buddhist background in *Growing up Canadian* are separated from the other Buddhist participants, we see their specific responses do not support the general conclusion of the study. Every single Sri Lankan Buddhist female participant in Bayer and team's study – i.e., Sanuthi (217), Nuveena (217), Chamika (222), and Nevinka (226) – comment on, and in some cases criticize, existing religious socialization/education. More importantly, they also display sophisticated knowledge about Buddhism. For example, one of them (Sanuthi?) compares the child-oriented Buddhist services of two Sri Lankan temples in Toronto (Carriere 2013, 276). The same respondent expresses her frustration with the way Buddhism is taught at her local temple in Scarborough, which almost caused her to give up her inherited Buddhist identity. It was not the temple's Sunday school but her father and grandmother who revived her interests in Buddhism (Martel-Reny and Beyer 2013, 219). That signifies the existence of not only institutional programs but also family-based traditions of Buddhist education within the Sri Lankan Buddhist community in Toronto. In addition to formal religious education, children and youths within Toronto's Sri Lankan Buddhist community also receive Buddhist religious socialization like summer meditation retreats, feeding the homeless (soup kitchens), distributing bare essentials to the poor, the annual Vesak celebration (the commemoration of the Buddha's birth, awakening, and passing away), and a day-long moral precept observation.

Figure 6.1   Dr Saranapala Bhikkhu leads the annual moral precept observation (*Sil*) program for youth

Source: The West End Buddhist Temple and Meditation Centre

Such forms of Buddhist education and socialization have facilitated the transmission of Buddhist knowledge and practices to the Canadian-born generation. The following quotation of another young Sri Lankan woman interviewed for *Growing up Canadian* demonstrates her sophisticated knowledge of Buddhist doctrine: "Buddhists believe that there is no 'you,' there is no 'me,' and there is no 'I.' And that the way to end suffering is through the Four Noble Truths: understanding where suffering comes from; knowing that there is suffering; and then you have to follow the Eightfold Path ... So it's basically knowing that there is suffering and that the Buddha taught how to get rid of suffering, which basically means being more aware of your thoughts and your feelings. That's the simplest way that I can put it" (BF25) (Martel-Reny and Beyer 2013, 222). These examples illustrate that Sri Lankan Canadian Buddhists have more than basic knowledge of Buddhism due to institutional and family-based Buddhist socialization. For many of them, Buddhism is not optional, as we have seen in the last chapter. Their diverging voices on the matters of religion are acknowledged; nevertheless, they are placed under the guidance of parents and monks in Buddhist socialization programs like dhamma education. In the following detailed discussion on Buddhism in the lives of the young generation of Sri Lankans in Toronto, the youth emerge as distinct Buddhists in their own right. To contextualize their diverse expressions of Buddhist identity, let me first describe the communal Buddhist encounters in Toronto in which young Buddhists form their identities.

COMMUNAL BUDDHIST ENCOUNTERS

Communal Buddhist encounters arguably characterize Buddhist experience in diaspora. Paul Numrich (1999) identifies two types of interactions among Buddhist communities across North America. Inter-Buddhist refers to religious interaction between Buddhists who belong to different denominations, while intra-Buddhist refers to interactions between Buddhists who share the same denominational beliefs and practices. Both types of interaction provide obstacles and opportunities, prospects and perils. The history of any Buddhist tradition would provide countless examples of such interactions, though they were more or less confined to individuals or small groups of people, such as missionaries, Buddhist students, and delegations. Unlike in the past, the contemporary Buddhist encounters in diaspora are not confined to interpersonal domains; instead, they also take communal forms as Buddhists representing diverse and intact Buddhist traditions interact with fellow Buddhists in the same city. In Toronto, for example, diverse Buddhist communities follow their own respective Buddhist traditions side by side. These communal expressions of Buddhist diversity are fortified through transnational networks. Janet McLellan's (1999) seminal work illustrates ethno-religious characteristics with five Asian Buddhist communities (Japanese, Tibetan, Vietnamese, Cambodian, and Chinese) in Toronto. Kay Koppedrayer and Mavis Fenn (2006) document the presence of Buddhism in the forms of Buddhist centres, communities, and free-floating ideas and symbols across the province of Ontario. Others (White 2010; Campbell 2011; and Verchery 2010) also add to the literature on Buddhism in Toronto with their work on Lao, Zen, and Chinese (Fo Guan Shan) Buddhism respectively. Such a rich and vibrant presence of Buddhist diversity in Toronto juxtaposes one particular Buddhist identity over and against the other Buddhist identities.

Underneath the Buddhist diversity expressed in many ethnicities, nationalities, and traditions, one can see a certain abstract commonness, such as the three foundations of the Buddhist tradition (the Buddha, Dhamma/Dharma, and Sangha). However, these common foundations are understood variously. In fact, this sense of commonness implies a loosely defined Buddhist identity, which forms the theme of unity within diversity in annual Vesak celebrations in Toronto. Buddhists in Toronto, and in other major metropolitan cities in the West for that matter, could be better described as a minority religious community of communities. This social reality poses a new set of challenges, including the transmission of a particular form of Buddhism. For example, Sri Lankan Buddhists in Toronto, in comparison to those in Sri Lanka, are less exposed to Buddhism. The little exposure they have is often diffused, inconsistent, and incoherent due to the vibrant presence of multi-ethnic Buddhists in Toronto.

Canadian-born Sri Lankan Buddhists in Toronto, like their parents, indicate that they have encountered various non-Sri Lankan forms of Buddhism through a variety of means. They have identified that books, the internet, and public media are major means through which they have encountered Tibetan, Zen, East Asian, and non-sectarian Buddhism. However, when it comes to more tangible means of encounters, such as temple visits and meetings with Buddhist teachers, non-Sri Lankan Theravāda Buddhism scores high, reflecting the participation of Burmese and Bangladeshi Theravāda monks in religious services within the community. Moreover both temples in this study occasionally organize Buddhist public talks and meditation retreats led by Caucasian Theravāda monks like Ajan Brahm, Ajan Viradhammo, and others from the Thai forest tradition. Under these circumstances, Buddhist practices within the community remain more or less intact as Theravāda.

However, the influence of non-Theravāda Buddhism on Sri Lankan Buddhists is also discernible in Buddhist knowledge, worldviews, and ultimately in the formation of Buddhist self-identity in Toronto. As Ananda Abeysekara (2002, 20) observes: "knowledges about what constitutes the self ... are produced in relation to, [and are] measured against the other ... persons, practices and institutions." A highly educated, middle-aged couple whom I interviewed together expressed how they were fascinated with the Mahayana concept of "Buddhanature." In response to my interview question "what do you think about other forms of Buddhism," they said: "[the husband:] Buddhism as a whole has the same essence. It is like 'the same cake with different icing' ... [the wife:] I don't think that there is anything wrong with any kind of Buddhism. However, I like the Mahayana concept of Buddhanature more than anything else in Theravāda, to be honest with you. We have to give credit to other people. We have a thing in Theravāda doctrine that we always look down upon others which I just don't like ... [the husband:] I find that Buddhanature is very interesting concept ... I think everyone has enlightenment within. Enlightenment is covered by all the defilements ... Everybody has it. It is the potential to be enlightened. [the wife:] It is like blooming of the lotus; that is how I look at Buddhanature. Just little by little, eventually it blossoms as a little flower" (personal interview 2009). The preceding testimony relates to a few important aspects associated with the inter- and intra-Buddhist encounters. As people are exposed to other forms of Buddhism, a non-sectarian appreciation of Buddhism replaces the historically prevalent sectarian rhetoric. In fact, this trend is more noticeable at the conceptual level than at the practical level. Although Sri Lankan Buddhists appreciate Mahayana and Vajrayana concepts, they rarely participate in Mahayana and/or Vajrayana temples or seek out non-Theravāda monks for spiritual guidance and merit-making ceremonies. In brief, Sri Lankan Buddhists remain Theravāda by practice, despite their exposure to, and fascination with, certain teachings derived from non-Theravāda Buddhism.

The couple interviewed also refers to a Buddhist eclecticism. They justify their appreciation of the non-Theravāda teaching of *Buddhanature* on the basis of an "essentialized" Buddhism, which is metaphorically referred to as "the same cake with different icing." What is implied in that metaphor is the same dhamma-culture distinction discussed in the preceding chapter. The impacts of inter- and intra-Buddhist encounters on Sri Lankan Buddhists, particularly their commitments to inherited tradition, vary. The majority of both generations acknowledge that their encounters with the "Buddhist other" have expanded their Buddhist knowledge. Parents (69 per cent), more than their children (47 per cent), find that newly expanded Buddhist knowledge has increased their beliefs in inherited Buddhism. Interestingly, the same number (30 per cent) of both generations believe that inter- and intra-Buddhist encounters made them critical of the Sri Lankan Buddhist tradition. This indicates the challenges and opportunities that Buddhist communal encounters in the diaspora have provided to a particular Buddhist tradition to contribute to the emerging general character of Buddhism as well as to get transformed by the encounters themselves. I briefly discuss an example that illustrates both incoming and outgoing influences of Theravāda Buddhism in Toronto.

Due to the fascination with popular concepts and practices associated with Buddhism in North America, such as Buddhanature and being vegetarian, some Sri Lankans find faults with their inherited Buddhism. Non-vegetarian meals of Theravāda monks often perplex (and in some cases annoy) non-Theravāda Buddhists and non-Buddhist observers. The following statement of a Buddhist youth indicates the influence of the popular misconception that all Buddhist monks are vegetarians. She says: "It bothers me how monks in Sri Lanka ... eat meat. I know that even for us [laity] it is better if you can be vegetarian even though there is no rule such like that. But when you become a monk you are agreeing that you become strict on what you follow, right? ... *if you are a monk you should follow it [vegetarianism] instead of ignoring it.* If you are lay people like us, you are free to eat whatever you like, right?" (personal interview, 2009). Being vegetarian is more of a personal choice than a monastic vow in Theravāda monasticism.

Traditionally, it is believed that the Buddha himself rejected a prominent monk's request to make vegetarianism an obligation for monks, because monks, out of humility, should rely on whatever food is offered to them. A strict vegetarian rule may exclude the non-vegetarian laity from participating in the food offering as monks go for morning alms around (*pindapāta*), as the assumption is that the laity offer to the monks a small portion of the same food that is already made for their everyday consumption. This Theravāda understanding or identity seems to be obscured in the above comment, which has been influenced by a stereotypical perception about Buddhist monks being vegetarian. This indicates the challenge of transmitting a particular form of Buddhism in a diaspora shared by numerous Buddhist traditions.

Nevertheless, the diaspora – with the presence of multiethnic and multicultural Buddhist forms – also provides an opportunity to each Buddhist denomination to go beyond a particular ethnic or national Buddhist audience. The medium of the English language facilitates reaching out to Buddhists from multiple ethnicities and cultures with a common denominational (i.e., Theravāda) interpretation, understanding, and practice of the Buddha's teachings. Buddhist services in English within the Sri Lankan community in Toronto have attracted Theravāda Buddhists from multiple ethnic backgrounds. People from various cultures – including Euro-Canadian, Sinhalese, Bangladeshi, Vietnamese, Singapore-Chinese, and other cultures – gather for Theravāda Buddhist teachings and practices. An English language-oriented group is visibly present at Mississauga's West End Buddhist Temple and Meditation Centre, which is not concerned with preserving particular ethno-cultural traits of Buddhism. Indeed a pan-Theravāda religious culture is slowly emerging from within the group. For example, some of the Buddhist practitioners from non-traditional Theravāda backgrounds greet the monks with bows and offer non-vegetarian meals to the monks. This group regularly meets for Pāli sutta studies and mindfulness meditation led by Bhikkhu Saranapala. The less-ethnic cultural tone of the group seems to appeal to the second-generation Buddhists, and some of them regularly participate in the dhamma discussion and meditation practice. Within such English-speaking Buddhist practices, the Canadian-born/raised generation has added a critical voice to the tradition passed on to them.

CRITICAL VOICES OF YOUNG BUDDHISTS

The critical voices of the second-generation Buddhists under discussion indicate their sense of creativity. The parent generation, as the transmitters of the Buddhist tradition, have exercised their rights in deciding what aspects of the Buddhist tradition should be transmitted, to whom, and how. Similarly, the second-generation Buddhists have also become creative receivers in receiving, reclaiming, and reinterpreting Buddhist teachings and practices. An overwhelming majority of them (95 per cent) agree that parents should educate them about Buddhism, and the majority of them consider their parents to be "more Buddhist" than themselves. This youthful acceptance of a subordinate position within the religion, however, does not deny them their particularities. In fact, they embrace their right to creative self-determination in religious matters. For example, 75 per cent of youths agree or even strongly agree: "youth may follow any religion they want." Even if we credit North American individualism and youth rebelliousness for the preceding sentiment, we cannot ignore the distinct sensibility of this second generation. Thus the youth perspective is a subordinate one, but it is also critical, and shapes the emergent Buddhist tradition.

Youths' perception of their parents' Buddhism delineates multiple tensions – namely, traditional vs modern Buddhist ideals, individual vs collective values, and participatory vs subjective practices. A few members of the second generation are quite vocal in criticizing how Buddhism is practiced by the first generation. One underlying criticism is that the parents are merely "traditional" Buddhists. A young man states: "My parents ... are not very devoted Buddhists. They ... you might call them common sense, traditional Sinhalese Buddhists. They go to the temple for social function. They may have a dāna [ritual of offering food to the monks] at our house once a year or so. Other than that they are very worldly people. They believe in the worldly values. And in fact they believe that money is the root of happiness and that is the primary goal of life, to attain money, to have family etc. ... I tried really, really hard to get them to meditate ... and move away their minds from money and materialism, but I find I am hitting a brick wall" (personal interview, 2009). This statement echoes a Theravāda perspective about who lay Buddhists are. In the traditional Theravāda Buddhism, the lay life relates to the *saṃsāra* (the cycle of life, death, and rebirth), while the monastic life symbolizes renunciation of the saṃsāra. In this distinction, the laity are worldly people, and their success is measured based on wealth, fame, prosperity, and power. The abundance of these things is celebrated, as long as it is accompanied by religious duty, which is often interpreted as supporting the Buddhist institution, the sangha, monastery, pilgrimage sites, sponsoring Buddhist festivals, etc. The happiness derived from these worldly gains is itself known as "*gihi sukha*," or "household happiness." This traditional justification of worldly life is increasingly being ignored, as the lay meditation movements have blurred the traditional monk-laity distinction. The youth's frustration over his failure to encourage his parents to meditate invokes the distinction between traditional vs modern lay Buddhists and their ideals, and gets expressed as an intergenerational tension.

The youth's comment also refers to a tension between two types of religious expressions: participatory vs subjective religious practices. Participatory religious expressions characterize active participation in collective religious practices, in which an individual practitioner is one of many participants. The participatory practitioners share a common goal and participate as a collective in order to achieve that goal. In contrast, subjective religious expressions highlight individual experience and meaning. As experiences are subjectively interpreted, the meanings derived from them are also individually determined. The Buddhist youth also favours the subjective religious expression, which in effect contradicts his parents' participatory expression of being Buddhist. A young woman laments: "Honestly, I don't think they [parents] understand deeply what their religion is. They know that there is Buddhism, and they follow it. They go to the temple and they pray. But there is no individual understanding and deeper understanding of what it is. I think it is just because you are born into it rather than trying to figure it out what it is." She correlates individual understanding to deeper understanding, so she believes that her parents follow Buddhism without knowing the meanings. The underlying assumption is that one should know the meaning first and then follow it. Meaning should lead to practice, not the other way around. A similar trend is noticed with the second-generation Buddhists within the Cambodian community in Ontario (McLellan 2009).

The second generation's comments on the first generation's religiosity often carry an individualistic judgment on collective religious expression. Ronald Grimes (2000, 115) argues that "individual-ism is not merely a belief in the value of individuals; it sets individual and community in opposition and then ranks individuality higher." Such hierarchical evaluation is apparent in the following statement of one seventeen-year-old girl, who says: "My father is a Buddhist obviously, but he is not into Buddhism or is not actually trying to understand it. He comes to the temple and helps out. He thinks that if he has pin [merit] he is good. I wish he [would] learn actual Buddhism a bit more ... he is more in building the temple. I think he should stop it [building temple] and actually attain something in his life ... My father looks for pin or pin weda [meritorious deeds], but I look for applicability of Buddhism in everyday life ... I tried [to get] my dad to be more Buddhist but it didn't work" (personal interview, 2009). The interviewee implies that her father is a nominal Buddhist, while she is an applied or practical Buddhist. She acknowledges that building the temple or working for the collective does benefit her father's Buddhist identity, but she downplays such collective religiosity as not being part of "actual" Buddhism. She questions how building a temple has anything to do with self-cultivation, although one could argue that it perfectly connects to altruism, a celebrated Buddhist virtue. For her, "actual" Buddhism means individualistic practices, such as self-cultivation through meditation and moral precept observation. These opinions cannot be totally generalized; nevertheless, they are instrumental to understanding the way that many second-generation Buddhists distinguish themselves from their parent generation in the process of constructing their own Buddhist identities.

The preceding critical voices of Sri Lankan Canadian Buddhist youths also allude to an intergenerational scuffle over a "better" way of being Buddhists. The sentences like "I find I am hitting a brick wall" and "I tried [to get] my dad to be *more Buddhist* but it didn't work" in the longer quotations mentioned above express some second-generation Buddhists' frustration over the failure of their efforts to improve parents' ways of practicing Buddhism. Meanwhile many parents in fact experience the reverse: the lack of youths' interest in their Buddhist rituals. Like youths, the parent participants in this research have not overtly expressed their frustration over their children's lack of engagement in Buddhism (which culturally would be interpreted as a failure in parenting). I have discussed the reasons for such lack of forthrightness on the parents' part in this book's introduction. The monks in the community know well the struggle parents face in making youths interested in Buddhist practices. A monk complains: "some Buddhist families do not inquire how the monks are doing, until someone dies in the family or one of their kids needs to be advised on the importance of parents and Buddhism." English-speaking monks in the community, as I discussed in the last chapter, are the parents' biggest allies in their efforts to engage youths in Buddhism. Parents not only arrange events like birthdays, high school graduation, and university entrance celebrations with the presence of monks, they also inform the monks in advance so that the latter can advise the youth effectively. English sermons in the community are often youth oriented. Thus both generations experience mutual and yet unparalleled pressure on the ways they perceive and practice Buddhism in the diaspora. Within this intergenerational persuasion, the following diverse ways of being Buddhist emerge and they demonstrate how the second generation exercises their sensibility over and against that of their parents.

DEVELOPING VS SELF-CLAIMING BUDDHISTS

All of the youth research respondents identify themselves as Buddhists, but to various degrees. Many of them are quite happy with their Buddhist identities and a few of them are quite proud of their Buddhist heritage. As discussed above, some youths find themselves more serious than their parents about Buddhist practices. One of my questions related to Buddhist identity was "What does being Buddhist mean to you?" Respondents came up with various answers, which indicated a spectrum from developing to self-consciously reclaiming Buddhist identity.

"Developing Buddhist" has repeatedly emerged as a self-identification of many young Buddhists. Like many identities, religious identity is under constant construction, characteristically so in the lives of youths. The following statement of a youth captures both the transiency of the identity and the multiple forces involved in its construction. Answering the interview question "how would you religiously identify yourself?" one young adult says: "I think I am a developing Buddhist in this society. I know the structure or teaching[s] of the Buddha, it is only now that I am learning to apply them in my life. Now I am trying more to integrate Buddhism into my life. For example, if I get angry, I am realizing that there is no point in holding onto certain things. I believe that I am a Buddhist, but I am not a dedicated Buddhist. I am learning to understand what Buddhism means to me as opposed to what others tell me to do" (personal interview, 2009). The interviewee relates the incipient nature of her religious identity to multiple loci: the ambient society, the "others," and the self. The "others" refers to the first generation, who often instruct the second generation on what Buddhism is and what Buddhists should do. The respondent clearly signifies that the second-generation youths do not indiscriminately receive what is told to them. Instead, they contextualize Buddhist knowledge and practices within the ambient North American society.

Moreover, the statement also reflects the stage of life – early twenties – when urges for independence are in a full swing. The term "developing Buddhist" captures the ongoing process in which youths tend to develop an individual identity that is distinguishable from that of others, in this case the first generation. The interviewee also juxtaposes the identity of a developing Buddhist with that of a dedicated Buddhist. The implied distinction between them is that the latter strives toward an integrated religious goal with a specific lifestyle, while the former learns to incorporate a Buddhist perspective into secular life. Explaining the developing Buddhist identity, the interviewee states, "it is just learning to understand life in a way that day by day things are starting to come your way. Learning to deal with situations in life, I learn stuff from Buddhism and try to apply it to the situations and how to maintain calm and things like that." The language of learning and progression toward a better commitment is embedded in the "developing Buddhist" identity.

The phrase also implies a cautionary sentiment that derives from youthful idealism, as well as self-claimed identity. A mother of two teenagers states: "what they learn in Buddhism they expect us to follow." These idealistic expectations derive from normative Buddhist education at dhamma schools, but they often get shattered as youths find the inconsistency between what they learn at dhamma classes and what their parents practice. A youth comments, "they [the parents] go to the temple a lot; they may meditate a lot; they can preach to us; but, they can be hypocritical about how they do things." This inconsistency of belief/practice is less tolerated in an individualistic society, as religious identity is considered an "individual choice" rather than an ascribed commitment. Individual choice carries individual responsibility. Thus youths who find themselves inconsistent with Buddhist teachings hesitate to claim Buddhist identity. One female interviewee shares her reluctance, "sometimes I would like to call myself Buddhist but sometimes I feel I do not deserve it. You can say you are a Buddhist ... but words really do not mean anything." When I asked, "If someone asks you what your religion is?" she replied, "I might call myself Buddhist, but I would rather call [it] seeking truth. When you say you are a Buddhist, it means you are already somewhere in your spiritual goal which I am not." The respondent perceives that being Buddhist is a spiritual identity rather than a religious or social identity, and as such it should accompany the inner transformation indicated in Buddhist teachings. This echoes the North American popular perception of Buddhism as a form of spirituality more than anything else. In fact 25 per cent of the second generation has identified Buddhism to be "a spirituality without restrictive beliefs and required practices."

The developing Buddhist identity also carries a sense of the plasticity of some youths' religious identity. It keeps the door open to explore what is available in other Buddhist and non-Buddhist traditions out of one's religious and spiritual temperament. For example, one university graduate expresses: "I just explore all possibilities of faith systems ... while keeping Buddhism as my primary reactor." For him, the non-Buddhist aspects are filtered through Buddhism. In other words, some youths are open to ideas and practices that they find complementary to a Buddhist identity. The survey data indicate that well over majority (70 per cent) of the second generation are open to inter-religious exploration. Such inter-religious curiosity sometimes accompanies peer pressure, resulting in a conversion to evangelical Christianity. One seventeen-year-old girl complains: "I have many Hindu [and] Christian friends. Actually, one of my Christian friends gave herself up to God and talks about God a lot. She tells me that 'you should give yourself up to God.' But I just try not to say anything. I don't say anything because I do not want to offend her. Then I do not want to explain my situation that I don't believe in God just again not to offend her" (personal interview, 2009). A few youths mentioned that some of their friends had abandoned Buddhism and/or converted to Christianity. A similar trend is observed in other studies on young Buddhists in Canada. In *Growing up Canadian*, Martel-Reny and Beyer (2013, 223) refer to a young Chinese-Vietnamese Buddhist who experienced constant peer pressure to convert to Christianity. McLellan (2009) also observes a similar trend within the Cambodian Buddhist community in Ontario. Buddhist education and socialization has enabled Sri Lankan Buddhist youths to thwart the evangelical pressure to conversion, but it has not prevented them from enquiring what is available in other religions. As such, some youths find that their inter-religious exploration does not prevent them from being developing Buddhists. As the preceding discussion illustrates, youths' self-identification as "developing Buddhists" captures multiple tropes of Buddhist affiliations characterized by ambiguity, circumspection, self-judgment, flexibility, and of course progression. The perception and understating of Buddhism could be characterized as "primarily diffuse," a description attributed to the second type of seekers identified in *Growing up Canadian*.

In contrast to developing Buddhists, a small but significant group of young Buddhists (approx. 30 per cent) have reclaimed their inherited Buddhist identity. They have not taken for granted what is passed on to them; inherited Buddhist identity does not satisfy them. Instead they have integrated Buddhism "in their own terms" – a trait associated with the third seeker group in Bayer and team's study. Exploring beyond initial Buddhist socialization, they have reclaimed their Buddhist identity in their own independent studies and committed practices. On the basis of their Buddhist learning and practices, they construct Buddhist identity. Referring to a confident statement "I am a Buddhist!," a young man says: "I am answering this way not because my parents told me, but because I have put many hours and years of struggling efforts to build up my Buddhist identity. And spiritually, that would be disgraceful, dishonourable, and disrespectful to all my efforts to say that I don't know who I am or whatever. So I honestly say that I am a Buddhist not because I have a tag that says I am a Buddhist, but when I look at my heart, all the experiences tell me that I have walked a Buddhist path and I consciously walked through that path and I have invested my own time and energy into it" (personal interview, 2009). The interviewee adamantly refuses to identify with a born-Buddhist identity. It is his own spiritual practice – rather than inheritance and beliefs in Buddhism – which he highlights, although the latter are also part of his Buddhist identity. He represents a minority, yet he is also part of an increasing group of young Buddhists who reclaim their inherited Buddhist identity through their practice – or, in the words of a youth, live "as much as possible according to the dhamma, according to what Buddha taught us like the Five Precepts and the Noble Eightfold Path." For them, Buddhist identity is not merely a birthright, but a conscious adult choice that is often distinguished from the cultural Buddhist identity of the first generation.

These self-claiming Buddhists, like their parents, kneel down in front of the Buddha statue, respect monks with bows, and take part in Buddhist rituals. They look for meaning in these practices and enquire how they relate or apply to overall Buddhist ways of living. The following statement by a young man captures the youth's integration of the intellectual, contemplative, and devotional aspects of the Buddhist tradition in his own terms. He says:

> I don't think that I would ever be interested in the ceremonial aspects of Buddhism, or the cultural aspects of Buddhism. I think they are catalysts. When we are in situations where our minds are going into unskillful path, they act like catalysts. They remind us where we are right now. They are external phenomena to click our mind ... I believe that every person at any moment of time can lose their mindfulness. I think meditators like myself even who are sure of themselves, can completely forget themselves saying that these kinds of ceremonials are not for them, and they can completely isolate themselves from ceremonial sides and find themselves gone ... only to realize that they have completely gone to a wrong direction. I think the ceremonial aspects or the show and dance aspects of Buddhism are good to ground us. They bring us to ground zero; they remind [us of] the basic lines. Until the enlightenment, we need the rituals. (Personal interview, 2009)

The interviewee at times contradicts himself. He seems to be torn between his urges to reject or accept Buddhist rituals. He simultaneously appreciates and depreciates the communal aspects of his inherited Buddhist tradition, but at the end he seems to have developed a nuanced appreciation of inherited Buddhist rituals. He identifies himself as a serious meditator who is less interested in collective expressions of Buddhism like rituals. He considered rituals as instrumental in order "to click our mind" into contemplative practices that lead to the ultimate goal of Buddhism: spiritual awakening. This creative integration of rituals and meditation alludes to a youth's perspective about what a ritual should be. He implies that a ritual should not be an end in itself. Rather, it is a means to an end – the establishment of mindfulness. Within this perspective, only those rituals associated with meditation are appreciated.

The heightened interest in meditation of this particular group distinguishes them from their parents. A young woman says: "my parents hardly meditate. I am very interested in meditation ... but sometimes I do get frustrated after a while, because I do not get the level of peacefulness. I guess I get distracted. But it is definitely something that I want to do." Similarly, another interviewee reveals that "I notice a lot of youths are getting interested in meditation. If it is done in an interesting way; like last summer, I went to a meditation that was done in a park. Something like that, youths find it interesting, because it is no longer inside a building and [it is] spending time in fresh air." The preceding statement renews an ancient Buddhist discourse that relates meditation to nature and establishes the connection between forest monks (*aranyawasi*) and meditation (*vipassanadhura*). Yet this time the discourse is not confined to monks. Instead it extends beyond the monk-lay division, as well as the gap between young and old.

With such development, a discourse shift is pending. The village-dweller (*gamawasi*) or town-dweller (*nagarawasi*) tradition – a popular form of Buddhist community in collective culture – seems to be dwindling in Toronto. Referring to one of two temples in this study, a youth complains: "It [temple] has become a sort of social gathering place. Sometimes people are in fundraising events, then, it becomes a money issue. When people turn into those things, then the temple becomes a gossip place. Then you know it is taking out the focus of religion. That's something I don't like. I wish the parents go there [temples] for the purpose it meant to be. They should make use of the opportunity" (personal interview, 2009). For the interviewee, the focus or intended purpose of religion – Buddhism – is to enhance one's individual character. Other things, like meeting friends or fundraising, are more rooted in secular or cultural things. Similarly, a first-year undergraduate suggests, "I think a temple should be a religious place not a social gathering place. We should have a Sri Lankan or Sinhalese community/cultural centre separate from the temple for non-religious or social gatherings." This indicates how the second-generation Buddhists have internalized the dhamma-culture rhetoric employed by their parents.

In addition to these two groups discussed above – developing and self-claiming Buddhists – a significant number of youth participants recognize their Buddhist heritage in a casual way. They may go to the temple once in a while with parents, take part in rituals at the annual merit-making ceremony at home, and attend public Buddhist talks in English. They do not independently seek Buddhist knowledge, practices, and wisdom beyond these casual expressions of their Buddhist identity within the family setting.

Sri Lankan Buddhist youths – regardless of their identifications as developing, re-claiming, or casual Buddhists – demonstrate, albeit to different degrees, a common pattern in constructing their Buddhist identity. This pattern could be called a "secular mode of being Buddhist," but this does not mean they have rejected religious beliefs and practices found in the Sri Lankan Buddhist tradition. They do take refuge in the Triple Gem, observe the Five Precepts in the Pāli language, and respect the Buddha and monks with bows. However, they do not consciously relate these Buddhist cultural practices to the construction of Buddhist identity. Instead, they highlight how they individually incorporate the Buddhist worldviews, values, and practices in everyday lives. The following statements of a few young people demonstrate a secular mode of being Buddhist.

Being Buddhist means having patience; like in grocery you do not rush and push everyone to get your things done. You can be Buddhist everywhere. It does not take that much to be a Buddhist. Being friendly, being good to others, helping others, respecting others and having good attitudes are all about being Buddhist.

Being Buddhist is taking things as they come. A lot of friends tell me that oh, you are calm and relaxed all the time even with stress of exams and family life.

I do not think too much about the future and past; Buddhism taught me living in the present. I have read different Buddhist books ... listened to *bana* [sermon] of different *hamudurowo* [monks] and practiced meditation. All of them one way or another helped me to live a simple life in the present.

To me, being Buddhist means being a better person, knowing how to handle situations, doing what you can do for the humanity, putting other people in front of you and not forgetting yourself and having a good balance [between affluence and poverty and the well-being of oneself and others]. (Personal interviews, 2009)

These statements indicate that, for many youths, being Buddhist means *being good* and *doing good*. One can discern that a Buddhist definition of "goodness" is expressed in these testimonies, but how that goodness is put into practice does not necessarily invoke a conventional way of being religious or a religious way of being Buddhist. A similar trend is noticed with the Sri Lankan Buddhist youth in London, UK. As Mahinda Deegalle (2008, 30) observes, "the second generation is more inclined to learn and practice the humanistic values in Buddhism." This mode of being Buddhist embodies the discourse of Buddhism as a way of life.

BUDDHISM IS A WAY OF LIFE: AN INTERGENERATIONAL (DIS)CONTINUITY

Canadian born and/or raised Sri Lankan Buddhists in Toronto, like their parents, prefer the interpretation of "Buddhism as a way of life" to other existing interpretations in Sri Lankan Buddhism, i.e., Buddhism as a religion, a philosophy, a spirituality, and/or an ethical system. For both generations, the "Buddhism is a way of life" discourse has been the first preference, followed by the spirituality discourse and then the philosophy discourse. Unlike the spirituality discourse, the way of life discourse maintains the integrity of the Buddhist tradition with clearly laid out worldviews and systematic practices. It also enables the reconciliation of the apparent contradiction between religious and scientific principles embedded in the philosophical discourse. Thus, the discourse of Buddhism as a way of life encapsulates the religious, philosophical, and practical aspects of the Buddhist tradition, and perhaps this broader scope or inclusivity has made the discourse attractive in the diaspora.

Moreover, the notion of Buddhism being a way of life also captures the postmodern imagination of cultural relativism as well as individualist religious expression. At least three underlying principles seem to be at work in the discourse. First, a way of life is culturally shaped, and, therefore, Buddhism needs to be culturally adapted. Second, Buddhism emphasizes practices more than anything else. Finally, in the context of an individualistic society, one is entitled to incorporate Buddhist teachings and practices as desired. In a multicultural, multireligious, and individualistic social setting like Toronto, it is not surprising that the discourse of Buddhism as a way of life is overriding other existing discourses about the Buddhist tradition.

The term "a way of life" is loaded with cultural connotations. When both generations define Buddhism as a way of life, they in fact refer to two distinct cultural expressions of Buddhist teachings. As I analyze how the first- and second-generation Sri Lankan Buddhists use the phrase, I contend that the first generation's Buddhist religiosity is more or less a matter of "cultural convention," in comparison to the second generation's "individual conviction" approach to Buddhism.[3] The former means that the first generation relates to Buddhism collectively, while the latter emphasizes that the second generation looks for individually convincing meaning before they commit themselves to Buddhist practices. For the first generation, the term includes living a life that conforms to collective norms and practices, supporting collective causes, and participating in collective practices. One middle-aged father articulates: "I have been participating in temple development project, giving dāna, listening to bana [sermon] like that. Other than that I am not doing much like poya-day [full-moon day] observation and meditation. I am hoping to do them when I am retired ... now I respect elders and maintain whatever Buddhist values like non-violence, dāna [offering food to the monks], pūja [rituals], and assisting the elders and other things. *We maintain a Buddhist way of life.* We also respect all other religions" (personal interview, 2009). The preceding statement denotes that, for the first generation, a Buddhist way of life is to engage in duty-bound Buddhist activities, which are often collectively performed. However, the following testimony of a youth invokes a different connotation of the phrase "Buddhism is a way of life." He articulates: "Buddhism is a way of life, something we do every day. It is all about finding inner peace in yourself, being independent and having your own sense of thought what is right or wrong. It is not reaching out to God or anything, but it is all about yourself. You are for yourself whatever you do right or wrong. It is for yourself" (personal interview, 2009). Phrases like "finding inner peace," "being independent," and "it's all about yourself," speak loudly of Buddhist spiritual individualism, a popular Buddhist discourse in North America.

It is interesting that some argue that Buddhism is also a way of life for Euro-American Buddhists.[4]

In the context of North American culture, the phrase "way of life" is often defined by an ethic of individualism. It implies that one is entitled to lead a life according to one's own preferences, needs, rights, and choices. Freedom to choose and practice is more compatible with the perception of Buddhism as a way of life, rather than Buddhism as a religion. As noted above, when youths define Buddhism to be a way of life they relate to the sense of personal choice and freedom found in Buddhism. They highlight some of the teachings of the Buddha that are compatible with the North American cultural values, such as being independent, being autonomous, taking control of one's life, and a sense of personal freedom. As we compare and contrast both generations' discourse around Buddhism as a way of life, we notice that the second generation picks up the discourse from their parents' generation, but they interpret it within the North American cultural setting.

The following statement encapsulates a few more important North American cultural features of the discourse. One twenty-seven-year-old interviewee, who was born in Sri Lanka and migrated to Canada at adolescence, explains: "*Buddhism is a religion* that I grew up with. Now I almost think *it is a way of life.* When I was growing up, as a kid, it was more rituals like offering flowers, lighting up candles, and you know, chanting, things like that. Then as I grew up probably after I came to Canada I really got more into Buddhism. I engaged more in meditation and how Buddhism can be used in life. Then I started reading more about Buddhism, and what Buddhism was all about and realized that it's much more than a religion. It really does teach you how to live your life. I think different parts of Buddhism really could be incorporated into your life" (personal interview, 2009, emphasis added). This particular interviewee clearly distinguishes *Buddhism as a way of life* from *Buddhism as a religion*, and she indicates where each comes into play in her own life. For her, religion contains rituals, such as the veneration of the Buddha (*buddhapuja*), while a way of life consists of meditation. She relates Buddhism as a religion to her childhood experience with Buddhism. As she grew up, she developed interests in what she calls a deeper side of Buddhism, i.e., meditation. She names her newly developed contemplative interest in Buddhism as a way of life. This shift in the perception of Buddhism comes with a new understanding and appreciation of Buddhism: the various Buddhist teachings could be integrated into one's life. The emphasis on the integration of Buddhism into everyday life is in fact what characterizes "Buddhism as a way of life." Moreover it is worth noting that she refers to not only the stages of life (from childhood to adulthood) but also the geographical changes (from Sri Lanka to Canada) that accompanied this perceptual shift about Buddhism.

The interpretation of Buddhism as a way of life also echoes – in content as well as purpose – the discourse of Buddhism as a philosophy. Since the late nineteenth century, the discourse of Buddhism as a philosophy has attracted Western-educated individuals within and beyond Asian Buddhist societies. One of the attractions was its assertion that Buddhist worldviews are compatible with those of modern science.[5] Buddhists have used the philosophical discourse to highlight the freedom of thought in Buddhist teachings. They have argued that Buddhism is scientific, so that it is not second to any religion, including Christianity. The discourse also has been used to distinguish – if not elevate – Buddhism from other religions. Similar tone, text, and purpose are discernable in the following arguments related to Buddhism as a way of life. Answering an interview question "what does Buddhism mean to you?" an undergraduate university student says: "Buddhism as I think of it is a way of life for me, like with friends who are not Buddhists there are many rules that are imposed upon them to follow. But when I compare them to Buddhism, I feel like rules are not imposed. They [five precepts] are more like my morals, which tell me if you want to know the right path do the right things. They are more kind of morals to me ... Buddhism gives you a lot of freedom; it does not impose [on] you; it lets you create your own opinions about it" (personal interview, 2009). The interviewee distinguishes Buddhism as a way of life from other religions. She contrasts the concept of religion to a way of life. For her, religion imposes rules and regulations on people, while a way of life allows people to make their own choices and decisions. The word "impose" presupposes hierarchy, authority, and external power. By saying that religion imposes rules upon people, she refers to the hierarchy, authority, and power involved in religion. It is implied that under religion, people are not free enough to do what they want or wish, as their lives are structured by the rules of the religion rather than by personal choice and freedom. The interviewee uses the term "a way of life" to highlight a sense of personal freedom and individual choice in leading one's life. She highlights that Buddhism as a "way of life" includes freedom and choice; it does not impose but guides; it does not control but gives space to develop a personal opinion about things. The intergenerational continuity and discontinuity expressed in the discourse of Buddhism as a way of life are also discernible in both generations' perceptions of the Buddha, their Buddhist aspirations and practices, and their Buddhist ethics and identities. Traditionally, the conception of the Buddha has been a classical denominator in identifying the Theravāda-Mahayana distinction. In addition to its denominational currency, the concept has also played a crucial role in mapping the historical development from the pre-modern to the modern period, cultural negotiations between Eastern and Western interpretations, and disciplinary navigation between intellectual and devotional perspectives. As I discussed earlier, the diaspora is the meeting ground of all these denominational, historical, cultural, and disciplinary encounters, and I use the concept of the Buddha to analyze the transmission of the Sri Lankan Buddhist tradition from the first to the second generation. Answering a survey question "who/what is the Buddha to you," an overwhelming majority of both generations favour a humanistic interpretation of the Buddha. This trend characterizes modern Buddhism. They first and foremost consider the Buddha to be a historical figure, and emphasize his role in teaching the way to enlightenment or cessation of suffering. The survey data also indicate that the second generation differs in the neo-traditional interpretation, in which the Buddha is perceived to be a supreme being with miraculous power and extraordinary virtues. In this particular context, a 16 per cent decrease is noticeable in relation to the second generation. The data also suggest that the non-Theravāda conception of the Buddha is still less popular. However, the second generation scores higher than their parents, reflecting their greater exposure to non-Theravāda Buddhism.

Moreover, a striking generational difference is noticeable in the ways in which both generations have expressed their religious/Buddhist goals as the following survey result indicates:

Table 6.1

The intergenerational (dis)continuity of religious goals/aspirations
of Buddhists

What is your Buddhist or religious goal in this very life?
Please mark only ONE of the following:

Answer options	First generation	Second generation
To become enlightened in this very life	13.5%	5.5%
To have a better life after death and eventually attain nirvanaya	31%	17.5%
To serve humanity and other beings to reduce suffering	29.5%	48.5%
To provide a good life for my family	26%	28.5%

Parents identify their preferred Buddhist goal as "having a better
life after death and eventually attaining nirvanaya." Such otherworldly goals do not resonate with the second generation. Instead,
almost half (49 per cent) of the youth generation identifies a very
this-worldly, social beneficial aspiration as their prioritized Buddhist goal: "to serve humanity and other beings to reduce suffering."
The survey data suggests that parents are almost equally divided
in perceiving this-worldly social benefits and otherworldly religious
aspirations as their Buddhist goals. Such a balanced distribution is
lacking among the second generation. This survey finding supports
the notion that a secular mode of being Buddhist or a humanistic
Buddhist identity is important to the second generation, which we
already saw from the interview data discussed above.

Both generations score high in relation to the engagement in
society and family with Buddhist morals and virtues. These preferences underscore the integration of Buddhism into everyday life
– the defining characteristic of Buddhism as a way of life. Socially
engaged Buddhism, more specifically sponsoring and supporting
humanitarian projects, has attracted both generations. Although
humanitarian efforts within the community could be characterized

as "ad hoc identity-based engagement" (Kniss and Numrich 2007), they also take institutionalized forms that reach out to beneficiaries beyond ethnic and religious boundaries. Both temples in this study have set up humanitarian and educational projects in Toronto and in Sri Lanka. For last the decade or so, the West End Buddhist Temple and Meditation Centre has organized the Buddhist Youths' Soup Kitchen at the Catholic Good Shepherd in downtown Toronto. The program has become a popular community service. More recently, the same Buddhist institution has also launched a seniors program, which provides social and spiritual support. The cultural group in the community sometimes goes to the senior homes in the region and entertains the residents with cultural dance and music.

The tsunami on 26 December 2004 in Sri Lanka heightened the humanitarian sentiments within the community. The community made significant contributions to post-tsunami rehabilitation projects by sending basic essentials like clothes, dry food, medicine, and other goods. The temples collected monetary donations and constructed homes for the tsunami victims. Even before the 2004 tsunami, monks and laity alike had been sponsoring school education for the poor and needy students in rural Sri Lanka – but these efforts were more organized after the tsunami. For example, the Toronto Mahavihara Scholarship Foundation was established in 2007 to support the children in the tsunami-affected area. The Tsunami Orphan Children's Program is another educational/humanitarian project popular within the community. Its management assures the community that "their hard earned money, however small or big, has gone to work and delivered a modern hostel building for an orphanage for Sri Lanka's tsunami-stricken, homeless children; a home and a roof over their heads worthy of the great virtue of man's humanity to man following the highest ideals of metta" (*Living Buddhism* 2008, 18). In addition to supporting these more organized projects, both generations variously engage in social and voluntary services in Toronto as well as in Sri Lanka. They participate in these activities with a sense of cultivating Buddhist virtues like loving kindness (mettā), compassion (karunā), generosity (dāna), and helping others (paropakāra).

Following the parent generation, the second-generation Buddhists have extensively admired socially engaged activities; they, however, hardly share parents' religious motivation. A young woman says, "when they [parents] are doing something they just do it in order to get good karma, whereas I would think of it as being nicer to

the person, right? That is the main way how I differ from them."
Overtly religious motivation like good karma is tempered with an
interpersonal secular ethics. The survey data also suggest that the
second generation's ethical behaviour, unlike that of their parents,
is less likely to be associated with religious motivations such as the
accumulation of good karmas for life after death or the purification
of one's mind for enlightenment. In this case, practice is continued
between the generations, but the first generation's religious motivation resonates less with the second generation.

Intergenerational continuity and difference is also noticeable in
the ways in which both generations express Buddhist self-identity.
Since the late 1980s, identification of Buddhists has dominated
the study of Buddhism in North America. A few theoretical frame-
works like "two Buddhisms" (Prebish 1988; Suguanasiri 2006) or
"three Buddhisms" (Nattier 1998; Seager 1999; Tweed 2002) have
emerged to categorize Buddhists in North America. Outlining the
limitations of these categories, Thomas Tweed (2002, 24) suggests
self-identification would be a preferred way to categorize Buddhists.
Accordingly, a survey question below asked the research respondents to self-identify within one of the categories available in the
repertoire of Sri Lankan Buddhism: Buddhist, Sinhalese Buddhist,
and Theravāda Buddhist. These categories overlap; nevertheless,
they connote the distinctive flavour of Buddhist identity. Like their
parents, the second-generation Buddhists prefer to identify themselves as simply being Buddhists, followed by an ethno-specific
(Sinhalese) Buddhist identity and a sectarian (Theravāda) Buddhist
identity. In the case of both generations, a generic Buddhist identity
overshadows the "Theravāda" denominational and ethno-specific
"Sinhala/Sinhalese" Buddhist identities. The tendency to associate
with a generic Buddhist identity jumps from 40 per cent to 70 per
cent in the case of the second generation. A second-generation young
woman says: "I would say I am a Theravāda Buddhist because of my
family background, but I strongly relate to Buddhism in general."
Such generalizations of Buddhist identity enable young Buddhists to
appreciate aspects of Buddhism across denominational boundaries.

These self-identification rates may vary according to a particular context. They allude to how others – including non-Buddhists
and non-Sri Lankan Buddhists – perceive the respondents. Wherever
particularity is concerned, the ethno-particularity – rather than
the denominational one – is highlighted. In a secular social setting,

ethnicity rather than religious denomination is prioritized. Even the academically abused term "ethnic Buddhist" presupposes the link between ethnicity and Buddhism, rather than denominational identity. However, as I have discussed in the first chapter, Buddhists from Sri Lanka in search of a particular identity highlight their connection to location (Sri Lanka) rather than to ethnicity (Sinhala/Sinhalese). The intergenerational (over 30 per cent) increase of non-specific Buddhist identity and the double-digit decrease in both ethnically and denominationally particularized identities indicate the generalization of Buddhist identity. This generalization might have derived from the minority status of Buddhism in Toronto. One might imagine a particularized identity would become heightened in a pluralistic society to differentiate oneself from others, in this case non-Sinhala Buddhists. However, the data show that there is a sharp decrease in particularized identification amongst the second generation in comparison to their parents. The preceding discussion on the discourse of Buddhism as a "way of life," the concept of Buddha, Buddhist goals, aspirations, and associated ethics all indicate intergenerational continuity and divergence within the Sri Lankan Buddhist community in Toronto. The second-generation Buddhists base their Buddhist identity within the religio-culture of their parents; nevertheless, they are not confined to it. Instead, they rather reach out beyond it. As such, they could be better defined as "religio-culturally based seekers" (Martel-Reny and Beyer 2013, 215).

CONCLUSION

I have employed *Growing up Canadian*'s (2013) phrase "religio-culturally based seekers" to contextualize and highlight the sensibility of Sri Lankan Canadian youths in processing transmitted Buddhism. The term "seekers" in the phrase captures the creativity of the youths, while the rest of the phrase ("religio-culturally based") indicates the continuity and retention of certain aspects of the parents' religio-culture. My discussion of the discourse of Buddhism as a way of life underscores how the second-generation youths have picked up the discourse from their parent generation and yet have interpreted it with individualist cultural underpinnings: individual conviction, personal freedom, and self-oriented benefits. What has been retained less are parents' collective cultural connotations of the discourse: cultural conventions, collective commitments, and community-oriented benefits. Thus I have argued that each generation's articulation that Buddhism is a "way of life" illustrates both the continuity and the discontinuity of intergenerational Sri Lankan Buddhism in Toronto.

I have also discussed the critical voices of youths that express displeasure about the ways Buddhism is practiced by the parent generation. The youth voices also disclose their frustration with their less-successful efforts in persuading parents to adopt a "better" way of being Buddhist. Although such efforts of reverse transmission are rare, they indicate not only a first-to-second generation transmission of Buddhism but also the cultural transformation that Buddhism itself has endured in the intergenerational transmission. An intercultural reconfiguration of Buddhism is variously displayed in the two ends of the youth Buddhist identity spectrum: developing vs self-claiming Buddhist. Such Buddhist identity expression simultaneously underlines both intergenerational transmission and intercultural reconfiguration of Buddhism. The latter relates to the sensibility of the youth generation. The former highlights the sensibility of the parent generation.

Conclusion: Making Sense of Reconfigured
Buddhism in Toronto

This book started with a vignette of dhamma education practice within the Sri Lankan Buddhist community in Toronto. It has examined and explained how Buddhism is transmitted from the community-centred first generation to its second generation, influenced by a culture of self-focus. This intercultural and intergenerational study has unpacked the translocal history, transmission strategies, and (un)intended outcome of dhamma education for laity in Sri Lankan Buddhism. In doing so, the book diversifies the Theravāda Buddhist education research hitherto dominated by monastic education (Dhammsami 2018; Borchert 2017; McDaniel 2008; Samuels 2004; Blackburn 2001). More importantly, it also recognizes Sri Lankan Buddhists' pioneering role in the development of a formal Theravāda Buddhist education for laity, and therefore their unique contribution to Buddhism in Canada. The minimal expectation of dhamma education has been, as expressed by dhamma teachers across time and place (discussed in chapter 3), to implant dhamma seeds into the fertile hearts and minds of young dhamma students. As the dhamma seeds – Buddhist teachings – have been fertilized with Canada's themes of multiculturalism, this book *Seeding Buddhism with Multiculturalism* demonstrates how dhamma seeds are prepared and presented to a young generation, who have internalized the dhamma seeds and transformed Buddhist beliefs and practices to suit their own lives.

All the people – monks, lay dhamma teachers, parents, and youths – involved in the project of Buddhist transmission emerge as innovators in their own right. The English-speaking monks have become intermediaries who advise both parents and children. With their tacit understanding of both collective and individualistic cultures, they have been able to intervene and mitigate the adverse effects of intergenerational tension and conflicts that also become intercultural issues in immigrant communities. More importantly, monks shine as cultural interpreters with their hermeneutic skills. Their cultural interpretation has made the inclusive, harmonious, and humanistic traits of Buddhism come to the fore. As these interpretations are enshrined in the dhamma education curriculum *Teaching Buddhism to Children*, lay dhamma teachers disseminate the redefined Buddhism to a new generation imagined as Sri Lankan Canadians. They have employed the dhamma-culture separation as a pedagogical strategy, a means that paid off by passing on more than a basic knowledge of Buddhist teaching, literature, and practices – but less so of Sinhalese ethnic identifiers like the Sinhalese language, literature, folk songs, and dance.

Parents, with the dedicated support from the monks and lay dhamma teachers, have become primary transmitters of Buddhist beliefs, values, and practices. They sometimes feel overwhelmed with the task, as neither extended families nor supportive cultural ambience are available in the diaspora to reinforce their collective cultural practices and moral values. Parents worry about the influence of secular worldviews, materialism, bad company, abuse of drugs, premature sex, non-Buddhist culture, and even conversion to Christianity. They find that the traditional hierarchical parent-child relationship is less effective in getting to know youths better. Therefore, some have adopted a friendship model to provide effective moral guidance to adolescent children. Thanks to these hermeneutic, pedagogical, and relational strategies of the first generation, the second generation has received Buddhist identities that simultaneously conform to and deviate from their parents' Buddhist identity.

Sri Lankan Canadian youths' Buddhist identity is generally subject-oriented, this-worldly rationalized, and intellectually exploratory. These traits differ noticeably from their parents' Buddhism, which is generally participatory, otherworldly motivated, and tradition-oriented. Two cultural appropriations of Buddhist principles and practices have fuelled these distinctive approaches to Buddhism. For instance, both generations consider Buddhism to be a way of life, but they define it differently. Due to collective cultural influence, for the parent generation a Buddhist way of life means doing Buddhist rituals, taking care of elderly parents, nursing grandparents, feeding monks, building temples, volunteering at the local dhamma schools, and serving on temples' boards of directors and on fundraising committees. They engage in these collective actions to accumulate good karmas with the hope of receiving karmic rewards in many lives to come. Youths hesitate to consider these community-oriented actions of their parents as particularly Buddhist. Some in fact wish that their parents would spend more time in personally "meaningful" and "beneficial" activities and less in these community-oriented services. Generally, Buddhist youths tend to think that ethical behaviour should be self-focused and driven by interpersonal trust and benevolence rather than expectation of a better life after death.

For many youths, a Buddhist way of life refers to doing mindfulness meditation; cultivating Buddhist virtues like loving kindness, compassion, appreciative joy, and equanimity; and leading a life congruous with the Five Precepts and Eightfold Path. These ethical ideals require an extraordinary moral stamina that is unrealistic in lay life. Since these stringent individualistic commitments and subjective experiences often characterize Buddhist identity for them, many youths therefore characterize themselves as "developing Buddhists" – a self-identity that frees them from self-criticism when they fall short of their own idealistic ethical commitments. On the other hand, a minority of youths have emerged as "self-claiming Buddhists" who are less satisfied with inherited Buddhism. They have in fact deepened an inherited Buddhist identity further with independent research and exploration, to the extent that they even expect more from the parent generation in terms of contemplative practices and moral commitment for self-cultivation. More importantly, Buddhist youths are open to conceptually seeking and exploring moral guidance beyond their parents' religious tradition. And yet their practical base remains within the inherited Sri Lankan Buddhist cultural domain. Therefore the phrase "religio-culturally based seekers" aptly describes many Sri Lankan Canadian Buddhists. As I discussed in chapter 6, they in fact live in an "intercultural domain" where their interactions with the parent generation display influences from both collective/hierarchical and individualistic/egalitarian cultures.

TWO METAPHORS: MOTHER CAT AND WHITE SWAN

The preceding story regarding the intergenerational transmission and intercultural reconfiguration of Buddhism identifies both generations as creative actors in their own right. In it, two metaphors have emerged indicating each generation's sense of creativity. Referring to her early life in Sri Lanka, a mother of three shares: "In Sri Lanka we used to have a domestic cat at home. I still remember how the mother cat took her kittens from place to place one after another as soon as she had felt danger to her kittens. It held the kittens in between its jaws with perfect pressure so that the kittens neither get hurt nor get dropped so that they reach to the safety. I try to be like the skillful mother cat [*laughs*] as I strive to nurture my children in goodness. It is not easy, but I sometimes ask myself if I am too strict or too lenient in disciplining my children" (personal interview 2009). The mother cat metaphor illustrates a "not too tight and not too loose" style of parenting.[1] The parenting insight indicates the heightened anxiety of raising children among immigrant families. Parents have often expressed concerns and difficulties in nurturing children within nuclear family settings, and they wish for the extended family support that they had enjoyed as they were growing up in a collective society in Sri Lanka. The mother cat metaphor also reflects the mother's move with her husband from war-torn Sri Lanka during the mid-1990s to Canada with their first child. It furthermore captures tender parental love and the heavy responsibility to provide children with a safe and secure environment as well as healthy moral upbringing. The latter in particular includes passing on Buddhist beliefs, values, and practices to the younger generation. In the interviews, parents often noted that passing Buddhist traditions on to their children was their parental obligation. The discussion of Sri Lankan Canadian youths' Buddhist identity, particularly in chapter 6, suggests that the skilful parental efforts have not been in vain. If the wise and caring mother cat exemplifies parents – the transmitters – the swan below represents youths, the receivers.

The West End Dhamma School's emblem displays a white swan holding an ola leaf book in its beak, and the swan is collaged into a red maple leaf. The 2008 *Dhamma School* magazine explains, "the swan symbolizes the student who learns the Dhamma. Swan is also a reflection of purity. It is capable of separating the 'good' from the 'bad,' a quality that a good citizen [rather student] should develop" (3). This book illustrates that youths indeed have exercised their discerning and distinguishing skills in retaining what they deem as "good" and applicable and leaving behind the aspects of their parents' Buddhism that appear to be impractical and unnecessary in their lives. It is worth remembering that the youths who have contributed to this study are single. As they eventually get married and raise their own children, they may come back to the inherited tradition with a fresh perspective. They may pick up a few aspects that they currently consider impractical and unnecessary; even then, though, this would not be the same as their parents' Buddhism.

BUDDHISM RECONFIGURED IN CANADA: WHO DOES CALL IT "CANADIAN BUDDHISM"?

This book exemplifies a reconfiguration of the Sri Lankan Buddhist tradition in Canada. Monastic reinterpretations of Buddhism echo Canadian multiculturalism. Dhamma teachers' dhamma-culture distinction encourages supplanting the collective Buddhist cultural values and practices with those of individualistic culture – albeit perhaps inadvertently. Parents' transmission strategies illustrate intercultural negotiation and integration. Youths' internalization of Buddhist beliefs and practices display the influence of both hierarchical and egalitarian cultures. In constructing the Sri Lankan Canadian Buddhist identity, Buddhist educators have argued that learning and practicing Buddhism turns students into good Canadian citi- zens. Being Buddhist thus means, among other things, upholding key Canadian values – namely, peaceful coexistence, appreciation of cultural diversity, and respect for secular and religious views and lifestyles. Do such assertions make Buddhism Canadian? They certainly do not, at least not from the perspective of Buddhist respondents in this research.

This study shows that making Buddhism Canadian has never been Sri Lankan Buddhists' intention or stated aim. It would be mere projection to consider the redefinition of Buddhism along the lines of multicultural themes to be a project of making Buddhism Canadian. Such a projection would also erroneously accuse Buddhists of designating Buddhism along the lines of a particular national identity. In referring to "Canadian Buddhism," Alexander Soucy (2014, 28) states: "I am questioning the usefulness and validity of the category of 'Canadian Buddhism,' and by extension 'American' and 'Western'

Buddhism. Furthermore, I am arguing against the academic enterprise, as distinct from claims by practitioners, for such a thing ... The impulse to define a Buddhism based on national identity may be understandable, particularly for practitioners; however, scholars need to be circumspect about where this discourse arises and avoid participation, if only because it is ultimately unfruitful." I agree with Soucy – except his reference to practitioners' impulse to define Buddhism as Canadian, American, or Western. I wonder whose interest it is to define Buddhism in this way. My experience with Sri Lankan Buddhists in Toronto, who have the best ingredients hitherto to lay a claim for "Canadian Buddhism," is that they resist making any such articulation. I trust that a robust study on the history of defining Buddhism along the line of national identities would confirm what Jonathan Smith (2004, 179–80) has to say about the term "religion" itself below: "Religion is not a native category. It is not a first-person term of self-characterization. It is a category [an anthropological one] imposed from the outside on some aspect of native culture. It is the other ... [scholars], who are solely responsible for the content of the term." Similar to the term "religion," the national or ethnic identifiers of the Buddhist tradition like Burmese, Sinhalese, and Thai Buddhism mushroomed – particularly in the anthropological studies that have proliferated since the 1970s. I have discussed in chapter 5 that Sri Lankan Buddhists have resisted the anthropological category – i.e., "Sinhala/Sinhalese Buddhism" in Toronto. They have replaced that ethno-specific reference with a geo-specific reference: "Sri Lankan Buddhism." The latter is a diasporic phenomenon with a heuristic purpose: to distinguish Buddhism and Buddhists from Sri Lanka from other forms of Buddhism/Buddhists who happen to live side by side in the same city like Toronto. As such, one hardly hears that self-reference in Sri Lanka. Furthermore, in reference to Buddhism beyond Sri Lanka, it is rarely defined by ethnic or national identities like "Indian," "Burmese," or "Thai" Buddhism. Instead, what we often hear is geo-specific references i.e., Buddhism/Buddhists in India, Burma, or Thailand. In the instances where Buddhism is qualified, the qualifying term highlights doctrinal differences i.e., Theravāda, Mahāyāna, and Vajrayāna Buddhism.[2]

Moreover one should discern the logic of using "Sri Lankan Buddhism" in Toronto and rejecting the term "Canadian Buddhism." Both terms qualify Buddhism with geo-specificity and national designations. But they invoke two opposing connotations. The use of the former in Toronto establishes the translocal connections; the latter undermines those lineage-recognizing connections. The former legitimates a tradition, and the latter questions its legitimacy indicating a rupture. Coherence and integrity are much more important for a religious community than are innovation and disruption. The Sri Lankan Buddhists' hermeneutic of adaptation and integration discussed in this book entails innovation on their part, but their constant historical and canonical references make their creativity inconspicuous and less pronounced. More importantly, their eclipsed creativity has enabled them to establish the coherence and integrity of inherited Buddhism. This does not mean that Sri Lankan Buddhism in Toronto remains static; it rather indicates the opposite. The Sri Lankan Buddhist tradition has evolved dynamically with Toronto's socio-political and cultural forces. Rather than resisting those forces as some Buddhist communities in Canada tend to do (Crowe 2014), Sri Lankan Buddhists have responded by redefining Buddhist concepts, practices, and institutions. Nevertheless, to claim that the redefined Buddhism in Toronto is "Canadian" is going against the wishes of the Buddhists themselves in this study.

Does the lack of emic reference to "Canadian Buddhism" prevent Buddhist respondents from using personal references like "Canadian Buddhist?" It certainly does not. Sri Lankan Buddhists may identify themselves as "Sinhalese Buddhists," although such ethno-specific reference is less noticeable in the public domain in Toronto. The nineteenth-century Indigenous Buddhist revivalist Anagarika Dharmapala popularized that term through a journal entitled *Sinhala Bauddhaya* [Sinhalese Buddhist] in 1906. Echoing that journal title, Sri Lankan Buddhists in Toronto have been publishing *Toronto Buddhist* since 1979. Similarly they have indeed alluded to a "Canadian Buddhist" in *Teaching Buddhism to Children*. Terms like "Toronto Buddhist" and "Canadian Buddhist" are readily available and in use among practitioners. This attribution of Canadian identity to qualify personal reference however does not translate into defining Buddhism. As such, we do not witness terms like "Canadian" or "Toronto Buddhism" being used to designate a type of Buddhism. In other words, Buddhist immigrants from Sri Lanka are eager to identify themselves as Canadians, but they do not show the same eagerness in defining Buddhism as Canadian. This (in)visibility of Canadian affiliation appears self-contradictory, and therefore requires an explanation regarding what drives such paradoxical claims.

I have argued that the visible "Toronto Buddhist" – and by extension "Canadian Buddhist" – identity speaks loudly about the purpose of the Buddhism-multiculturalism dialogue discussed in this book: making Canada home for Buddhists. Sri Lankan monks in Toronto have refurbished or reshuffled the constituents of their tradition to expand and extend Canadian identity. The examples of Buddhist interpretation, integration, and internalization discussed in the preceding chapters demonstrate a mutual exchange between an incoming immigrant religious community and a receiving, multicultural Canada. They convey that Buddhism does not threaten but rather strengthens Canadian values. The pervasive discourse of multiculturalism in Toronto and the individualistic secular public ethos in Canada propel Sri Lankan Buddhists to highlight the aspects of their religious tradition that correspond to the law of the land where they have chosen to live. In doing so, Sri Lankan Buddhists claim that they and their religion – the redefined Buddhism – belong to Canada. The Buddhism-multiculturalism dialogue has interpenetrated the discourses of Buddhism as well as those of Canada. Consequently, it has reconstructed both Buddhist and Canadian identities. And yet, the urge to maintain coherence across different times and spaces does not encourage the Buddhists to articulate the emerging reconfigured Buddhism as "Canadian." Therefore, the expressions like "Toronto Buddhism" and/or "Canadian Buddhism" remain invisible.

Particularly in chapter 4, I have argued that Sri Lankan Buddhists in Toronto have engaged in a hermeneutic of adaptation and integration. Such characterization in fact goes against the following caution for scholars in Canada from Paul Crowe (2014, 167–8): "When we read the history, organization, and social dynamics of immigrant religious communities through a hermeneutic of adaptation and integration, we risk creating their stories in terms that assume a distance between 'those communities' and 'the rest of us' and contributing to the polarizing language currently affecting public discourse in this country [Canada]." I could not agree more with Crowe that, as scholars, we alone should not invoke "a hermeneutic of adaptation and integration" to analyze immigrant groups as that may fuel the fear-mongering, divisive discourse that advocates or even imposes assimilation. The risks certainly increase if such analysis is applied to immigrant communities such as the Chinese Buddhists of Crowe's study in Vancouver, who prioritize the translocal history, religious mission, and effective organization of their religious institutions. I would, however, argue that if "a hermeneutic of adaption and integration" becomes an emic (as opposed to etic) phenomenon or discursively emerges *within* the immigrant religious community in question, then our scholarship/research becomes a venue to express the marginalized voice of immigrants. As the preceding chapters have demonstrated, Sri Lankan Buddhists in Toronto have spoken in the language of adaptation and integration, defining their actions as "intelligent adaptation." By bringing such immigrant voices and actions of adaptation and integration to the front and centre, this book in fact resists the polarizing discourse in contemporary Canada. It also suggests that Canada's multiculturalism policy encourages immigrant communities to localize their traditions, cultures, and religions. In response to that call, the Sri Lankan Buddhists of Toronto examined in this study have engaged in a process of localization that includes Canada but also goes beyond Canada.

(G) LOCALIZATION AND FUTURE RESEARCH DIRECTIONS ON SRI LANKAN BUDDHISM IN DIASPORA

In relation to the eighteenth-century localization of an imported monastic lineage in Sri Lanka, Anne Blackburn observes that "new historical models and methods are required to accommodate an imported lineage within a locally intelligible teleology ... At the same time, a locally acceptable history must be created for the imported lineage" (2003, 139). Being a foreign tradition in Canada, Buddhism needs "a locally intelligible teleology" to establish its claim to belong to Canada. I suggest that Canada's discourse of multiculturalism provides that essential teleology. By interpreting Buddhist concepts and practices in a way that will resonate with the values of multiculturalism, Sri Lankan Buddhists, and particularly the monks in Toronto, have initiated "a locally acceptable history." Canada's multiculturalism policy has become Sri Lankan Buddhists' "interpretative discourse" that has been missing in some Buddhist communities in Canada (McLellan 2009, 115). To connect Buddhism to multiculturalism sounds new, but it echoes the historical models and methods that are essential in the localizing process.

The recent history of Sri Lankan Buddhism provides ample insights into how to go about redefining the Buddhist tradition in a particular time and space. The eighteenth-century introduction of the Siyam Nikaya exemplifies a model and method of localizing an imported Thai monastic lineage by reviving an Indigenous literary genre (Blackburn 2001). The late nineteenth-century Buddhist reformers illustrate how to connect the traits of modernity to the teachings of the Buddha. They dove into the earliest Pāli sutta texts by overlooking the Pāli commentaries and vernacular literature. The mid-twentieth century Buddhist majority discourse in independent Sri Lanka displays a socio-political particularization of Buddhism by selectively reviving certain aspects of premodern Buddhism for a postcolonial political agenda (Bond 1988; Gombrich and Obeyesekere 1988). Sri Lankan Buddhists in Toronto are privileged to be able to draw from these historical models and methods as they strive to ground their Buddhist tradition in Toronto. At their discretion, they have revived certain models and methods from their tradition's repertoire while leaving others that they deem inappropriate and unhelpful. These historical reconfigurations demonstrate that Buddhists have oscillated between particularization and universalization depending on what was limiting their ability to transmit, exist, and thrive.

In Toronto it was the ethnically particularized Sinhala/Sinhalese Buddhism that was initially challenging the transmission. To overcome that obstacle, the Buddhism-ethnicity separation was adopted as a transmission strategy. This distinction highlights the cultural transferability of Buddhist teachings, which resulted in the reconfiguration of Buddhism as an inclusive and harmonious religion. In Theravāda Buddhism, localization becomes authoritative and legitimate if it is connected to and congruent with its history. Localizers have to convincingly make a case for a historical connection. At the very least innovation must appear to be repeating history in some sense, so that it does not truly look like an innovation at all. History-making is not linear; it is rather discursive and reflective. The localization or reconfiguration witnessed in this book is just a part of making history discursively and reflectively.

The term "glocalization"[3] refers to a trend that interpenetrates the boundaries of both being global and being local. It often shapes contemporary society, particularly that of immigrants. Within this context, the reinterpreted Buddhism and redefined Buddhist identity that we have observed in Toronto are simultaneously local/Canadian as well as global/Sri Lankan. It is arguably global in both narrow and wider senses. Its Sri Lankan characteristics may reflect those of Sri Lankan Buddhists dispersed across the globe, including Sri Lanka. Its features resonate with the characteristics of what scholars call "Buddhist modernism" (McMahan 2008). In reference to Buddhist groups (both Asian and non-Asian) in Canada, Soucy (2010, 8) asserts that "every adaptation is both an example of the global becoming local, and the local going global." The hyphenated "Sri Lankan-Canadian" Buddhist identity, reimagined in *Teaching Buddhism to Children*, simultaneously captures the local and global references. However, we should not ignore the obvious: its spatial reference to Canada, where it has been reconfigured.

The societal construction of Buddhism and its academic study in North America has recently received academic scrutiny. Despite the fact that the term "American Buddhism" has been around for a few decades, what it constitutes and what it characterizes remain elusive. Jeff Wilson blames the macro reference of the term and users' ambition to employ a regional Buddhist phenomenon across a national landscape. He therefore suggests applying regionalism as an interpretative paradigm of analysis in the study of Buddhism in North America. He observes: "Yet in 2012 we find that major forms of interpretation such as regionalism from one primary related discipline – American religious history – remain nonetheless widely neglected. Among the implications of this inattention to regional phenomena is the possibility that we may know less about 'American Buddhism' than we think we do – we may, rather, know mainly about West Coast, Northeastern, or Midwestern Buddhism, not American Buddhism per se" (Wilson 2012, 18). This critique of the misnomer "American Buddhism" applies equally to "Canadian Buddhism." Wilson's observation and methodological suggestion are instructive. A regional focus may keep the local construction of Buddhism front and centre. Uncritical use of it, however, may prevent us from discerning the socio-cultural and even economic Buddhist networks that go beyond a local region and yet shape local Buddhism visibly and invisibly. Alexander Soucy (2014, 37) intervenes into the discussion with the following suggestion: "in order to understand Buddhism in Canada and the West, we need a model for understanding Buddhism at a global level. That is, we need to think about the idea of a Buddhist globalism that interacts with and influences local Buddhisms." This debate on regionalism vs globalism is worth pondering, as both sides of the camp in fact reflect the nature of contemporary Buddhism – it is both regional as well as global.

This book strikes a balance between regionalism and globalism. By tracing back the history of dhamma education in Toronto
to the late nineteenth and twentieth century, this book reminds us
that Buddhism in Canada, and by extension in the West, needs to
be studied within its modern history. This is particularly true of
those Buddhisms practiced in Asian Buddhist diasporas. From a
more methodological point of view, it also suggests that a translocative observation is essential to comprehend the reconfiguration of
Buddhism in Canada. For instance, fieldwork in Toronto as well as
in Colombo has enabled me to discern how dhamma education in
Toronto lacks the Sinhala Buddhist discourse in its counterpart in
Sri Lanka. Moreover, it also explains why Sri Lankan Buddhists,
unlike other Theravāda Buddhists in Toronto, heavily rely on formal
dhamma education to transmit Buddhism to their Canadian-born
children. Others have also observed the necessity and merits of setting
up research on Buddhism in Canada in relation to their respective
Asian countries (Hori 2010, 36). The outcome of the translocative
observation indicates that Buddhism in Toronto remains Sri Lankan
yet with a Canadian multicultural flavour.

With a detailed discussion and analysis of Sri Lankan Buddhism in
Toronto as a religion in diaspora, this book relates to two meta-dis-
courses in cultural studies. First, it reminds us that no culture is
static. It has enabled us to see the dynamic nature of culture that
evolves with time and space. Religion in diaspora highlights that
religio-culture is in fact a process rather than a static, fixed entity.
This "processual view of culture" (Vertovec 2011, 250) is epitomized in this study of Buddhism in the diaspora. Second, the book
with intercultural and intergenerational analyses also questions the
popular structural-functionalism, which suggests that cultural values, practices, and institutions form an integrated and coherent system that mutually interdepends on its parts. That means a culture
comprised of inherent values that are enforced with certain practices
and institutions. When one aspect – i.e., supporting institutions like
extended family structure – is absent, the other interdependent cultural aspects like values and practices would fall apart. Contrary
to that perspective, the collective-individualist cultural negotiation
in Toronto indicates that Buddhist immigrant families and community do not necessarily fall apart as Buddhists selectively integrate
certain aspects of both cultures. The research shows that intercultural negotiation rather enables Sri Lankan Buddhists to thrive as a

dynamic community evidenced by significant new developments in the community.

In 2006 two more temples have branched out from the two existing temples studied in this book. The Brampton Buddhist Mission Centre and the Buddha Meditation Centre of Greater Toronto seem to have capitalized on two Buddhist interests – namely, humanitarian service and contemplative practices. Moreover, the Waterloo Wellington Buddhist Cultural Association was added in 2011. These new institutions have intensified the multiplication of Buddhist resources noted in chapter 2; likewise intensified is the sense of competition for Sri Lankan Buddhists' time, attention, and of course donations. Within this context, the differentiation of one institution from others through distinct services and discourses may become crucial. Such developing community dynamism may demand future research observing how the character of Sri Lankan Buddhism in Toronto evolves.

One such area of future observation would be the absence of deity worship. Compared to its counterpart in Sri Lanka, the absence of deity worship stands out in Toronto. Deity worship is ubiquitous in Buddhism in Sri Lanka and yet absent in Sri Lankan Buddhism in Toronto. As happened elsewhere in the Sri Lankan diaspora – specifically in London, UK – the missing deity worship might eventually get introduced in Toronto. The Sri Saddhatissa International Buddhist Centre (SSIBC) in London, UK – a breakaway temple from the first Tharavāda Buddhist temple in Europe, the London Buddhist Vihara (est. 1926) – introduced deity worship in 1993. Addressing the question, "what does make the SSIBC distinctive?" Mahinda Deegalle (2008, 25) observes: "the most innovative aspect of the SSIBC is its *Devale*, literally 'abode of god(s).'" Testing the community reaction, the SSIBC first introduced a portable *devale*[4] that secured a permanent place in 1998 within the temple itself, like many temples in Sri Lanka. Deegalle notes: "the worship of deities is by no means without controversy because some Buddhists think that this kind of devotional practice towards deities is not a part of what the Buddha taught." This sentiment has been strong with the monastic tradition of the Toronto temples studied; therefore, we have not seen deity worship become an institutional part of Sri Lankan Buddhism in Toronto. The absence also might have been due to the community's emphasis on the intergenerational transmission of Buddhism. Deegalle details an intergenerational conflict over the issue in London.[5]

Future research might offer not only new findings, but also fresh nuance to the observations offered here. For example, this research has captured a moment of time when multiculturalism as a diversity managing political tool is working well and celebrated as quintessentially Canadian. Sri Lankan Buddhists in Toronto have rightly used the popular policy to express who they are and how they belong to Canada. A cynical observer could argue that Toronto's local discourse of multiculturalism has been employed for a translocal purpose. In fact according to Arjun Appadurai (2006, 178), the term locality in a globalized world is not confined to spatial reference; it also connotes "relational and contextual" locations beyond particular geographical boundaries. In that sense, the inclusive and harmonious Buddhism that emerged in Toronto can be read in a "relational and contextual" language. Such a reading may enable the cynical observer to infer the wider implications and even motivations of that positive image of Buddhism and Sri Lankan Buddhists. Here I refer to Sri Lankan Buddhists' double minority status in relation not only to the Canadian society but also to the Tamil Sri Lankans in Toronto. Particularly the latter's presence in Toronto and their campaign against the Sinhalese Buddhist rhetoric in Sri Lanka have brought the Sinhalese-Tamil ethnic tension to the fore. Within this context, one could argue that the reinterpreted Buddhism helps Sri Lankan Buddhists to distance themselves from the civil war in Sri Lanka. Thus a localized interpretation of Buddhism in Toronto is also about Sri Lanka. With no evidence to make that assertion, this book has not pursued that line of argument. As the military phase of the Tamil-Sinhalese ethnic conflict ceased in 2009, one possible future research focus would be to discern if and how the multicultural Buddhist discourse persists.

Another future research thread of Sri Lankan Buddhism in Toronto would be to follow the translocal institutional ties of the Buddha Meditation Centre of Greater Toronto. The latter belongs to a rapidly proliferating Sri Lankan Buddhist movement with concurrent emphases on devotional and contemplative practices. In one decade it has established four branches in Canada, including a Buddhist Nuns' Centre in Milton (in southwest Ontario). Its mother institute, the Mahamevnawa Buddhist Monastery, was founded only in 1999. In less than two decades it has had tremendous institutional growth, and opened more than seventy centres. Many of them are located across Sri Lanka, but a significant number are established beyond Sri Lanka

– including five centres in Canada, six in the US, four in Australia, seven in Europe, two in South Korea, and one in India. It also has an effective and coordinated publication in Sinhala, English, and Tamil along with audio, video, and online presence. In addition to an effective male monastic community, a female monastic community called Anagarika Maniyan Wahanses has made the movement outstanding. Future research on this dynamic Sri Lankan newcomer to Toronto's Sri Lankan Buddhist landscape would definitely nourish the research seed planted in *Seeding Buddhism with Multiculturalism*.

First-Generation Buddhists

1. Research Information and Your Consent

1. This study centres in and around the first generation Sri Lankan Buddhists in Toronto. To qualify for this research, you MUST be aged of 30+, and participant at LEAST occasionally at the services organized by the Sri Lankan temples in Toronto.

Are you qualified for this research?

◯ Yes

◯ No .

2. I have read the information letter and understood my rights as a research participant and consent to use the data provided.

◯ Yes, and wish to continue

◯ I do not wish to continue

2. General Information

3. Gender/ Sex:

◯ male   ◯ female

Other (please specify)

[   ]

4. Please circle your age category:

◯ 30-36   ◯ 49-54   ◯ 67-72

◯ 37-42   ◯ 55-60   ◯ 73+

◯ 43-48   ◯ 61-66

5. What is your marital status?

◯ Single   ◯ Married   ◯ Divorced   ◯ Widower/widow   ◯ Dating someone   ◯ Common Law

6. What is the highest level of education you have completed?

○ Have not finished high school   ○ Some graduate work

○ High school graduation   ○ Masters

○ College degree   ○ PhD

○ University graduate

Other (please specify)

7. What is your occupation?

☐ Unemployed   ☐ Trades person (e.g., electrician, plumber etc.)   ☐ Student

☐ Professional (e.g., teacher, lawyer, etc.)   ☐ Service industry   ☐ Manufacturing

☐ Business   ☐ Monastics   ☐ Civil servant

☐ Stay at home parent   ☐ Self employed

Other (please specify)

8. What is your family composition?

○ Nuclear (parents+children)

○ Extended with 2 generations (parents, uncle/aunt, children)

○ Extended with 3 generations (grandparents, parents, children)

○ Not applicable

9. Do children or young adult live at your household? If yes, please identify their age ranges below by marking categories as many as needed.

☐ 0-6   ☐ 7-12   ☐ 13-18   ☐ 19-24

3. Buddhism in Your Life

10. How would you religiously identify yourself?

○ A Buddhist   ○ A Theravada Buddhist   ○ A Sinhalese Buddhist

Other (please specify)

11. To be Sinhalese means to be a Buddhist.

○ Agree   ○ Strongly agree   ○ Disagree   ○ Strongly disagree

12. Which are you?

◯ Monastic   ◯ Upasaka   ◯ Upasika   ◯ Lay supporter

Other (please specify)

[   ]

13. What is your Buddhist or religious goal in this very life? Please mark only ONE of the following:

◯ To provide a good life for my family

◯ To become enlightened in this very life

◯ To serve humanity and other beings to reduce suffering

◯ To have a better life after death and eventually attain nirvanaya

Other (please specify)

[   ]

14. What is your spouse's religion?

☐ Buddhism   ☐ Christianity   ☐ Hinduism   ☐ Islam   ☐ Judaism

Other (please specify)

[   ]

15. How often do you go to the temple?

◯ Once a week   ◯ A few times a month   ◯ Less than once a year

◯ Twice a week   ◯ A few times a year

◯ Once a month   ◯ Once a year

16. Please identify three of your main reasons for going to the temple. Please mark only ONE choice per row:

	To maintain/renew social connections	To gain merits	To be a better person	To visit the monks	To maintain ethnic identity	To learn/practice Buddhism	To maintain Buddhist identity
First choice	◯	◯	◯	◯	◯	◯	◯
Second choice	◯	◯	◯	◯	◯	◯	◯
Third choice	◯	◯	◯	◯	◯	◯	◯

Other (please specify)

[   ]

17. Please indicate how much you like the following temple activities:

	Like most	Like	Like somewhat	Don't like	Don't like at all
Poya Day service	○	○	○	○	○
Weekly meditation	○	○	○	○	○
Weekly sutra studies	○	○	○	○	○
Dharma education/Daham pasela	○	○	○	○	○
Dharma discussion for the parents of Dharma students	○	○	○	○	○
Monks' home visit (acceptance dana)	○	○	○	○	○
Pirit chanting	○	○	○	○	○
Social support (soup kitchen)	○	○	○	○	○
Cultural events	○	○	○	○	○
Social networking	○	○	○	○	○
Private counseling with monks	○	○	○	○	○
Preservation of ethnic identity and language	○	○	○	○	○
Other	○	○	○	○	○

Other (please specify)

18. Please list your top three favourite Buddhist activities.

One

Two

Three

19. What else can the temple do for you?

☐ Family counseling   ☐ Celebration of youth's educational achievement

☐ Summer camps for children and youth   ☐ Youth leadership workshop

☐ Organizing cultural educational trip to Sri Lanka for youth   ☐ Fund raising for the needy and poor

Other (please specify)

20. Do you believe that one has to be a monk to realize Nirvanaya?

○ Yes   ○ No   ○ Not sure

21. Which of the following spiritual forces or beings who, you believe, can intervene in your every day life. Please tick all that apply.

☐ Creator God   ☐ Buddhist saints (Rahatan Wahanse)   ☐ Deceased relatives (Malagiya Neayo)

☐ Sai Baba   ☐ The Gaothama Buddha   ☐ Gods (i.e., Vishnu, Kataragama)

☐ Boddhisattva (i.e., Maithree)   ☐ Ista devata (personal deity)

22. Worshiping gods is a part of Buddhism.

◯ Strongly agree   ◯ Agree   ◯ Somewhat agree   ◯ Disagree   ◯ Strongly disagree

23. The following personal challenges increased your Buddhist faith:

	Strongly agree	Agree	Somewhat agree	Disagree	Strongly disagree
Emotional challenges	◯	◯	◯	◯	◯
Loneliness	◯	◯	◯	◯	◯
Parenthood	◯	◯	◯	◯	◯
Migration from Sri Lanka	◯	◯	◯	◯	◯
Life crises (death of loved one)	◯	◯	◯	◯	◯
Personal trouble	◯	◯	◯	◯	◯

Other (please specify)

[   ]

24. How important are the following Buddhist activities to you?

	Extremely important	Important	Somewhat important	Not important	Not important at all
To accumulate good karmas for life after death	◯	◯	◯	◯	◯
To purify my mind for enlightenment	◯	◯	◯	◯	◯
To give material supports to Buddhism	◯	◯	◯	◯	◯
To support the needy and poor	◯	◯	◯	◯	◯
To defend Buddhism against non-Buddhist influences	◯	◯	◯	◯	◯
To model good virtues	◯	◯	◯	◯	◯
Other	◯	◯	◯	◯	◯

Other (please specify)

[   ]

4. Dhamma Education

25. Identify relevent boxes related to your participation in Dhamma education. Please tick all that apply.

☐ I currently teach at Dhamma school in Toronto ☐ I have taught at Dhamma school in Sri Lanka ☐ I have never been to Dhamma school ☐ I have learned Buddhism at Dhamma school ☐ I have learned Buddhism at public school

26. Did or does Dhamma School meet your expectations in terms of the following:

	Yes	Somewhat	No
My moral and spiritual development	○	○	○
Become a better citizen	○	○	○
Strengthening Buddhist identity	○	○	○
Philosophical understanding	○	○	○
Insight into religious truths	○	○	○
Friendship with other fellows	○	○	○
Other	○	○	○

Other (please specify)

27. Please explain to what extent Dhamma School has influenced in your:

	Greatly influenced	influenced	Somewhat influenced	Not influenced	Not influenced at all
Moral behaviour	○	○	○	○	○
Buddhist knowledge	○	○	○	○	○
Buddhist identity	○	○	○	○	○
Better citizen	○	○	○	○	○
Sense of self	○	○	○	○	○
Other	○	○	○	○	○

Other (please specify)

28. What do you think is/was missing in Dhamma education?

One	
Two	
Three	

5. Encounter with Other Buddhist Tradition(s)

29. If you have been exposed to other types of Buddhism, please identify how:

	Through books and internet	Educational setting	Friendship	Relationship	Dhamma School	Visit to temple	Meeting with Buddhist teachers	Public media
East Asian Buddhist traditions	☐	☐	☐	☐	☐	☐	☐	☐
Zen Buddhism	☐	☐	☐	☐	☐	☐	☐	☐
Tibetan Buddhism	☐	☐	☐	☐	☐	☐	☐	☐
Non-Sinhalese Thevarada Buddhism	☐	☐	☐	☐	☐	☐	☐	☐
Non-sectarian Buddhism	☐	☐	☐	☐	☐	☐	☐	☐
Other	☐	☐	☐	☐	☐	☐	☐	☐

Other (please specify)

30. Contact with other forms of Buddhism has:

	Yes	No	Not sure
Increased my belief in my inherited Buddhism	○	○	○
Expanded my Buddhist knowledge	○	○	○
Inspired me to know more about my inherited Buddhism	○	○	○
Made me critical of my inherited Buddhism	○	○	○
Not made any change	○	○	○

31. How responsible do you hold each of the following for passing the Buddhist tradition on to the future generation?

	Extremely responsible	Responsible	Somewhat responsible	Not responsible	Not responsible at all
School teachers	○	○	○	○	○
Monks/nuns	○	○	○	○	○
Parents/grandparents	○	○	○	○	○
Lay dharma teachers	○	○	○	○	○
Government	○	○	○	○	○
The dharma students themselves	○	○	○	○	○
Other	○	○	○	○	○

Other (please specify)

32. Please identify what aspects of Buddhism you find interesting?

	Very interesting	Interesting	Somewhat interesting	Not interesting	Not interesting at all
Buddhist metaphysical beliefs (i.e., heavens and hells)	○	○	○	○	○
Buddhist rituals (i.e., Buddhapuja, Sanghika dana etc.)	○	○	○	○	○
Buddhist ethics (5 and 8 precepts)	○	○	○	○	○
contemplative practices (i.e., meditation)	○	○	○	○	○
Social services (i.e., soup kitchen)	○	○	○	○	○
Philosophical issues (i.e., sutra study, dharma talks)	○	○	○	○	○
Other	○	○	○	○	○

Other (please specify)

33. If you have a choice, would you send your child(ren) to a Buddhist Day School similar to a Catholic School?

○ Yes   ○ No

34. How effective are the following ways to pass Buddhist tradition on to the next generation?

	Highly effective	Effective	Somewhat effecive	Not effective	Not effective at all
Separate Buddhist schools	○	○	○	○	○
Buddhist practices at home and at the temple	○	○	○	○	○
Sunday Dhamma schools	○	○	○	○	○
Let the children decide themselves	○	○	○	○	○

35. What is Buddhism to you? Please mark ONLY one of the following: Buddhism is:

○ A way of life that claims to reduce suffering

○ A moral/ethical system

○ A religion with rituals, metaphysical beliefs, and practices

○ A philosophy without dogmas

○ A spirituality without restrictive beliefs and required practices

Other (please specify)

36. Who/what is the Buddha to you? Please mark only ONE of the following:

○ Buddha was no more no less than a human being who taught how to end suffering

○ Buddha is/was a supreme being with miraculous power and extraordinary virtues who teaches the path to Nirvana

○ Buddha is/was a manifestation of the universal moral and spiritual force that governs order of the universe and can intervene in everyday life

○ Buddha was spiritual teacher who came to reveal the way to Enlightenment

○ Buddha is a divine being who can help humans

Other (please specify)

[   ]

37. What does "Sangha" mean to you? Please mark only ONE.

○ The order of monks only   ○ The monastic and lay followers of the Buddha

○ Buddhist monks and nuns   ○ The community

Other (please specify)

[   ]

38. Do children related to you go to Dhamma School?

☐ Your child(ren)   ☐ Your grand children   ☐ Cousins/Nephews/Nice   ☐ None

39. As parents and elders, to what extent do you expect the following from the Dhamma School?

	Greatly expected	Expected	Somewhat expected	Not expected	Not expected at all
Moral and spiritual development	○	○	○	○	○
Better citizen	○	○	○	○	○
Transmission of Sinhalese Buddhist identity	○	○	○	○	○
Knowledge of Buddhism	○	○	○	○	○
Socialization of children among Buddhist peers	○	○	○	○	○
Other	○	○	○	○	○

Other (please specify)

[   ]

40. Please rate how important the following material sources of Buddhist knowledge or inspiration are to you:

	Very important	Somewhat important	Not important	N/A
Published materials on Buddhism in Sinhala	O	O	O	O
Published materials on Buddhism in English	O	O	O	O
Published materials on Buddhism in other languages	O	O	O	O
Multimedia (TV, films)	O	O	O	O
Internet	O	O	O	O
Courses on Buddhism (school, college, university)	O	O	O	O
Other	O	O	O	O

Other (please specify)

41. How influential are the following people in terms of understanding and living a Buddhist way of life?

	Extremely influential	Influential	Somewhat influential	Not influential	Not Influential all all	N/A
Parents	O	O	O	O	O	O
Grandparents	O	O	O	O	O	O
Monks/nuns	O	O	O	O	O	O
School teacher	O	O	O	O	O	O
Dhamma teacher	O	O	O	O	O	O
Relatives	O	O	O	O	O	O
Friends	O	O	O	O	O	O
Other	O	O	O	O	O	O

Other (please specify)

42. When faced with a question about your Buddhist practice or belief you:

	Strongly agree	Agree	Somewhat agree	Disagree	Strongly disagree
Consult lay Buddhist who knows/practices Buddhism	O	O	O	O	O
Refer to Buddhist texts	O	O	O	O	O
Visit Buddhist internet sites	O	O	O	O	O
Consult Buddhist monks or nuns	O	O	O	O	O
Look for the interpretation in tradition	O	O	O	O	O
Reflect on self-experience	O	O	O	O	O
Talk to friends	O	O	O	O	O
Discuss with family	O	O	O	O	O

6. Migration and Cross-cultural Issues

43. From where did you migrate to Canada?

○ Directly from Sri Lanka   ○ Migrated from other country

44. When did you migrate to Canada or the USA?

○ Pre-1966   ○ 1967-1983   ○ 1984-1993   ○ 1994-2004   ○ 2005-Present

45. Please explain how much the following reasons motivated you to migrate to North America:

	Very decisive	Decisive	Somewhat decisive	Not decisive
Political reasons/crises in Sri Lanka	○	○	○	○
Economic opportunity in N.America	○	○	○	○
Higher education	○	○	○	○
Better life for your family	○	○	○	○
Other	○	○	○	○

Other (please specify)

46. Overall, how satisfied or dissatisfied are you with your migration decision?

○ Extremely dissatisfied   ○ Dissatisfied   ○ Somewhat satisfied   ○ Satisfied   ○ Extremely satisfied

47. Please identify how challenging are the issues mentioned below.

	Extremely challenging	Challenging	Somewhat challenging	Not challenging	Not challenging at all
Maintenance of North American living standard	○	○	○	○	○
Passing on ethnic and religio-cultural identity	○	○	○	○	○
To practice and uphold Buddhist values	○	○	○	○	○
Raising children with religio-cultural values	○	○	○	○	○
To maintain family and community ties	○	○	○	○	○
Other	○	○	○	○	○

Other (please specify)

48. Please identify to what extent the following Buddhist cultural values are being compromised or enhanced.

	Extremely compromised	Compromised	Extremely enhanced	Enchanced	Neither compromised nor enhanced
Family and communal consensus	○	○	○	○	○
Collective accountability and responsibility	○	○	○	○	○
Simple and moderate life style	○	○	○	○	○
Age and spiritual hierarchy	○	○	○	○	○
Self reliance and self responsibility	○	○	○	○	○
Buddhist contemplative practices (meditation)	○	○	○	○	○
Buddhist doctrines (i.e, impermanence etc.)	○	○	○	○	○
Buddhist ritualistic practices	○	○	○	○	○
Other	○	○	○	○	○

Other (please specify)

[   ]

49. Are the following values affecting your Sinhalese cultural values?

	Compromising	Not compromising	Enhancing	Not enhancing	Not affective at all
Personal freedom and preference	○	○	○	○	○
Concern with material well-being	○	○	○	○	○
Interest in other religions and cultures	○	○	○	○	○
Gender and social equality	○	○	○	○	○
Educational opportunity	○	○	○	○	○
Other	○	○	○	○	○

Other (please specify)

[   ]

50. What do you think about the following Buddhist beliefs and practices in relation to religious life in North America?

	Highly relevant	Relevent	Needs motivation to make relevent	Irrelevant	N/A
marriage rituals	○	○	○	○	○
Offering material needs to the monks	○	○	○	○	○
Belief in heaven and hell	○	○	○	○	○
Beliefs in karma	○	○	○	○	○
Living according to the 5 precepts	○	○	○	○	○
Pali chanting	○	○	○	○	○
Sitting on the floor	○	○	○	○	○
Meditation	○	○	○	○	○
Education about other Buddhist traditions	○	○	○	○	○
Chairs or pews for temple service	○	○	○	○	○
Other	○	○	○	○	○

Other (please specify)

51. What do you think about the following roles and organizations within the North American context?

	Highly relevant	Relevant	Somewhat relevant	Irrelevant	N/A
Hierarchically defined lay and monastic roles	○	○	○	○	○
Lay preachers	○	○	○	○	○
Order of nuns (Bhikkhuni)	○	○	○	○	○
Temporary ordination for a few days/weeks to develop Buddhist knowledge and understaning	○	○	○	○	○
Multi-ethnic Buddhist organization	○	○	○	○	○
Other	○	○	○	○	○

52. How important is it that your child(ren) gets married to

	Very important	Important	Somewhat important
Buddhist	○	○	○
Sri Lankan	○	○	○
Theravada Buddhist	○	○	○

53. Please respond to the following statements:

	Strongly agree	Agree	Disagree	Strongly disagree
Parents should not impose, but educate the youth	◯	◯	◯	◯
Youth can selectively choose what Buddhist traditions to follow	◯	◯	◯	◯
Youth should follow their parents' religion as it is	◯	◯	◯	◯
Youth may follow any religion they want	◯	◯	◯	◯
Parents should not intervene in youth religiosity	◯	◯	◯	◯

7. Thank you

Thank you very much for your kind consideration and participation in this research!

APPENDIX TWO
Second-Generation Buddhists

1. This study centres in and around the Sri Lankan Buddhist community in Toronto. To qualify for this research, you MUST be between the age of 16-30, and participant at LEAST occasionally at the services organized by the Sri Lankan temples in Toronto.

Are you qualified for this research?

◯ Yes

◯ No

2. I have read the information letter and understood my rights as a research participant and consent to use the data provided.

◯ Yes, and wish to continue

◯ I do not wish to continue

3. Gender/ Sex:

◯ male   ◯ female

4. What is your age range?

◯ 16-19   ◯ 20-24   ◯ 25-30

5. What is your relationship status?

◯ Single   ◯ Dating someone   ◯ Married   ◯ Divorced   ◯ Common Law

6. What is the highest level of education you have completed?

◯ Have not finished high school   ◯ Some graduate work

◯ Completed high school   ◯ Masters

◯ College degree   ◯ PhD

◯ University graduate

Other (please specify)

[   ]

7. What is your occupation?

☐ Student ☐ Manufacturing ☐ Trades person (e.g., electrician, plumber etc.)

☐ Self-employed ☐ Service industry ☐ Professional (e.g., teacher, lawyer, etc.)

☐ Civil servant ☐ Business

☐ Unemployed ☐ Stay at home parent ☐ Monastic

Other (please specify)

8. What is your family composition?

○ Nuclear (parents+children)

○ Extended with 2 generations (parents, uncle/aunt, children)

○ Extended with 3 generations (grandparents, parents, children)

○ Not applicable

9. When asked, how do you present your religious identity? Please tick one:

○ A Buddhist ○ A Theravada Buddhist ○ A Sinhalese Buddhist

Other (please specify)

10. To be Sinhalese means to be Buddhist.

○ Strongly agree ○ Agree ○ Somewhat agree ○ Disagree ○ Strongly disagree

11. Which are you?

○ Monastic ○ Upasaka ○ Upasika ○ Lay supporter

Other (please specify)

12. What is Buddhism to you? Please mark ONLY one of the following:
Buddhism is:

○ A spirituality without restrictive beliefs and required practices

○ A way of life that claims to reduce suffering

○ A philosophy without dogmas

○ A religion with rituals, metaphysical beliefs, and required practices

○ A moral/ethical system

Other (please specify)

13. What is your Buddhist/religious goal in this very life? Please mark only ONE of the following:

○ To provide a good life for my family

○ To become enlightened in this very life

○ To serve humanity and other beings to reduce suffering

○ To have a better life after death and eventually attain nirvanaya

Other (please specify)

[   ]

14. I consider religion a decisive factor when choosing friends:

○ Strongly agree   ○ Agree   ○ Somewhat agree   ○ Disagree   ○ Strongly disagree

15. If in a relationship, what is your girl/boy friend's /partner's /spouse's religion?

☐ Theravada Buddhism   ☐ Mahayana Buddhism   ☐ Other Buddhism   ☐ Christianity   ☐ Hinduism   ☐ Islam   ☐ Judaism

Other (please specify)

[   ]

16. How often do you go to the temple?

○ Once a week   ○ A few times a month   ○ Less than once a year

○ Twice a week   ○ A few times a year

○ Once a month   ○ Once a year

17. Please identify three of your main reasons for going to the temple. Please mark only ONE choice per row.

	To see friends	To please parents/family obligation	To gain merit	To be a better person	To maintain ethnic identity	To learn/ practice Buddhism	To maintain a Buddhist identity
First reason	○	○	○	○	○	○	○
Second reason	○	○	○	○	○	○	○
Third reason	○	○	○	○	○	○	○

18. Please indicate how much you like the following temple activities:

	I really like it	I like it	I like it somewhat	I do not like it	I strongly dislike it
Poya Day service	○	○	○	○	○
Weekly meditation	○	○	○	○	○
Weekly Sutra studies	○	○	○	○	○
Dharma education/Daham pasela	○	○	○	○	○
Monks' home visit (acceptance dana)	○	○	○	○	○
Pirit chanting	○	○	○	○	○
Social support (soup kitchen)	○	○	○	○	○
Cultural events	○	○	○	○	○
Social networking	○	○	○	○	○
Private counseling with monks	○	○	○	○	○
Preservation of ethnic identity and language	○	○	○	○	○
Other	○	○	○	○	○

Other (please specify)

19. Please list your top three favourite Buddhist activities.

One

Two

Three

20. What else can the temple do for you?

☐ Family counseling ☐ Celebration of youth's educational achievement

☐ Summer camps for youth ☐ Youth leadership workshop

☐ Organizing cultural educational trip to Sri Lanka for youth ☐ Fund raising for the poor and needy

Other (please specify)

21. Do you believe that one has to be a monk to realize Nirvanaya?

○ Yes ○ No ○ Not sure

22. Which of the following spiritual forces or beings who, you believe, can intervene in your every day life? Please tick all that apply.

☐ Gods (i.e., Vishnu, Kataragama) ☐ The Gauthama Buddha ☐ Boddhisattva (i.e., Maithree)

☐ Deceased relatives (Malagiya Neayo) ☐ Ista devata (personal deity) ☐ Creator God

☐ Buddhist saints (Rahatan Wahanse) ☐ Sai Baba

23. Worshiping gods is a part of Buddhism.

◯ Strongly agree   ◯ Agree   ◯ Somewhat agree   ◯ Disagree   ◯ Strongly disagree

24. The following personal challenges increased your Buddhist faith:

	Strongly agree	Agree	Somewhat agree	Disagree	Strongly disagree
Emotional challenges	◯	◯	◯	◯	◯
Life crises (death of loved one)	◯	◯	◯	◯	◯
Loneliness	◯	◯	◯	◯	◯
Migration from Sri Lanka	◯	◯	◯	◯	◯
Parenthood	◯	◯	◯	◯	◯
Personal trouble	◯	◯	◯	◯	◯

Other (please specify)

[   ]

25. How important are the following Buddhist activities to you?

	Extremely important	Important	Somewhat important	Not important	Not important at all
To accumulate good karmas for life after death	◯	◯	◯	◯	◯
To purify my mind for enlightenment	◯	◯	◯	◯	◯
To give material supports to Buddhism	◯	◯	◯	◯	◯
To support the needy and poor	◯	◯	◯	◯	◯
To defend Buddhism against non-Buddhist influences	◯	◯	◯	◯	◯
To model good virtues	◯	◯	◯	◯	◯
Other	◯	◯	◯	◯	◯

Other (please specify)

[   ]

26. Have you been in contact with any of the forms of Buddhism listed below? If so, please share how it happened.

	Through books and internet	Education setting	Friendship	Relationship	Dhamma school	Visits to temples	Meeting with Buddhist teachers	Public media
East Asian Buddhist traditions	☐	☐	☐	☐	☐	☐	☐	☐
Tibetan Buddhism	☐	☐	☐	☐	☐	☐	☐	☐
Zen Buddhism	☐	☐	☐	☐	☐	☐	☐	☐
Non-Sinhalese Theravada Buddhism	☐	☐	☐	☐	☐	☐	☐	☐
Non-sectarian Buddhism	☐	☐	☐	☐	☐	☐	☐	☐
Other	☐	☐	☐	☐	☐	☐	☐	☐

Other (please specify)

[   ]

27. Contact with other forms of Buddhism has:

	Yes	No	Not sure
Increased my belief in my inherited Buddhism	◯	◯	◯
Expanded my knowledge of Buddhism	◯	◯	◯
Not make any change	◯	◯	◯
Inspired me to know more about my inherited Buddhism	◯	◯	◯
Made me critical of my inherited Buddhism	◯	◯	◯

28. Please rate how important the following material sources of Buddhist knowledge and inspiration are to you:

	Very important	somewhat important	not important	N/A
Published materials on Buddhism in Sinhala	◯	◯	◯	◯
Published materials on Buddhism in English	◯	◯	◯	◯
Published materials on Buddhism in other languages	◯	◯	◯	◯
Multimedia (TV, films etc.)	◯	◯	◯	◯
Internet	◯	◯	◯	◯
Courses on Buddhism (school, college, university)	◯	◯	◯	◯
Other	◯	◯	◯	◯

Other (please specify)

29. How influential are the following people in terms of understanding and living a Buddhist way of life?

	Extremely influential	Influential	Somewhat influential	Not influential	Not Influential all all	N/A
Parents	◯	◯	◯	◯	◯	◯
Grandparents	◯	◯	◯	◯	◯	◯
Monks/nuns	◯	◯	◯	◯	◯	◯
School teacher	◯	◯	◯	◯	◯	◯
Dhamma teacher	◯	◯	◯	◯	◯	◯
Relatives	◯	◯	◯	◯	◯	◯
Friends	◯	◯	◯	◯	◯	◯
Other	◯	◯	◯	◯	◯	◯

Other (please specify)

30. Do you go or have you been to Dhamma School?

◯ Yes, I have been or go to Dhamma School in Toronto   ◯ Yes, I have been to Dhamma School in Sri Lanka   ◯ I have never been to Dhamma School

31. Did or does Dhamma School meet your expectations in terms of the following:

	yes	somewhat	no
My moral and spiritual development	◯	◯	◯
Become a better citizen	◯	◯	◯
Strengthening Buddhist identity	◯	◯	◯
Philosophical understanding	◯	◯	◯
Insight into religious truths	◯	◯	◯
Friendship with other Buddhists	◯	◯	◯
Other	◯	◯	◯

Other (please specify)

32. Please explain to what extent Dhamma School has influenced you in your:

	Greatly influenced	influenced	Somewhat influenced	Not influenced	Not influenced at all
Moral behaviour	◯	◯	◯	◯	◯
Buddhist knowledge	◯	◯	◯	◯	◯
Buddhist identity	◯	◯	◯	◯	◯
Better citizen	◯	◯	◯	◯	◯
Sense of self	◯	◯	◯	◯	◯
Other	◯	◯	◯	◯	◯

Other (please specify)

33. What do you . think is missing in Dhamma education?

One

Two

Three

34. Which are you?

◯ Born in Canada or the USA   ◯ Migrated to Canada or the USA before age of 13

35. Is it important for you to have friends who are:

	Extremely important	Important	Somewhat important	Not important	Not important at all
Buddhist	◯	◯	◯	◯	◯
Sinhalese	◯	◯	◯	◯	◯
South Asian	◯	◯	◯	◯	◯

36. Please explain whether the issues mentioned below are challenging.

	Extremely challenging	Challenging	Somewhat challenging	Not challenging	Not challenging at all
To have friends who share your ethnic and religious backgrounds	◯	◯	◯	◯	◯
To practice and uphold Buddhist values	◯	◯	◯	◯	◯
To relate to my parents' cultural values and practices	◯	◯	◯	◯	◯
To get accurate Buddhist knowledge and interpretation	◯	◯	◯	◯	◯
Other	◯	◯	◯	◯	◯

Other (please specify)

[   ]

37. Relative to your parents' Buddhism, you do:

	Strongly agree	Agree	Somewhat agree	Disagree	Strongly disagree	Not sure
Place greater emphasis on meditation	◯	◯	◯	◯	◯	◯
Engage in other forms of Buddhism	◯	◯	◯	◯	◯	◯
Tend to separate Buddhism from culture	◯	◯	◯	◯	◯	◯
Emphasize meanings over beliefs and practices	◯	◯	◯	◯	◯	◯
Prefer individualistic practices instead of communal ones	◯	◯	◯	◯	◯	◯
Think Buddhism governs your parents' lives more than yours	◯	◯	◯	◯	◯	◯
Have more egalitarian (gender, spiritual, age) values than them	◯	◯	◯	◯	◯	◯
Consider yourself more Buddhist than your parents	◯	◯	◯	◯	◯	◯
Emphasize Buddhist identity over Sinhalese ethnic identity	◯	◯	◯	◯	◯	◯
More interested in Buddhist philosophy	◯	◯	◯	◯	◯	◯
Tend to be less concerned with required Buddhist practices	◯	◯	◯	◯	◯	◯
Place more emphasis on ritual	◯	◯	◯	◯	◯	◯

38. To what extent do you and your parents agree on the following issues?

	Strongly agree	Agree	Somewhat agree	Disagree	Strongly disagree	Not sure/no opinion
Personal freedom and independence	○	○	○	○	○	○
Social equality	○	○	○	○	○	○
Gender equality	○	○	○	○	○	○
Concern for material well-being	○	○	○	○	○	○
Interest in learning	○	○	○	○	○	○
Relationship with friends and dating	○	○	○	○	○	○
Interest in other religions and cultures	○	○	○	○	○	○
Emphasis on tradition	○	○	○	○	○	○
Compassion or concerns for others	○	○	○	○	○	○
Other	○	○	○	○	○	○

Other (please specify)

39. What do you think about the following Buddhist beliefs and practices in relation to religious life in North America?

	Highly relevant	Relevant	Needs modification to make relevant	Irrelevant	N/A
Marriage rituals	○	○	○	○	○
Caring for the monks' material needs	○	○	○	○	○
Belief in heaven and hell	○	○	○	○	○
Belief in Karma	○	○	○	○	○
Living according to the 5 precepts	○	○	○	○	○
Pali chanting	○	○	○	○	○
Sitting on the floor	○	○	○	○	○
Meditation	○	○	○	○	○
Education about other Buddhist traditions	○	○	○	○	○
Chairs or pews for the temple service	○	○	○	○	○
Other	○	○	○	○	○

Other (please specify)

40. What do you think about the following roles and organizations within the North American context?

	Highly relevant	Relevant	Somewhat relevant	Irrelevant	N/A
Hierarchically defined lay and monastic roles	○	○	○	○	○
Lay preachers	○	○	○	○	○
Order of nuns (Bhikkhuni)	○	○	○	○	○
Temporary ordination for a few days/weeks to develop Buddhist knowledge and understaning	○	○	○	○	○
Multi-ethnic Buddhist organization	○	○	○	○	○
Other	○	○	○	○	○

Other (please specify)

41. How important for you is it to marry a:

	Very important	Somewhat important	Not important
Buddhist	○	○	○
Sri Lankan	○	○	○
Theravada Buddhist	○	○	○

42. Please respond to the following statements:

	Strongly agree	Agree	Disagree	Strongly disagree
Parents should not impose but educate the youth	○	○	○	○
Parents should not intervene in youth religiosity	○	○	○	○
Youth can selectively follow all Buddhist traditions	○	○	○	○
Youth may follow any religion they want	○	○	○	○
Youth should follow parents' religion as it is	○	○	○	○

Thank you very much for your kind consideration and participation in this research!

Notes

1 I use the terms "diaspora" and "resettlement" in this study to refer to those who have migrated to North America since the mid-1960s. These terms preceded by "the" refer to Sri Lankan Buddhists in Toronto; otherwise they refer to wider immigrant and refugee communities to highlight the broader implications of this study.

2 "Dhamma education" (*Daham Adhyapanaya* in Sinhala) in Sri Lankan Buddhism refers to formal Buddhist religious education designed for children and youths. From the late nineteenth century, dhamma education developed in two streams: Buddhist education in public schools and the weekly Sunday dhamma schools at local Buddhist temples. With occasional reference to the former, this study concentrates on the latter.

3 Every other temple service – such as protective Pāli chanting, full-moon day precept observation, or weekly sutra studies – scored lower than dhamma education.

4 In relation to the second generation, the 1.5 generation speaks and understands the Sinhala language with less difficulty. They are more appreciative of Sinhala culture, and they expressed that they would like to go back to Sri Lanka to contribute to the country where they were born. Although a bicultural and bilingual identity characterizes the 1.5 generation, there is no consensus about the time of immigration. For example, Won Moo Hurh (1993, 50) defines 1.5 generation as those who came to the USA between the ages of eleven and sixteen. However, Khyati Y. Joshi (2006, 7) uses the term 1.5 generation to refer to those who migrated to the USA after age five but prior to age twelve. Bilingualism (ability to speak and understand both ethnic and dominant languages) and biculturalism

(familiarity with both ethnic and ambient dominant cultures) or lack of them are not determined by the time of initial arrival in the country of current residence; instead, they depend rather on frequent or infrequent visits to ancestral lands (Joshi 2006, 7). I would add that bilingualism and biculturalism also derive from the other factors such as the size of the ethnic community and the efficacy of formal and informal intercultural transmission strategies put in place within each community.

5 For example, only eight of 116 youths who contributed to the survey belong to 1.5 generation. More about my research methodology will be discussed later in the chapter.

6 See the conclusion of this book for more on the ongoing debate on "Canadian Buddhism."

7 The research focus, data collection, and data analysis of this study strongly resonate with the research methodological tradition of ethnography (Creswell 1998, 65). However, they also bear some characteristics of two other research methodological traditions – namely phenomenology, and the case study (Creswell 1998, 65). For example, this study describes, analyzes, and explains the experience of being Buddhist (phenomenology) of a cultural group (ethnography) through an in-depth examination of dhamma schools and education (a case study).

8 In almost all cases, parents wanted me to talk about the importance of the parent-child relationship, respect for parents and grandparents, the association of good friends, and importance of the excellence in education. In fact, I have noticed that these same issues are the recurring themes of English dhamma talks in the community.

9 Susantha Goonatilake (2001) criticizes Sri Lanka based anthropological studies conducted by the following anthropologists: Richard Gombrich (Oxford), Gananath Obeyesekere (Princeton), Bruce Kapferer (London), and S.J. Tambiah (Harvard).

10 In fact, initially I thought that I would research the interreligious identity of children who grow up with interreligious socialization. Later on, I realized that such project would be unfeasible for research in robes due to the lack of cooperation from the community. Consequently, I switched to the dhamma education and the transmission of the tradition.

11 An analogy related to lay-monk relation in Buddhism. Dhammaapada Verse #49.

CHAPTER TWO

1 For a robust discussion on the politics of Tamil organizations in Toronto, refer to the second chapter of *Pain, Prode and Politics* (Amarsingam 2015).

2 Ven. Piyadassi Thera, as also known as the travelling missionary monk, belonged to the Bambalapitiya Vajirarama Monastic tradition in Sri Lanka that had strong links with Vietnamese Theravāda Buddhists in 1960s.

3 Please see Coleman (2001) and McLellan (1999) for the socio-economic conditions of Buddhists with Caucasian and Asian origins respectively.

4 However, in the late 1980s the Toronto Mahavihara received a small grant (approximately CAD $700.00) from the Buddhist Affairs Department of Sri Lankan Ministry of Culture (*Toronto Buddhist*, November 1987, 5). In 2010, the Toronto Mahavihara and the Brampton Buddhist Mission Centre received $43,000 and $8,000 respectively to strengthen the temple security systems after arson attacks (Milley 2010).

5 In 1980, a pamphlet entitled "Mahavihara School of Buddhist Studies" announced twelve courses with seven staff members who were monks and lay people of Sinhalese and Caucasian origin.

6 An account of authors' transcribed interviews conducted during 1984–85 with a few early Buddhist leaders in Toronto, including Bhante Punnaji.

7 In Sri Lanka, temple property is considered as an inherited property in the teacher-disciple generational lines (*guru-sishya sampradaya* or *parampara*). The first disciple often inherits it. If there are no students, the related monastic fraternity (nikāya) claims the property.

8 It is indeed a sacred practice conducted within clearly marked boundaries (*sima*) where only Buddhist monastic Sangha participate.

9 Unlike Sri Lankan Buddhists, Bangladeshi, Indian, and Caucasian Buddhist practitioners invite monks to bless bride and groom at wedding ceremony itself. In such cases, monks invoke blessings for the couple but never sign the marriage certificate. None of the monks hold legal authority to do so.

10 In the language of the market (Finke and Smith 2001), clients, suppliers, and products are multiplied; however, the niche has remained more or less the same. In such scenarios, market monopoly is undermined and clients share multiple options. This prompts a sense of competition, creativity, and commitment from the suppliers' side to better serve the consumers.

CHAPTER THREE

1 He served as the chairperson of the Dhamma School Examination
  Syndicate in the late 1950s. His influence on the Sinhala Buddhist discourse in *Daham Pasela* is discussed later in this chapter.

2 This discourse is also referred to as Sn 1.8 (Pāli Text Society).

3 By the early twentieth century, Olcott's *Buddhist Catechism* had enjoyed
  its fortieth edition and been printed in many languages. The *Bauddha
  Adahilla*, on the other hand, received only a second edition, and was
  printed only in Sinhala.

4 In Sri Lanka, like India, Christian missionaries are accused of luring the
  poor, needy, and destitute with material and worldly gains for proselytizing Christianity. Lately certain Islamic organizations are also accused of
  doing the same. Such non-Buddhist proselytizing missions are dubbed
  "unethical conversions" in Sri Lanka and have been used to justify monks
  becoming members of the parliament in order to pass legislations that
  would make "unethical conversion" illegal.

5 Olcott refers to the *Mahavamsa*'s report of the King Vijaya's arrival in the
  island as an evidence of historical presence of the Buddha. *Mahavamsa*
  says King Vijaya arrived in the island on the day of the Buddha's
  parinibbāna.

6 The Sinhalese term "Jatiya" means both "ethnicity" and "nationality."

7 It says in Sinhala: "*Budu Sasuna Bebalewa, Sinhala Jatiya Diyunu veva*"
  (May Buddhism shine, and may the Sinhala race/ethnicity progress).

8 In July 1959, the commission suggested a series of recommendations
  under nine themes including Buddhist education for monks and laity.

9 2 Dhamma schools should be established in the areas where they
    don't exist (21 June 1958).
  3 Dhamma schools should be made a government organization with a
    motion at the Parliament (21 June 1958).
  4 The issues for the consideration of curriculum committee (5 July 1958).
  5 The establishment of dhamma schools in the areas where they don't
    exist (12 July 1958).
  6 Dhamma knowledge and the ethical development (19 July 1958).

10 Some of the books used prior to dhamma school textbooks are
  *Dhammapada, Loweda Sangarava, Jataka Sangrahaya,
  Saddharmachandrika*, and *Budugunalankaraya*.

11 Here I refer to "*Bauddha Sanskrutiya*," which simply means "Buddhist
  Culture." It is one of the four textbooks recommended for the final examination of Dhamma School.

12 In March 2010, I witnessed a rare but intact *Bodhipuja* led by a recently arrived monk.

13 The verses are translated as follows in an assigned textbook:
"You brought me up with loving care
Introducing me to important people everywhere
You have wonderful qualities, which are so rare
To me, you have always been very fair
So my dear father, I kiss your feet and say:
'To displease you, I'll never dare.'"

"For ten long months you bore me
Risking your own life;
Fed me, nursed me, showering with love
Throughout day and night.
You were always behind me,
Never letting me out of your sight.
You taught me more than anyone else
What really is proper and right.
So my dear mother,
Lovingly kissing your feet, I say:
'As before, please show me the way.'"
(Nanayakkara [Step two] 1993, 52–3).

14 This relates to ethno-religious nationalism as opposed to civic nationalism.

15 In this influential manual, Buddhism is defined as a science and a philosophy. This definition underscores a detached, objective, and intellectual mastery of Buddhism, rather than any subjective, ritualized, or emotional commitment to Buddhism. A cognitive mode of Buddhist religiosity has been prioritized to the extent that the emotional understanding or affective approach to Buddhism is glossed over. Gombrich and Obeyesekere (1988) observe that "to be on the path to *nirvana* is no longer to be prey to any human emotion" (Gombrich and Obeyesekere 1988, 251).

16 Except in a few instances, students are not credited for the practices of dhamma. In fact, it is a pedagogical concern how to evaluate and credit the subjective learning of Buddhism in a formal Buddhist education. If the character formation is the main claim of dhamma education, educators need to prioritize the practical side of Buddhism.

17 Although factual knowledge (expressed in who, what, when, where, and which questions) dominates dhamma education, integrative knowledge (expressed in the "how" question) of the Buddhist tradition appears in higher classes. For example, the *Daham Pasela* requires grade ten pupils in

Sri Lanka to engage with the teachings and to integrate Buddhist principles in their lives. Subsequently, the 2007 Young Members Buddhist
Association examination for dhamma school students in Sri Lanka asks
students to identify leadership qualities in the Buddha's biography that
they can emulate in their own lives (YMBA examination 2007).

CHAPTER FOUR

1 In the Sri Lankan monastic tradition, monks' personal names are preceded
   by the names of their birthplaces and followed by honourary monastic
   titles like himi, nahimi, sthavira, etc. Well-known monks are often referred
   to with their birthplaces followed by their monastic titles, and their personal names are omitted. As such, Palene Sri Vajiragnana Nahimi is often
   known as Palene Nahimi.
2 Interestingly the Pāli term *bāla* (immature) is used to refer to children as
   well as to those spiritually less developed.
3 The relationship between Buddhism and Western psychology was first
   established by Carl Jung (Meckel and Moor 1992) and by Walpula Rahula
   (1956).
4 Notice the word Brahma echoes the creator God in the Hindu tradition.
5 It is also noteworthy that in the circles of converted Buddhists in the West,
   the term Sangha is widely used to refer to Buddhists in general.
6 The Five Precepts definition invokes the religious-secular ethical difference. Secular ethics prioritizes a this-worldly orientation. Its rationality
   is based on ordinary, commonsensical, and verifiable principles. What is
   verifiable by human faculties constitutes the parameters of secular ethics.
   In contrast, religious ethics are not confined to verifiable parameters, and
   transcend this-worldly reasoning. More importantly, the otherworldly
   rationality of religious ethics distinguishes it from its secular
   counterpart.
7 This particular reference is also cited as AN X. 206 (Pāli Text Society).
8 This Pāli discourse is referred as to DN 16 (Pāli Text Society).
9 This Pāli discourse is referred to as MN 18 (Pāli Text Society).
10 The other two are universal health care and the international peacekeep-
   ing mission.
11 Dr Charles Hobart, an American sociologist from the University of
   California, who later taught at the University of Alberta, used the word
   "multiculturalism" in his address to the Canadian Council of Christians
   and Jews in Winnipeg in 1963 (Stevenson 2014, 215–16).

12 Elke Winter (2014) suggests that in the 2000s "there is a new-found consensus among politicians and media representatives in favour of a 'thick'
republican notion of citizenship, which includes Aboriginal people, English
Canadians, and French Canadians unconditionally, admitting newcomers
and second- or third-generation immigrants only on the condition that
they at least partially give up their heritage cultures and assimilate to 'our'
values and ways of life" (69).

13 The first two stages are also known as "symbolic multiculturalism" and
"structural multiculturalism" (Winter 2014, 54).

14 For a detailed account please see "Education about religion in Ontario
Public Elementary Schools" (Choquette, Vachon, and Wideman). It is
available at the official website of the Ontario Ministry of Education at
http://www.edu.gov.on.ca/eng/document/curricul/religion/religioe.html.
Accessed 10 May 2010.

15 David Seljak (2005, 185) reports that there are thirty-two Jewish day
schools, thirty-one Muslim schools, and also some Sikh schools in the
province of Ontario. Certain Jewish and Muslim groups with independent
religious schools argue that their charter rights are undermined by the fact
that their community schools receive no public funds, while Catholic
schools do. For this reason, they have taken legal actions against the
Ontario's provincial government, but they have been less successful in
their demand for equal right in education (Zine 2008, 38).

16 The Shambhala School in Halifax, Nova Scotia, is the only day school in
Canada established by a Buddhist community (in 1993). It denies an
exclusive connection to Buddhism; rather it identifies as "a non-religious
school that believes all students possess natural intelligence and curiosity
as well as a desire to belong to a harmonious community" (Shambhala
School) available at http://www.shambhalaschool.org/about.html.
Accessed 1 May 2010.

17 Paul Numrich (2009) identifies the same three reasons for the absence of
parochial schools among Japanese-American Buddhists, the earliest established Buddhist community in North America (198–9).

18 Sugunasiri (2001, 160) notes: "Spirituality is ... not the same as religion.
They [religion and spirituality] may overlap, but [the latter] includes spiritual orientations not traditionally included, such as Secular Humanism. I
now define spirituality as a genetic potential for discriminating between
skilled and unskilled states of mind and behaviour, in relation to oneself
and others."

19 This Pāli discourse is referred to as MN 18 (Pāli Text Society).

CHAPTER FIVE

1 The Sigāla Sutta (DN 31) dominates the list of laity-oriented Pāli canonical discourses labelled as "*gihivinaya*" in Sri Lankan Buddhism. Formal and informal Buddhist education – i.e., sermons, wall paintings, and vernacular literary works – are abstracted from the *Gihivinaya* to illustrate Buddhist perspectives on individual and communal responsibilities, interpersonal relationships, wealth creation and management, etc. Such ubiquitous Buddhist practices are often marginalized and overshadowed by the sheer number of canonical discourses on celibacy and the renunciation of monastic Buddhism, resulting in misconceptions of Buddhism: "The historical Buddha asked of his adherents something quite radical ... abandon your station, your duty, your relationships" (Scheible 2013, 429).

2 One particular verse in the Dhammapada (Dhp. 24 [Pāli Text Society]) is repeatedly mentioned. It says to succeed in life one has to be diligent, mindful, well disciplined, considerate of oneself and others, spiritual/ religious, and perseverant.

3 As the name Theravāda (the way of senior monks) suggests, monastic presence is very important in establishing the Buddhist tradition.

4 The tensions between the first and second generations are often interpreted as the influence of the dominant culture of each generation.

5 Steven Collins also argues that Pāli is the one and only true pan-Theravāda identity shared by all Theravāda Buddhists across different cultures (2014, Keynote Speech at the Theravāda Civilization Project, Asian Studies Association, Philadelphia).

6 Sri Lankan Buddhist parents in Toronto do want to pass their Sinhalese ethnic culture to their Canadian-born children. That desire, however, is tempered by pragmatism and overshadowed by the overtly expressed desire of passing on Buddhism. For example, English rather than Sinhala has become the language of instruction in dhamma education.

7 Asanga Thilakeratne (2006) interprets monks' involvement in the Sinhalese-Tamil problem as a calling to the social and national obligation.

8 The value of adopting a friendship model of interaction to teach Buddhist values to children is also acknowledged among non-Asian Buddhist circles in North America. In the 2008 fall issue of *Tricyle*, Mary Talbot writes: "If we can position ourselves to be those friends to children – our own or other people's – we are providing a great service ... we live in the first-ever historical period when children look more to their peers and the media for

their social cues than to their elders. If we don't want Hannah Montana and Iron Man serving as our kids' only role models, we need to earn and maintain their respect" (in Scheible 2013, 441).

CHAPTER SIX

1 This could be 80 per cent, if we also include the fourth female participant who is adamant about passing her inherited Buddhist tradition to her prospective children (Martel-Reny and Beyer 2013, 226).
2 In relation to the religious socialization of young Buddhist men, who did worse than their female counterparts, Beyer notes "these [Buddhist] parents either did not engage in expressly teaching their children Buddhism or did not to any great extent insist that their children follow them on their religious path" (Beyer 2013, 200).
3 I develop these terms from Samuel H. Reimer's (2006, 56) terms "social convention" and "personal conviction" respectively.
4 Gary Storhoff and John Whalen-Bridge (2010) entitled their edited book *American Buddhism as a Way of Life.*
5 In order to combat the nineteenth-century Christian missionary propaganda that Buddhism was an outdated religion, Olcott argued that Buddhism accords with science. As Olcott succeeded in his effort, he also juxtaposed and rejected any premodern religious expression of the Buddhist tradition. What Olcott had rejected was later reintroduced to the tradition by the neo-traditional Buddhists during the mid-1950s in postcolonial Sri Lanka (Bond 2004). This Buddhist scientific rhetoric has persisted in Sri Lankan Buddhism with traditional Buddhist beliefs and practices, making the Buddhist tradition a paradox: a philosophy (science) with religious beliefs and practices, i.e., beliefs in life after death and karmas.

CHAPTER SEVEN

1 A few parents compared their children to absorbent sponges that suck in any liquids (harmful and harmless) around them. They, as parents, try to distance their children from bad companions while exposing them to a "healthy environment"; the latter refers to accompanying their children to temples and religious services in the community as well as inviting monks and performing Buddhist rituals at home. Referring to nurturing her teenage children, another mother states, "we try our best. Not too tight not too loose. It is like tenderly holding a wet, slippery soap bar. If you hold it too tight, it slips away. If you hold it too loose, it does not get lifted."

2 Vajranana Buddhists' self-reference of "Tibetan Buddhism/Buddhists" is a special case due to its socio-political and cultural connotations. I wonder how often Buddhists in Tibet use (or are allowed to use) such nationally/ethnically defined self-reference.

3 The original use of this term means selectively localizing what had been globalized earlier (Robertson 2005). It refers to the similar argument that the constituting components of modernity – originating in Europe and then later globally dispersed – have been selectively and strategically adopted by Indigenous actors in other regions to serve their diverse agendas (Chakrabarty 2000; McMahan 2008). However, I am using Robinson's term "glocalization" to highlight the interpenetrating nature of local and global boundaries. Perhaps it would be better termed "inter-glocalization."

4 Deegalle (2008, 25) notes, "When a Sri Lankan wants to make a puja (offering) for a deity, an altar is set up with paintings of the deity, ritual implements, lamps, flowers and incense. After the puja is performed, paintings and other objects are stored in a safe place to be used in the next occasion."

5 "With regard to the worship of deities by Buddhists, one can see occasional conflicts between the first and second generation of Sri Lankans. While the elder generation born in Sri Lanka fail to distinguish the deity worship from the Buddhist worship, the younger generations who are growing up in Britain and often read English materials for learning Buddhism are not willing to follow the same beliefs and practices of the parents. In one case, a Sri Lankan teenage girl born and bred in the UK was arguing with her mother insisting that her mother was mixing Hinduism and Buddhism. The mother was tying to make her own point that it was the tradition of Sri Lankan Buddhism" (Deegalle 2008, 26).

References

Abeysekara, Ananda. 2002. *Colors of the Robe: Religion, Identity, and Difference*. Studies in Comparative Religion. South Carolina: University of South Carolina Press.

Abrahams, Caryl, and Lisa Steve. 1990. "Self-Perceived Success of Adjustment by Sri Lankan Immigrants in Metropolitan Toronto: A Preliminary Report." Polyphony: Bulletin of the Multicultural History Society of Ontario 12.

Abu-Laban, Yasmeen. 2014. "Reform by Stealth: The Harper Conservatives and Canadian Multiculturalism." In *The Multiculturalism Question: Debating Identity in 21st Century Canada*, edited by Jack Jedwab, 149–72. Montreal and Kingston: McGill-Queen's University Press.

Amarasingam, Amarnath. 2015. *Pain, Pride, and Politics: Social Movement Activism and the Sri Lankan Tamil Diaspora in Canada*. Athens, GA: University of Georgia Press.

Anderson, Benedict. 1983. *Imagined Communities: Reflections on the Origin and Spread of Nationalism*. London and New York: Verso.

Anderson, Carol S. 2003. "'For Those Who Are Ignorant' A Study of the Bauddha Adahilla." In *Constituting Communities Theravāda Buddhism and the Religious Cultures of South and Southeast Asia*, edited by John Holt, Jacob N. Kinnard, and Jonathan S. Walters, 171–88. SUNY Series in Buddhist Studies. Albany: State University of New York Press.

Anonymous. n.d. "Buddhist Mahavihara, Malaysia." Buddhistmahavihara. com. Accessed 24 May 2009. http://www.buddhistmahavihara.com/.

– n.d. *Daham Pasal Kalamanakaranaya*. Colombo.

– n.d. "Shambhala Buddhism." Shambhalaschool.org. Accessed 1 May 2010. http://www.shambhalaschool.org/about.html.

– n.d. *Toronto Buddhist: A Canadian Buddhist Journal*. Scarborough: Toronto Mahavihara Society.

– 2004. *Temporary (Two Weeks) Ordination, a Timely Concept: To Understand and Realize a Great Philosophy*. Dehiwela: Buddhist Cultural Centre.

– 2005. "Citizenship and Immigration Statistics." Library and Archives Canada, Electronic Collection, lac-bac.gc.ca., Citizenship and Immigration Canada, Minister of Public Works and Government Services, Canada. Accessed 20 June 2008. http://epe.lac-bac. gc.ca/100/202/301/immigration_statistics-ef/index.html.

– 2008. "Living Buddhism: A Canadian Buddhist Journal" 1 (May).

Asad, Talal. 1986. *The Idea of an Anthropology of Islam*. Washington, DC: Georgetown University.

– 1993a. *Genealogies of Religion: Discipline and Reasons of Power in Christianity and Islam*. Baltimore: Johns Hopkins University Press.

– 2003. *Formations of the Secular: Christianity, Islam, Modernity*. Stanford, CA: Stanford University Press.

Assaji, Ganthune. 1993a. *Daham Pasela Grade 9*. Colombo: The Department of Buddhist Affairs.

– 1993b. *Daham Pasela Grade 10*. Colombo: The Department of Buddhist Affairs.

Athukorala, Daya Rohana. 1986. *Daham Pasalin Sadachara Samajayak*. Colombo: The Department of Buddhist Affairs.

Attygalle, Randima. 2009. "Where East Brings Solace to the West." *Nation Eye*, 8 February 2009.

Bankston, Carl L., and Danielle Antoinette Hidalgo. 2008. "Temple and Society in the New World: Theravada Buddhism and Social Order in North America." In *North American Buddhists in Social Context*, edited by Paul David Numrich, 51. Leiden and Boston: Brill.

Bartholomeusz, Tessa J. 1994. *Women under the Bō Tree: Buddhist Nuns in Sri Lanka*. Cambridge Studies in Religious Traditions 5. Cambridge and New York: Cambridge University Press.

Bechert, Heinz. 1978. "Contradictions in Sinhalese Buddhism." In *Religion and Legitimation of Power in Sri Lanka*, edited by Bardwell L. Smith, 188–98. Chambersburg, PA: ANIMA Books.

Berkwitz, Stephen C. 2004. *Buddhist History in the Vernacular: The Power of the Past in Late Medieval Sri Lanka*. Brill's Indological Library, v. 23. Leiden and Boston: Brill.

Berry, John W. 2014. "Multiculturalism: Psychological Perspective." In *The Multiculturalism Question: Debating Identity in 21st Century Canada*, edited by Jack Jedwab, 225–40. Montreal and Kingston: McGill-Queen's University Press.

Beyer, Peter. 2006. "Buddhism in Canada: A Statistical Overview from Canadian Censuses, 1981–2001." *Canadian Journal of Buddhist Studies* 2: 83–102.

– 2013a. "Growing Up Canadian: Systemic and Lived Religion." In *Growing up Canadian: Muslims, Hindus, Buddhists*, edited by Peter Beyer and Rubina Ramji, 3–20. Montreal and Kingston: McGill-Queen's University Press.

– 2013b. "Maybe, in the Future: Buddhist Men." In *Growing up Canadian: Muslims, Hindus, Buddhists*, edited by Peter Beyer and Rubina Ramji, 192–212. Montreal and Kingston: McGill-Queen's University Press.

Beyer, Peter, and Marie-Paule Martel-Reny. 2013. "Fluid Boundaries of a Tolerant Religion: Buddhist Women." In *Growing up Canadian: Muslims, Hindus, Buddhists*, edited by Peter Beyer and Rubina Ramji, 213–34. Montreal and Kingston: McGill-Queen's University Press.

Biles, John, Humera Ibrahim, Paul Bramadat, and David Seljak. 2005. "Religion and Public Policy: Immigration, Citizenship, and Multiculturalism – Guess Who's Coming to Dinner?" In *Religion and Ethnicity in Canada*, 154–77. Toronto: Pearson Education Canada Inc.

Blackburn, Anne M. 2001. *Buddhist Learning and Textual Practice in Eighteenth-Century Lankan Monastic Culture*. Princeton, NJ: Princeton University Press.

– 2003. "Localizing Lineage: Importing Higher Ordination in Theravadin South and Southeast Asia." In *Constituting Communities Theravāda Buddhism and the Religious Cultures of South and Southeast Asia*, edited by John Holt, Jacob N. Kinnard, and Jonathan S. Walters, 131–49. SUNY Series in Buddhist Studies. Albany: State University of New York Press.

Bodhi, Bhikkhu, and Nyanaponika Thera, eds. 1999. *Numerical Discourses of the Buddha: Aṅguttara Nikāya: An Anthology of Suttas from the Aṅguttara Nikāya*. Walnut Creek, CA: AltaMira Press.

Boisvert, Mathieu. 2005. "Buddhists in Canada: Identity and Commitment." In *Religion and Ethnicity in Canada*, edited by Paul Bramadat and David Seljak, 69–88. Toronto: Pearson Education Canada Inc.

Bond, George Doherty. 1988. *The Buddhist Revival in Sri Lanka: Religious Tradition, Reinterpretation, and Response*. Columbia, SC: University of South Carolina Press.

– 2004. "Two Reconstructions of Buddhism in Sri Lanka." In *The Comity and Grace of Method: Essays in Honor of Edmund F. Perry*, edited by Thomas Ryba, George Doherty Bond, and Herman Wayne Tull, 235–62. Evanston, IL: Northwestern University Press.

Borchert, Thomas A. 2017. *Educating Monks: Minority Buddhism on China's Southwest Border*. Honolulu: University of Hawai'i Press.

Bowlby, Paul. 2014. "Canadian Social Imaginaries: Re-Examining Religion and Secularization." In *Religion in the Public Sphere: Canadian Case Studies*, edited by Solange Lefebvre and Lori G. Beaman, 25–43. Toronto: University of Toronto Press.

Bramadat, Paul. 2005. "Beyond Christian Canada: Religion and Ethnicity in a Multicultural Society." In *Religion and Ethnicity in Canada*, edited by Paul Bramadat and David Seljak, 1–29. Toronto: Pearson Education Canada Inc.

Brown, Karen McCarthy. 2001. *Mama Lola: A Vodou Priestess in Brooklyn*. Berkeley: University of California Press.

Cadge, Wendy. 2005. *Heartwood: The First Generation of Theravada Buddhism in America*. Chicago: University of Chicago Press.

Campbell, Patricia Q. 2010. "Transforming Ordinary Life: Turning to Zen Buddhism in Toronto." In *Wild Geese: Buddhism in Canada*, edited by Alexander Duncan Soucy, Victor Sōgen Hori, and John S. Harding, 187–209. Toronto and Ithaca: McGill-Queen's University Press.

Carrière, Kathryn. 2013. "Growing Up in Toronto: Muslims, Hindus, Buddhists." In *Growing up Canadian: Muslims, Hindus, Buddhists*, edited by Peter Beyer and Rubina Ramji, 262–89. Montreal and Kingston: McGill-Queen's University Press.

Casanova, José. 1994. *Public Religions in the Modern World*. Chicago: University of Chicago Press.

Chakrabarty, Dipesh. 2000. *Provincializing Europe: Postcolonial Thought and Historical Difference*. Princeton: Princeton University Press.

Chandler, Stuart. 2005. "Spreading Buddha's Light: The Internationalization of Foguang Shan." In *Buddhist Missionaries in the Era of Globalization*, edited by Linda Learman, 162–84. Honolulu: University of Hawai'i Press.

Chandrasekère, Sarath. 2008. "Inventing the Sri Lankans: Construction of Ethnic Identity by Immigrants to Ontario." PhD diss., University of Toronto.

Chandrasekera, Swarna. 2001. *Teaching Buddhism to Children: A Curriculum Guide to Dhamma School Teachers*. Mississauga: Halton-Peel Buddhist Society.

Chandrasekhar, Sripati, ed. 1986. *From India to Canada: A Brief History of Immigrants Problems of Discrimination, Admission, and Assimilation.* La Jolla, CA: Population Review Books.

Chau, Thich Minch (The Venerable). 1958. "How to Impart Buddhism to Children." In *Buddhist Sunday School Lessons,* edited by Sumangalo The Venerable, xi–xxii. Penang: The Penang Buddhist Association.

Choquette, Robert, Andre E. Vachon, and Ron Wideman. 2007. "Education about Religion in Ontario Public Elementary Schools." Ontario Ministry of Education. Accessed 25 May 2008. http://www.edu.gov.on.ca/eng/document/curricul/religion/religioe.html.

Coleman, James William. 2001. *The New Buddhism: The Western Transformation of an Ancient Tradition.* Oxford and New York: Oxford University Press.

Collins, Steven. 2010. *Nirvana: Concept, Imagery, Narrative.* Cambridge: Cambridge University Press.

Corea, J.C.A. 1969. "One Hundred Years of Education in Ceylon." *Modern Asian Studies* 3, no. 2: 151–75.

Crowe, Paul. 2014. "Dharma on the Move: Vancouver Buddhist Communities and Multiculturalism." In *Flowers on the Rock: Global and Local Buddhisms in Canada,* edited by Victor Sōgen Hori, John S. Harding, and Alexander Duncan Soucy, 150–72. Montreal and Kingston: McGill-Queen's University Press.

De Alwis, Malathi. 2009. "'Disappearance' and 'Displacement' in Sri Lanka." *Journal of Refugee Studies* 22, no. 3: 378–91.

De Silva, Lynn A. 1974. *Buddhism: Beliefs and Practices in Sri Lanka.* [Colombo: De Silva].

De Silva, Premakumara. 2006. "Anthropology of 'Sinhala Buddhism.'" *Contemporary Buddhism: An Interdisciplinary Journal* 7, no. 2: 165–70.

Deegalle, Mahinda. 1996. "The Moral Significance of Buddhist Nirvana." In *Pāli Buddhism,* edited by Frank J. Hoffman and Mahinda Deegalle, 105–16. Richmond: Curzon.

– 1997. "A Bibliography on Sinhala Buddhism." *Journal of Buddhist Ethics* 4: 216–56.

– 2008. *Dharma to the UK: A Centennial Celebration of Buddhist Legacy.* London: World Buddhist Foundation.

Dharmadasa, K.N.O. 1992a. "The People of the Lion: Ethnic Identity, Ideology and Historical Revisionism in Contemporary Sri Lanka." *Ethnic Studies Report* 10, no.1: 37–59.

– 1992b. "The People of the Lion: Ethnic Identity, Ideology and Historical Revisionism in Contemporary Sri Lanka." *Sri Lanka Journal of the Humanities* 15, nos 1–2: 1–35.

Dhammasami, Khammai. 2018. *Buddhism, Education and Politics in Burma and Thailand: From the Seventeenth Century to the Present.* London: Bloomsbury.

Dhammawasa, Ven. K. 2013. "Message from Most Venerable K. Dhammawasa Nayaka Thera, Abbot Incumbent, West End Buddhist Temple and Meditation Centre," 2013.

Dharmapala, Anagarika. 1965. "A Message to the Young Men of Ceylon." In *Return to Righteousness: A Collection of Speeches, Essays and Letters of the Anagarika Dharmapala*, edited by Ananda W. P. Guruge, 501–18. Colombo: Anagarika Dharmapala Birth Centenary Committee, Ministry of Education and Cultural Affairs, Ceylon.

Dip, Kamal, Ian Donaldson, and Brittany Turcotte. 2008. "Integration and Identity in Canada: The Importance of Multicultural Common Spaces." *Canadian Ethnic Studies* 40, no. 1: 161–87.

Doobinin, Peter. 2008. "Tough Lovingkindness." *Tricycle* (Fall): 74–7, 116.

Ebaugh, Helen Rose Fuchs, and Janet Saltzman Chafetz, eds. 2002. *Religion across Borders: Transnational Immigrant Networks.* Walnut Creek, CA and Lanham, MD: AltaMira Press; Rowman & Littlefield.

Evers, Hans-Dieter. 1968. "Buddha and the Seven Gods: The Dual Organization of a Temple in Central Ceylon." *Journal of Asian Studies* 27, no. 3: 541–50.

Foster, Cecil. 2014. *Genuine Multiculturalism: The Tragedy and Comedy of Diversity.* Montreal: McGill-Queen's University Press.

Gibson-Graham, J.K. 1994. "'Stuffed If I Know!': Reflections on Post-modern Feminist Social Research." *Gender, Place and Culture* 1, no. 2: 205–24.

Gombrich, Richard F. 1971. *Precept and Practice: Traditional Buddhism in the Rural Highlands of Ceylon.* Oxford: Clarendon Press.

Gombrich, Richard F., and Gananath Obeyesekere. 1988. *Buddhism Transformed: Religious Changes in Sri Lanka.* Princeton, NJ: Princeton University Press.

Goonatilake, Susantha. 2001. *Anthropologizing Sri Lanka: A Eurocentric Misadventure.* Bloomington: Indiana University Press.

Gowans, Christopher W., and Alasdair C. MacIntyre, eds. 2000. "The Rationality of Traditions." In *Moral Disagreements: Classic and Contemporary Readings*, 204–16. London and New York: Routledge.

Grant, Peter R. 2007. "Sustaining a Strong Cultural and National Identity: The Acculturation of Immigrants and Second-Generation Canadians of

Asian and African Descent." *Journal of International Migration and Integration* 8: 89–116.

Gunaratne, K.S. 1986. "Buddhist Education for Children." *Toronto Buddhist* 8, no. 1: 11–12.

Gunawardena, R. 1990. "The People of the Lion: The Sinhala Identity an Ideology in History and Historiography." In *Sri Lanka: History and the Roots of Conflict*, edited by Jonathan Spencer, 45–86. London and New York: Routledge.

Gunawardena, R.A.L.H. 1979. "The People of the Lion: The Sinhala Identity an Ideology in History and Historiography." *Sri Lanka Journal of the Humanities* 1, no. 2: 1–36.

– 1984. "The People of the Lion: Sinhala Consciousness in History and Historiography." In *Ethnicity and Social Change in Sri Lanka: Papers Presented at a Seminar Organised by the Social Scientists Association, December 1979*, edited by Social Scientists Association of Sri Lanka, 1–41. Colombo, Sri Lanka: Social Scientists' Association.

Guruge, Ananda W.P. 1965. *Return to Righteousness: A Collection of Speeches, Essays and Letters of the Anagarika Dharmapala*. Colombo: Anagarika Dharmapala Birth Centenary Committee, Ministry of Education and Cultural Affairs, Ceylon.

– 1993. *An Agenda for the International Buddhist Community*. Colombo: Karunaratne & Sons Ltd.

Hallisey, Charles. 1995. "Roads Taken and Not Taken in the Study of Theravada Buddhism." In *Curators of the Buddha: The Study of Buddhism under Colonialism*, edited by Donald S. Lopez, 31–61. Chicago: University of Chicago Press.

Hansen, Randall. 2014. "Assimilation by Stealth: Why Canada's Multicultural Policy Is Really a Repackaged Integration Policy." In *The Multiculturalism Question: Debating Identity in 21st Century Canada*, edited by Jack Jedwab, 73–88. Montreal and Kingston: McGill-Queen's University Press.

Harris, Elizabeth J. 2006. *Theravāda Buddhism and the British Encounter: Religious, Missionary and Colonial Experience in Nineteenth-Century Sri Lanka*. London and New York: Routledge.

Hemasara, Kitalagama. 1992. *Daham Pasela Grade 6*. Colombo: The Department of Buddhist Affairs.

Hershock, Peter D. 2006. *Buddhism in the Public Sphere: Reorienting Global Interdependence*. London and New York: Routledge.

Hori, Victor Sōgen. 1994. "Sweet and Sour Buddhism." *Tricycle* (Fall): 48–52.

– 2010. "How Do We Study Buddhism in Canada?" In *Wild Geese: Buddhism in Canada*, edited by Alexander Duncan Soucy, Victor Sōgen Hori, and John S. Harding, 3–10. Montreal and Kingston: McGill-Queen's University Press.

Hori, Victor Sōgen, John S. Harding, and Alexander Duncan Soucy, eds. 2014. *Flowers on the Rock: Global and Local Buddhisms in Canada*. Montreal and Kingston: McGill-Queen's University Press.

Hori, Victor Sōgen, and Janet McLellan. 2010. "Suwanda H.J. Sugunasiri: Buddhist." In *Wild Geese: Buddhism in Canada*, edited by Alexander Duncan Soucy, Victor Sōgen Hori, and John S. Harding, 377–99. Montreal and Kingston: McGill-Queen's University Press.

Hurst, Lynda. 2007. "Multiculturalism Policy Falling behind the Times." 29 May 2007. Accessed 24 May 2013. http://www.thestar.com/article/218666--multiculturalism-policy-falling-behind-the-times.

Jayasooriya, L. 2004. *How School Books Destroyed Buddha Dhamma in Sri Lanka*. Nawinna: Tharanjee Prints.

Jayaweera, Swarna. 1968. "Religious Organizations and the State in Ceylonese Education." *Comparative Education Review* 12, no. 2: 159–70.

Johns, Ernest L. 1985. "A Report on Publicly-Funded Schools in Canada: Policies and Issues." In *Religious Education Belongs in the Public Schools*, edited by Ernest L. Johns, 96–106. Toronto: The Ecumenical Study Commission on Public Education.

Josephides, Lisette. 1997. "Representing the Anthropologist's Predicament." In *After Writing Culture: Epistemology and Praxis in Contemporary Anthropology*, edited by Allison James, Jennifer Lorna Hockey, and Andrew H. Dawson, 16–33. ASA Monographs 34. London and New York: Routledge.

Karunadasa, W.M. 2004. "The Saga of the First Buddhist School." Buddhist Channel. Accessed 15 April 2009. TV. http://www.buddhist-channel.tv/print.php.

Kemper, Steven. 2005. "Dharmapala's Dharmadhuta and the Buddhist Ethnoscape." In *Buddhist Missionaries in the Era of Globalization*, edited by Linda Learman, 22–50. Honolulu: University of Hawai'i Press.

Kent, Brad. 2008. "Sean O'Faolain and Pierre Elliott Trudeau's Midcentury Critiques of Nationalism." *New Hibernia Review* 12, no. 1: 128–45.

Khantipalo, Pra. 1990. "The Limits of Theravada Buddhism." *Buddhist Studies Review* 7, nos 1–2: 25–37.

Kiblinger, Kristin Beise. 2005. *Buddhist Inclusivism: Attitudes towards Religious Others*. Aldershot, UK and Burlington, VT: Ashgate.

Knight, Margaret Lisa. 2008. *Morals in the Life Story of the Buddha*. Pennsylvania: International Buddhist Society of Pennsylvania.

Kniss, Fred Lamar. 2007. *Sacred Assemblies and Civic Engagement: How Religion Matters for America's Newest Immigrants*. New Brunswick, NJ: Rutgers University Press.

Kurien, Prema A. 2001. "Religion, Ethnicity and Politics: Hindu and Muslim Indian Immigrants in the United States." *Ethnic and Racial Studies* 24, no. 2: 263–93.

– 2007. *A Place at the Multicultural Table: The Development of an American Hinduism*. New Brunswick, NJ: Rutgers University Press.

Kymlicka, Will. 2004. "Marketing Canadian Pluralism in the International Arena" 59, no. 4: 829–52.

Landres, J. Shawn. 2002. "Being (in) the Field: Defining Ethnography in Southern California and Central Slovakia." In *Personal Knowledge and Beyond: Reshaping the Ethnography of Religion*, edited by James V. Spickard, J. Shawn Landres, and Meredith B. McGuire, 100–12. New York: New York University Press.

Leadbeater, C.W. 1902. *The Smaller Buddhist Catechism*. Translated by C. Jinarajadasa. Colombo: The Buddhist Theosophical Society.

Lefebvre, Solange, and Lori G. Beaman. 2014. "Introduction." In *Religion in the Public Sphere: Canadian Case Studies*, edited by Solange Lefebvre and Lori G. Beaman, 3–22. Toronto: University of Toronto Press.

Lopez, Donald S. 2008. *Buddhism & Science: A Guide for the Perplexed*. Chicago: University of Chicago Press.

MacIntyre, Alasdair C. 1981. *After Virtue: A Study in Moral Theory*. Notre Dame, IN: University of Notre Dame Press.

Madanayake, Bandu. 2010. "Sri Lankan and Myanmar Buddhism." In *Asian Religions in British Columbia*, edited by Daniel L. Overmyer, Don Baker, and Larry DeVries, 124–40. Vancouver: UBC Press.

Mahalekam, Seneviratne. 1991. *Bauddha Sanskrutiya*. Colombo: The Department of Buddhist Affairs.

– 1992. *Daham Pasela Grade 7*. Colombo: The Department of Buddhist Affairs.

Mahathanthrige, Gunasena. 1993. *Daham Pasela Grade 8*. Colombo: The Department of Buddhist Affairs.

Malalgoda, Kitsiri. 1976. *Buddhism in Sinhalese Society, 1750–1900: A Study of Religious Revival and Change*. Berkeley: University of California Press.

Matthews, Bruce. 1995. "University Education in Sri Lanka in Context: Consequences of Deteriorating Standards." *Pacific Affairs* 68, no. 1: 77–94.

– 2005. "Preface." In *Buddhism in Canada*, edited by Bruce Matthews, xvi–xxii. London and New York: Routledge.

McDaniel, Justin. 2008. *Gathering Leaves & Lifting Words: Histories of Buddhist Monastic Education in Laos and Thailand.* Seattle: University of Washington Press.

McLellan, Janet. 1999. *Many Petals of the Lotus: Five Asian Buddhist Communities in Toronto.* Toronto: University of Toronto Press.

– 2005. "Buddhism in the Greater Toronto Area: The Politics of Recognition." In *Buddhism in Canada*, edited by Bruce Matthews, 65–104. London and New York: Routledge.

– 2008. "Themes and Issues in the Study of North American Buddhists and Buddhism." In *North American Buddhists in Social Context*, edited by Paul David Numrich, 19–50. Leiden and Boston: Brill.

– 2009. *Cambodian Refugees in Ontario: Resettlement, Religion, and Identity.* Toronto: University of Toronto Press.

McLellan, Janet, and Marybeth White. 2005. "Social Capital and Identity Politics among Asian Buddhists in Toronto." *Journal of International Migration and Integration* 6, no. 7: 235–53.

McMahan, David L. 2008. *The Making of Buddhist Modernism.* Oxford and New York: Oxford University Press.

– ed. 2012. *Buddhism in the Modern World.* New York: Routledge.

Milley, Danielle. n.d. "Toronto Maha Vihara Society Temple Now More Secure." Accessed 28 April 2011. http://www.insidetoronto.com/print/853225.

Nanakirti Himi, Ganegama. 2008. *Bauddha Daham Pasal Adhyapanaya Ha Daham Guruwaraya.* Dehiwela: Buddhist Cultural Centre.

Ñāṇamoli, Bhikkhu, and Bhikkhu Bodhi, eds. 1995. *The Middle Length Discourses of the Buddha: A New Translation of the Majjhima Nikāya.* Kandy, Sri Lanka and Boston: Buddhist Publication Society.

Nanayakkara, Sanath. 2006. *Buddhism: A Graduated Course (Step Two).* Dehiwela: The Buddhist Culture Centre.

Narada. 1964. *The Buddha and His Teachings.* Kuala Lumpur: Buddhist Missionary Society.

– 1993. *The Dhammapada.* Taipei: The Corporate Body of the Buddha Educational Foundation.

Norman, K. R. 1978. "The Role of Pāli in Early Sinhalese Buddhism." In *Buddhism in Ceylon and Studies on Religious Syncretism in Buddhist*

Countries: Report on a Symposium in Göttingen, edited by Heinz
Bechert, 28–47. Abhandlungen Der Akademie Der Wissenschaften in
Göttingen: Philologisch-Historische Klasse; Folge 3, Nr. 108 1.
Göttingen: Vandenhoeck & Ruprecht.

Numrich, Paul David. 1996. *Old Wisdom in the New World:
Americanization in Two Immigrant Theravada Buddhist Temples.*
Knoxville: University of Tennessee Press.

– 2003. "Two Buddhisms Further Considered." *Contemporary Buddhism*
4, no. 1: 55–78.

– 2004. "Schism in the Sinhalese Buddhist Community in Los Angeles." In
*The Comity and Grace of Method: Essays in Honor of Edmund F.
Perry*, edited by Thomas Ryba, George Doherty Bond, and Herman
Wayne Tull, 304–18. Evanston, IL: Northwestern University Press.

– 2009. "Immigrant Parochial Schools: Religion, Morality and
Citizenship." In *Children and Childhood in American Religions*, edited
by Don S. Browning and Bonnie J. Miller-McLemore, 194–209. The
Rutgers Series in Childhood Studies. New Brunswick, NJ: Rutgers
University Press.

Obeyesekere, Gananath. 1963. "The Great Tradition and the Little in the
Perspective of Sinhalese Buddhism." *Journal of Asian Studies* 22:
139–53.

– 1970. "Religious Symbolism and Political Change in Ceylon." *Modern
Ceylon Studies* 1: 43–63.

– 1975. "Sinhalese Buddhist Identity in Ceylon." In *Ethnic Identity:
Cultural Continuities and Change*, edited by George De Vos and Lola
Romanucci-Ross, 231–58. California: Mayfield Publishing Company.

– 1984. *The Cult of the Goddess Pattini.* Chicago: University of Chicago
Press.

– 2006. "Thinking Globally about Buddhism." In *The Oxford Handbook
of Global Religions*, edited by Mark Juergensmeyer, 69–82. Oxford:
Oxford University Press.

Olcott, Henry Steel. 1885. *A Buddhist Catechism, According to the Canon of
the Southern Church.* The Biogen Series, no. 3. Boston: Estes and Lauriat.

Ong, Aihwa. 2003. *Buddha Is Hiding: Refugees, Citizenship, the New
America.* Berkeley, CA: University of California Press.

Overmyer, Daniel L., Don Baker, and Larry DeVries. 2010. *Asian
Religions in British Columbia.* Vancouver: UBC Press. http://site.ebrary.
com/id/10438675.

Padgett, Douglas M. 2002. "The Translating Temple: Diasporic Buddhism
in Florida." In *Westward Dharma: Buddhism beyond Asia*, edited by

Charles S. Prebish and Martin Baumann, 201–17. Berkeley, CA: University of California Press.

Pannasiha M.N. Thera, Madihe. 1995. "Dhamma Schools and Their Development." *The Buddhist: Dhamma Schools Centenary Issue* 66 (2 June–July): 4–5.

Pearson, Anne Mackenzie. 2004. "Being Hindu in Canada: Personal Narratives from First and Second Generation Immigrant Hindu Women." *Journal of Theology and Religion* 23, no. 1: 55–88.

Prebish, Charles. 1993. "Two Buddhisms Reconsidered." *Buddhist Studies Review* 10, no. 2: 187–206.

Prebish, Charles, and Martin Baumann. 2002. "Introduction: Paying Homage to the Buddha in the West." In *Westward Dharma: Buddhism beyond Asia*, edited by Charles S. Prebish and Martin Baumann, 1–13. Berkeley: University of California Press.

Prothero, Stephen R. 1996. *The White Buddhist: The Asian Odyssey of Henry Steel Olcott*. Bloomington: Indiana University Press.

Quli, Natalie E.F. 2010. "Laicization in Four Sri Lankan Buddhist Temples in Northern California." California: Graduate Theological Union.

Reimer, Samuel H. 2006. "A Look at Cultural Effects on Religiosity: A Comparison between the United States and Canada." In *Religion and Canadian Society: Traditions, Transitions, and Innovations*, 54–70. Toronto: Canadian Scholars' Press Inc.

Reynolds, Frank E. 1972. "From Philology to Anthropology: A Bibliographical Essay on Works Related to Early Theravāda and Sinhalese Buddhism." In *The Two Wheels of Dhamma; Essays on the Theravada Tradition in India and Ceylon*, edited by Gananath Obeyesekere, Frank Reynolds, and Bardwell L. Smith. Chambersburg, PA: American Academy of Religion.

Robertson, Roland. 1995. "Glocalization: Time-Space and Homogeneity-Heterogeneity." In *Global Modernities*, edited by Mike Featherstone, Scott Lash, and Roland Robertson, 25–44. London and Thousand Oaks, CA: Sage Publications.

Rose, Gillian. 1997. "Situating Knowledges: Positionality, Reflexivities and Other Tactics." *Progress in Human Geography* 21, no. 3: 305–20.

Ryan, Phil. 2014. "Our Multiculturalism: Reflections in the Key of Rawls." In *The Multiculturalism Question: Debating Identity in 21st Century Canada*, edited by Jack Jedwab, 89–106. Montreal and Kingston: McGill-Queen's University Press.

Saddhatissa, H. 1978. "The Saddha Concept in Buddhism." *Eastern Buddhist* 11, no. 2: 137–42.

Salgado, Nirmala S. 2013. *Buddhist Nuns and Gendered Practice: In Search of the Female Renunciant*. New York: Oxford University Press.

Samuels, Jeffrey. 2004. "Toward an Action-Oriented Pedagogy: Buddhist Texts and Monastic Education in Contemporary Sri Lanka." *Journal of the American Academy of Religion* 72, no. 4: 955–71.

Saram, P.A.S. 1999. "Weberian Buddhism and Sinhalese Buddhism." *Social Compass* 23: 355–82.

Saranapala, Bhante. 2013. "Message from Chair." Presented at the Buddha's Birthday Celebration: Blessings on the City, the Nation and the World, Mississauga Celebration Square, June.

Saranapala, Bhikkhu. n.d. "Mindfulness: Key to Getting Rid of Stress." In *The 'Secret' to Happiness: Ajahn Brahm in Toronto 2008*, 5–6. Mississauga: Holton Peel Buddhist Society.

Sasson, Vanessa R. 2013. "Introduction: Charting New Territory: Children and Childhoods in Buddhist Texts and Traditions." In *Little Buddhas: Children and Childhoods in Buddhist Texts and Traditions*, edited by Vanessa R. Sasson, 1–16. New York: Oxford University Press.

Scheible, Kristin. 2013. "'Give Me My Inheritance': Western Buddhists Raising Buddhist Children." In *Little Buddhas: Children and Childhoods in Buddhist Texts and Traditions*, edited by Vanessa R. Sasson, 428–52. New York: Oxford University Press.

Scott, David. 1994. *Formations of Ritual: Colonial and Anthropological Discourses on the Sinhala Yaktovil*. Minneapolis: University of Minnesota Press.

Seager, Richard Hughes. 2002. "American Buddhism in the Making." In *Westward Dharma: Buddhism beyond Asia*, edited by Charles S. Prebish and Martin Baumann, 106–19. Berkeley: University of California Press.

Seljak, David. 2005. "Education, Multiculturalism, and Religion." In *Religion and Ethnicity in Canada*, edited by Paul Bramadat and David Seljak, 178–200. Toronto: Pearson Education Canada Inc.

Seneviratne, H.L. 1999. *The Work of Kings: The New Buddhism in Sri Lanka*. Chicago: University of Chicago Press.

Shiu, Henry. 2010. "Buddhism after the Seventies." In *Wild Geese: Buddhism in Canada*, edited by Alexander Duncan Soucy, Victor Sōgen Hori, and John S. Harding, 84–110. Montreal and Kingston: McGill-Queen's University Press.

Smith, Jonathan Z. 2004. *Relating Religion: Essays in the Study of Religion*. Chicago: University of Chicago.

Smith-Hefner, Nancy Joan. 1999. *Khmer American: Identity and Moral Education in a Diasporic Community*. Berkeley: University of California Press.

Snodgrass, Judith. 2007. "Defining Modern Buddhism: Mr and Mrs Rhys Davids and the Pāli Text Society." *Comparative Studies of South Asia, Africa and the Middle East* 27, no. 1: 186–202.

– 2009. "Discourse, Authority, Demand: The Politics of Early English Publications on Buddhism." In *TransBuddhism: Transmission, Translation, Transformation*, edited by Nalini Bhushan, Jay L. Garfield, and Abraham Zablocki, 21–42. Amherst, MA: University of Massachusetts Press, in association with the Kahn Liberal Arts Institute of Smith College.

Soucy, Alexander Duncan. 2010. "Asian Reformers, Global Organizations: An Exploration of the Possibility of a 'Canadian Buddhism.'" In *Wild Geese: Buddhism in Canada*, edited by Alexander Duncan Soucy, Victor Sōgen Hori, and John S. Harding, 39–60. Montreal and Kingston: McGill-Queen's University Press.

– 2014. "Buddhist Globalism and the Search for Canadian Buddhism." In *Flowers on the Rock: Global and Local Buddhisms in Canada*, edited by Victor Sōgen Hori, John S. Harding, and Alexander Duncan Soucy, 25–54. Montreal and Kingston: McGill-Queen's University Press.

Soucy, Alexander Duncan, Victor Sōgen Hori, and John S. Harding. 2010a. "Introduction." In *Wild Geese: Buddhism in Canada*, edited by Alexander Duncan Soucy, Victor Sōgen Hori, and John S. Harding, 3–10. Montreal and Kingston: McGill-Queen's University Press.

– eds. 2010b. *Wild Geese: Buddhism in Canada*. Montreal and Kingston: McGill-Queen's University Press.

Southwold, Martin. 1983. *Buddhism in Life: The Anthropological Study of Religion and the Practice of Sinhalese Buddhism*. Manchester, UK: Manchester University Press.

Stark, Rodney. 2000. *Acts of Faith: Explaining the Human Side of Religion*. Berkeley: University of California Press.

Stevenson, Garth. 2014. *Building Nations from Diversity: Canadian and American Experience Compared*. Montreal and Kingston: McGill-Queen's University Press.

Storhoff, Gary, and John Whalen-Bridge, eds. 2010. *American Buddhism as a Way of Life*. Albany: State University of New York Press.

Sugunasiri, Suwanda H.J. 2008. *Thus Spake the Sangha: Early Buddhist Leadership in Toronto*. Toronto: Nalanda Publishing Canada.

– 2001. *Towards Multicultural Growth: A Look at Canada from Classical Racism to Neomulticulturalism*. Toronto: Village Publishing House.

Suh, Sharon A. 2004. *Being Buddhist in a Christian World: Gender and Community in a Korean American Temple*. Seattle: University of Washington Press.

Susila Himi, Kompitiye Sri. 1995. *Sri Lankave Daham Pasel Adhyapanaya*. Colombo, Sri Lanka: S. Godage saha Sahodarayo.

Sweet, Lois. 1997. *God in the Classroom: The Controversial Issue of Religion in Canada's Schools*. Toronto: McClelland & Stewart Inc.

Tambiah, Stanley Jeyaraja. 1970. *Buddhism and the Spirit Cults in North-East Thailand*. Cambridge, UK: Cambridge University Press.

– 1992. *Buddhism Betrayed?: Religion, Politics, and Violence in Sri Lanka*. Chicago: University of Chicago Press.

Taylor, Charles. 1992. "The Politics of Recognition." In *Multiculturalism and the Politics of Recognition: An Essay*, 25–74. Princeton, NJ: Princeton University Press.

Tedlock, Barbara. 1991. "From Participant Observation to the Observation of Participation: The Emergence of Narrative Ethnography." *Journal of Anthropological Research* 47, no. 1: 69–94.

Tilakaratne, Asanga. 2006. "The Role of Buddhist Monks in Resolving the Conflict." In *Buddhism, Conflict and Violence in Modern Sri Lanka*, edited by Deegalle Mahinda, 210–25. London and New York: Routledge.

– 2007. *Madihe Maha Nahimi: Charitaya ha Chintanaya*. Maharagama: Sasana Sevaka Samitiya.

Tran, Kelly, Jennifer Kaddatz, and Paul Allard. 2005. "South Asians in Canada: Unity through Diversity." *Canadian Social Trends* 78: 20–5.

Triandis, Harry Charalambos. 1995. *Individualism & Collectivism*. Boulder, CO: Westview Press.

Tsomo, Karma Lekshe. 2009. "Global Exchange: Women in the Transmission and Transformation of Buddhism." In *TransBuddhism: Transmission, Translation, Transformation*, edited by Nalini Bhushan, Jay L. Garfield, and Abraham Zablocki, 151–66. Amherst, MA: University of Massachusetts Press, in association with the Kahn Liberal Arts Institute of Smith College.

Tweed, Thomas A. 1992. *The American Encounter with Buddhism, 1844–1912: Victorian Culture and the Limits of Dissent*. Bloomington, IN: Indiana University Press.

– 1997. *Our Lady of the Exile: Diasporic Religion at a Cuban Catholic Shrine in Miami*. New York: Oxford University Press.

– 2006. *Crossing and Dwelling: A Theory of Religion.* Cambridge, MA: Harvard University Press.

Verchery, Lina. 2010. "The Woodenfish Program: Fo Guang Shan, Canadian Youth, and a New Generation of Buddhist Missionaries." In *Wild Geese: Buddhism in Canada,* edited by Alexander Duncan Soucy, Victor Sōgen Hori, and John S. Harding, 210–35. Montreal and Kingston: McGill-Queen's University Press.

Vertovec, Steven. 2000. *The Hindu Diaspora: Comparative Patterns.* London and New York: Routledge.

– 2011. "The Cultural Politics of Nation and Migration." *Annual Review of Anthropology* 40: 241–56.

Walpola, Piyal. 2008. "The Rise of Buddhism in Canada: Eastern Spiritual Path Gaining Ground." In *The 'Secret' to Happiness: Ajahn Brahm in Toronto 2008,* 3–4. Mississauga: Holton Peel Buddhist Society.

Walshe, Maurice. 1996. *The Long Discourses of the Buddha: A Translation of the Digha Nikaya.* Kandy: Buddhist Publication Society.

Warusawithana, Srima, ed. 2007. *Our Daham Pasela.* Maharagama: Siri Vajiragnana Daham Pasela.

White, Marybeth. 2005. "Lao Buddhism in Toronto: A Case Study of Community Relations." In *Buddhism in Canada,* edited by Bruce Matthews, 105–19. London and New York: Routledge.

– 2010. "That Luang: The Journey and Relocation of Lao Buddhism in Canada." In *Wild Geese: Buddhism in Canada,* edited by Alexander Duncan Soucy, Victor Sōgen Hori, and John S. Harding, 168–86. Montreal and Kingston: McGill-Queen's University Press.

Wijesundara, Himale. 2008. "The West End Buddhist Centre Dhamma School: Then & Now." In *Dhamma School: West End Buddhist Centre.* Mississauga: West End Buddhist Centre.

Williams, Raymond Brady. 1988. *Religions of Immigrants from India and Pakistan: New Threads in the American Tapestry.* Cambridge, UK and New York: Cambridge University Press.

– 2004. *Williams on South Asian Religions and Immigrant: Collected Works.* Burlington, VT: Ashgate.

Wilson, Jeff. 2012. *Dixie Dharma: Inside a Buddhist Temple in the American South.* Chapel Hill: University of North Carolina Press.

Winslow, Deborah. 1984. "A Political Geography of Deities: Space and the Pantheon in Sinhalese Buddhism." *Journal of Asian Studies* 43, no. 2: 273–91.

Winter, Elke. 2014. "Multiculturalism in the 1990s: The Smallest Common Denominator in Defining Canadian National Identity." In *The*

Multiculturalism Question: Debating Identity in 21st Century Canada,
edited by Jack Jedwab, 53–72.

Zhou, Min. 2006. "Negotiating Culture and Ethnicity: Intergenerational
Relations in Chinese Immigrant Families in the United States." In
Cultural Psychology of Immigrants, edited by Mamaswami
Mahalingam, 315–36. New Jersey: Lawrence Erlbaum Associates
Publishers.

Zine, Jasmin. 2008. *Canadian Islamic Schools: Unravelling the Politics
of Faith, Gender, Knowledge, and Identity*. Toronto: University of
Toronto Press.

Index